DISCOVERIES, MISSIONARY EXPANSION AND ASIAN CULTURES

ABOUT THE EDITOR

Teotonio R. de Souza (b. 18.2.1947). He is the Founder-Director of the Xavier Centre of Historical Research, Goa since 1979. He is the author of *Medieval Goa* and edited *Indo-Portuguese History: Old Issues, New Questions* (1985), *Essays in Goan History* (1987), *Goa through the Ages: An Economic History* (1990), *Jesuits in India: In Historical Perspective* (1992). He has also written extensively on Indo-Portuguese History and Church History in various academic and cultural journals in India and abroad. He is post-graduate teacher and Ph.D. research guide of the Goa University, and is Life-Member and Fellow of various associations of Historians, including Indian History Congress and the Portuguese Academy of History. He has convened national and international seminars since 1981, including the Third International Seminar on Indo-Portuguese History (ISIPH-3). He has convened the 7th Seminar of the same series for January 1994.

DISCOVERIES, MISSIONARY EXPANSION AND ASIAN CULTURES

Edited by
Teotonio R. de Souza
Director
Xavier Centre of Historical Research
Goa

Foreword by
Gregory Naik, S.J.

CONCEPT PUBLISHING COMPANY, NEW DELHI 110059

ISBN 81-7022-497-7

First Published 1994

Published and Printed by
Ashok Kumar Mittal
Concept Publishing Company
A/15-16, Commercial Block, Mohan Garden
NEW DELHI 110059 (India)

Lasertypeset by
Printing Express
H-13, Bali Nagar,
NEW DELHI 110015

FOREWORD

The origin and spread of the activities of the Society of Jesus worldwide are connected historically with the Iberian "Discoveries" and expansion worldwide. The 450th anniversary of the arrival of the Spanish Jesuit St. Francis Xavier in Portuguese-controlled Goa in 1542 was commemorated by the Goa Jesuits by calling a group of historians and social science scholars to discuss the event and its impact on Asian cultures in a national seminar. This was seen as a relevant and enlightened exercise in the context of the strong feelings of the peoples of the underdeveloped nations of the Third World against the triumphalism marking the celebrations of the 500th anniversary of the "discovery" of the New World by Columbus.

The "missionary" role was closely associated with the colonial expansion that followed "discoveries", and the political leaders and critical thinkers of the Third World countries continue resenting this association and what they see as disastrous consequences of it to the cultural and economic lives of their peoples. Such feelings were expressed, for instance, by the Peruvian Indian leaders to Pope John Paul in 1985: "Take back your *Bible* and return it to our oppressors. They need its moral precepts more than we, because, since the arrival of Christopher Columbus, America has had imposed on it, by force, a culture, a language, a religion and values which belong to Europe" (David Willey, *God's Politician,* London, Faber and Faber, 1992: 227). Closer in India, Sardar Panikkar voiced similar feelings that drew wide publicity and attention of Church leaders and Western countries in the wake of India's independence. He wrote in *Asia and Western Dominance:* "A large-scale attempt was made to effect a mental and spiritual conquest as supplementing the political authority already enjoyed by Europe". He points to the Society of Jesus as the most characteristic expression of this drive, and adds: "Though the results were disappointing in the extreme from the missionary point of view, this assault on the spiritual foundations of Asian countries has had far-reaching consequences in the religious and social reorganisation of the peoples" (London: George Allen and Unwin, 1953: 481). Mahatma Gandhi had some hard feelings of this kind, and many leaders and thinking citizens of India and other nations of the Third World share the same till today.

It was thought vital for the Jesuits at large, and for the Goa Jesuits in particular, to be critically aware of the historical context and developments to which they are called upon to contribute with the "mission" of Christ, rather than with the "mission" of the Western nations or any other vested interests. It was with this purpose in mind that the Jesuits of Goa and Pune have backed the research efforts of the Xavier Centre of Historical Research since its establishment fifteen years ago. Its various publications have given a proof of this scholarly and critical spirit that has not been apologetic, but on the contrary unsparing in constructive critique of the roles of religion and religious institutions in the course of history. Its recent publication entitled *Jesuits in India: In Historical Perspective* (Macau, Instituto Cultural de Macau, 1992) is a clear instance of such a bold enterprise, and we are grateful for this ongoing contribution of the Xavier Centre of Historical Research and its team of scholars and collaborators under the direction of Dr. Teotonio R. de Souza. We are happy once again that this book too endorses the same spirit of pursuit of truth with love and concern for God's presence in our Asian cultures, and with determination to expose whatever seeks to undermine it or compromise it with forces of injustice and oppression.

Jesuit House
Panjim, Goa
26 January 1993

Gregory Naik, S.J.
Superior
Goa Region S.J.

CONTENTS

INTRODUCTION

To commemorate the 450th anniversary of the arrival of St. Francis Xavier on the Indian soil in Goa on 6th May, 1542, the Xavier Centre of Historical Research undertook on behalf of the Goa-Pune Jesuits to organise a national seminar to discuss the event as a part of a series of events that led to the *Discoveries* and to consequences that are celebrated with enthusiasm and triumphalism in some parts of the world, while they are seen differently in the Third World, which is a creation of that process.

Missionary expansion was not unknown in times prior to the Discoveries, but it gained a special significance in the context of Discoveries and the ethos generated by it. The impact of these events has been different in different parts of the globe. Asian cultures seem to have met more successfully the challenge than the cultures of the Americas or of Africa, where entire populations were decimated beyond hopes of recovery. The Asian success is reflected in the insignificant percentage of adherence that western Christianity could win in the continent. However, the impact of the western missionaries and the socio-political structures backing them have not been negligible. The question about gains and losses is open to debate and this seminar has not failed to make its own contribution to it.

Over twenty historians and scholars in other social sciences from India and three from Europe accepted our invitation to present their views and to take part in the discussions. The results are now presented to the public, and we hope that they will stimulate further reflection and motivate action that could redress or at least mitigate the more unsavoury aspects of the colonial legacy inaugurated by the "Colombus Project" or by the "Vasco da Gama" epoch. It may appear that the focus of this seminar and its published proceedings has overemphasised the role of the Portuguese and their rule in Goa. However, this is not unwarranted, considering the fact that the Portuguese initiated and dominated the first phase of the process of the western dominance in Asia, and it was at the headquarters of their

Estado da India that one could feel the pulse of the system at work. Goa served also as a laboratory for evolving missionary methods for Asia, or even for the rest of the Third World. Hence, it was only proper that the Portuguese and their religious policies in Goa-centred *Estado da India* took a lion's share of the seminar attention. Not all the presentations made at the seminar are included in this volume. Those that have been selected could be grouped under three themes:

(1) Asian reaction to the phenomenon of the "Discoveries" and the colonial aftermath, challenging some of the essentials of the western viewpoints. In this category we have the contributions of Claude and Norma Alvares, Teotonio R. de Souza, Anthony da Silva, William da Silva and Rowena Robinson, and Bailon de Sa. Claude and Norma Alvares give us an insight into what they term "the Colombus Project" of the West. They probe into the history of the formation of the distorted European vision of the world that is being imposed on the rest of the world with tragic success. The new world has "discovered" as a result a ruthless incarnation of Christ through Europe. Teotonio de Souza delves further in the same theme, relating the "missionary waves" emanating from certain regions of the west from time to time to the socio-economic upheavals there. He sees such missionaries as "social rejects" of the west, but who served as convenient tools for the cultural domination of the new colonies and as early marketing agents of the western industry. The Christianity they exported was one such monopoly product of the west, and despite the post-colonial conciliatory strategy represented by Vatican II, the process is on and not just a past history. Anthony da Silva gives us insights into the psychology of the discoverers and the discovered, illustrating this in the context of the Portuguese-Goan encounter. He stresses the fact that the Portuguese never considered making India their home as the Muslims in India did. As a result of such an attitude the Portuguese nurtured a superior image of themselves that did not permit them to accept even the Christianised Goans as their equals in any respect. He concludes with a warning to the present generation to eschew from such mentality of the discoverers, who had nothing to learn from other cultures. William da Silva and

Rowena Robinson have attempted to define *conversion* in sociological terms. They do not see it as an exclusive characteristic of the west. Conversion is explained also in terms of the break-down of traditional social values, and the Portuguese policies towards the orphan girls and widows, towards non-Christian places of worship and interference with the food habits of the Hindus seem to have contributed towards such a crisis of social organisation and relations, subverting them from within. Bailon de Sa discusses the motivations behind the Portuguese discoveries, and while conceding their scientific contribution and trade benefits, chastises the religious fanaticism that accompanied them making a mockery of the Gospel values. He deprecates the blindness of the Portuguese in this respect. Despite the cultural vandalism of the Portuguese in Goa, including attempts to destroy the native language of the people, the Goans have remained receptive to the wider world, while rooted firmly in the soil.

(2) Missionary expansion with special reference to the missionary methods of conversion engaged several participants of the seminar, such as P.P. Shirodkar, Joseph de Barros, A. R. Kulkarni, Adi H. Doctor, Rudolf C. Heredia and Benny Aguiar. P.P. Shirodkar describes the harrowing experiences of the natives against the Portuguese Inquisition and other methods of forced conversions in India. He is not satisfied with the attitude of those who today explain away such horrors as a thing of the past, and would like to see justice done just as in the case of the crimes of Nazi Germany. Joseph de Barros presents a viewpoint that may appear somewhat jarring in the general framework of this volume. However, it reflects the feelings of a section of the natives, and as such it cannot be ignored or wished away. It mirrors the internal contradictions of a society and for that reason it has found a place in this volume. A.R. Kulkarni points out to the failure of the book religions, like Christianity and Islam to make a serious dent in India despite questionable methods adopted to win converts. He discusses at length the Hindu response to conversions in the form of purification rituals evolved to welcome the converts back into the Hindu fold. He does not see it as a burning issue of our days, but the readers are certainly left with questions about issues that are not entirely unrelated in the wake

of the Ayodhya crisis. Adi H. Doctor examines the missionary strategy to undermine Hinduism in the 19th century in British India, particularly through the educational institutions and by exposing the superstitious beliefs of Hinduism. However, there arose Hindu reformers who counter-exposed the Christian superstitions in the context of the Reformation and Enlightenment in Europe, thereby blunting the edge of the missionary attacks. Rudolf C. Heredia treats the issue of Catholic educational institutions as agents of evangelisation in India. Rather than pursuing an anti-Hindu stand, these efforts were aimed at meeting the challenge of the Protestant counterparts and at equipping the Catholic middle class to have a share in the benefits of the British dispensation. Heredia challenges those reponsible for the Catholic educational institutions to be more socially and politically conscious in a prophetic way, rather than perpetuating a bourgeois paternalistic pattern of education inherited from the foreign missionaries. Finally Benny Aguiar confirms the ongoing colonial legacy that retains its hold upon the Catholic Church in India. He illustrates it with the resistance to efforts at inculturation of liturgy and the slow evolution of a more relevant rite and theology. However, he sees ferment at work and its promise to bear fruit.

(3) The third and last category of presentations may appear to be a mixed bag, but they reflect directly or indirectly the impact of the discoveries and missionary expansion on various organisational and cultural aspects, including trade, education, sports, movements of people and goods. Artur Teodoro de Matos discusses the financial resources of the missionaries in Goa, particularly the Jesuits. In addition to fixed subsidies from the State, they were very resourceful in raising funds for their many activities through profitable investments in landed estates and in trade. Philomena Antony explores the missionary links between Goa and Brazil and a fruitful exchange of agricultural products that resulted from these. She also extends her analysis to non-missionary contacts, particularly many who came to Goa as *exiles* and mingled with the local population and made Goa their home. Maria de Jesus dos Mártires Lopes gives us a comparative picture of the contribution made by the Jesuits and the native Oratorians to the

educational development in Goa in the late 18th century. R.K. Kochhar pays tribute to the scientific contribution of several Jesuits in India, and how their contribution was turned by the British and the French to good effect for promoting their imperial interests. Anirudha Gupta seeks to expose historical pretentions. He takes the case of the British anti-slavery campaign under an ostensibly edifying cover of missionary indignation. But all through, roguery and morality went hand-in-hand at the service of British commercial interests in East Africa. Finally, M.D. David deals with the Christian contribution to the development of sports through Young Men's Christian Association (YMCA) and the induction of India into the Olympic Games for the first time in 1924. The movement also promoted health education and hygiene. All this was considered essential to keep the youth morally and spiritually healthy.

We hope that our readers will appreciate the frankness of the views expressed by our various contributors. We are indebted to them for their willingness to do so. The convenors of the seminar and the editor do not personally endorse all the views put forth in this volume, but we respect them all as an expression of search for truth and a courage to question even certain inherited dogmas of western thought and expectations.

We wish to acknowledge the generous financial support of the Goa-Pune Jesuit Province for the organization of the seminar and the publication of the proceedings. We feel further encouraged by the endorsement of our efforts by the regional superior of the Goa Jesuits, Fr. Gregory Naik, S.J. Our grateful thanks also to the Director of the Baga Retreat House, Fr. Fermin D'Souza, whose generous hospitality made the Baga seminar a memorable experience. And finally, it is due to the selfless and dedicated collaboration of my colleague Dr. Charles Borges that this volume has been made more readable, while Ms. Ernesta Bhobe handled patiently and efficiently the earlier stages of wordprocessing.

TEOTONIO R. DE SOUZA

LIST OF CONTRIBUTORS

Msgr. Benny Aguiar, Editor, *The Examiner*, 5, Convent Street, Bombay 400 039.

Dr. Claude Alvares, Journalist and Social Activist, Almeida Vaddo, Parra, Goa 403 510.

Norma Alvares, Journalist and Social Activist, Almeida Vaddo, Parra, Goa 403 510

Mrs. Philomena S. Antony, Head, Department of History, Chowgule College, M-2, Govt. Housing Colony, Vidyanagar, Margao, Goa 403 601.

Dr. Joseph de Barros, Historian, Ph.D. guide, Goa University, Instituto Menezes Braganza, P.O. Box 221, Panaji, Goa 403 001

Dr. M. D. David, Professor and Head, Department of History, Wilson College, Bombay 400 007.

Dr. Adi H. Doctor, Professor and Head, Department of Political Science, Goa University, P.O. Bambolim Complex, Goa 403 202.

Dr. Anirudha Gupta, Professor in International Studies, 151, Uttarakhand, New JNU Campus, New Delhi 110 067.

Dr. Rudolf C. Heredia, Research Head, Indian Social Institute, 10 Institutional Area, Lodi Road, New Delhi 110 003.

Dr. R.K. Kochhar, Professor, Indian Institute of Astrophysics, Koramangala, Bangalore 560 034.

Dr. A. R. Kulkarni, Emeritus Professor of History, 'Shri', 992/993-23, Rajendra Nagar, Pune 411 030.

Dra. Maria de Jesus dos Martires Lopes, Historian, Rua Americo Durão, n. 4, 2o Dto, 1900 Lisboa, Portugal.

Dr. Artur Teodoro de Matos, Professor of History, Universidade Nova de Lisboa, Rua Americo Durão, n. 4, 2o Dto, 1900 Lisboa, Portugal.

Ms. Rowena Robinson, Research student, c/o Mrs. Celine Santos, Tamdeg Vaddo, Carmona, Goa.

Dr. P.P. Shirodkar, Director, Directorate of Archives, Archaeology, and Museum, Junta House, 4th Floor, Flat 3, Lift 2, Panaji, Goa 403 001.

Dr. Anthony da Silva, Professor of Psychology, De Nobili College, Pune 411 014.

Dr. William da Silva, Reader and Head, Department of Sociology, Goa University, P.O. Bambolim Complex, Goa 403 202.

Dr. Teotonio R. de Souza, Director, Xavier Centre of Historical Research, Alto Porvorim, Goa 403 521.

Dr. Bailon de Sá, President, Institute Menezes Braganza, Corlim, Ilhas, Goa 403 110.

SECTION I

1

THE CHRISTIAN AND THE WILD

CLAUDE ALVARES and NORMA ALVARES

Introduction

On 12th October, 1992, at Santo Domingo, Pope John Paul II, joined the quincentennial celebrations to mark the arrival of Christopher Columbus in the Americas. The Pope paid tribute to Columbus for helping plant the seeds of Christianity in the new world. "We are gathered in front of this Columbus lighthouse built in the form of a cross, to symbolize the cross of Christ planted on this earth in 1492," he said.

It is doubtful if the more than 100 million Amerindians and Africans who lost their lives on both the continents of North and South America as a result of the brutal interventions and havoc wreaked by this so-called explorer called Columbus and his successors would have felt the same way.

The failure of Christianity, not its implantation, is the issue to be examined. If it were indeed a superior religion, then human beings are at a loss for the rejection. If not, then the failure should be welcomed. Also important is an examination of the complicity of this religion that claimed to originate with the Prince of Peace with deeds commonly associated with the Prince of Darkness.

The quincentennial is a good occasion for the examination simply because Columbus was a reasonably good exemplar of what the Christian missionary was about. His Christian mission was fairly clear. As Thomas Suarez has observed: "Columbus' ultimate goal was to reclaim the Holy Land for Christendom. He grew to perceive himself as one with a divine destiny in the preparation for the coming of the Antichrist and the end of the world." He in fact looked upon the "discovery" as some form of crusade. A Jew converted to Catholicism, he expected to find the earthly Paradise and even though he had eventually found it on his third voyage.

Papal Bulls: Bullying the Non-Christians

In 1492, the Roman Catholic Europe was wholly preoccupied with overturning Muslim dominance in European affairs. This was a persistent medieval European objective that could legitimize any kind of action. Both Spain and Portugal also had a conceptual and legal framework for such ventures in the form of a series of Papal Bulls that provided the context to European expansion and to Europe's relationship with the non-Christian world.

These Bulls allowed the European monarchs to legitimize their activities and to stake their respective claims to possession and rights in the international sphere. The monarchs then subcontracted the pursuit of their vision to their clients. All voyages into Atlantic waters had to be licensed by monarchs: royal warrant was the only means to protect and lay secure claim to whatever marketable resource one might acquire, whatever its nature.

The Papal Bull *Dum Diversas* of 1452, for instance, authorised the King of Portugal to attack, conquer and subdue "Saracens", pagans and other unbelievers who were inimical to Christ; to capture their goods and their territories; to reduce their persons to perpetual slavery, and to transfer their lands and properties to the King of Portugal and his successors. The Papacy itself in the second half of the fifteenth century was an increasingly weak institution. Nevertheless, the Bulls represented the quintessence of European understanding, a function of its essential way of seeing the world.

The Papal Bull *Romanus Pontifex* of 1455 specifically credits the Portuguese king with seeking to circumnavigate Africa to make contact with the Indies where, it was hoped, they would find Prester John, a Christian monarch. Throughout the Middle Ages Prester John figured in European literature and was deemed to reside on the other side of the Muslim lands, somewhere out east. Together with this potential ally, the Bull expected Portugal to prosecute the struggle against the 'Saracen' and other enemies of Christ.

A Distorted Christian Vision of the World

The geographical perspective of Columbus can be gauged somewhat from medieval maps circulating at the time. Thus the great Mappa Mundi of Hereford, made around 1280, is decidedly circular. It is both a representation of geographical information and a map of ideas and ideology. It shows a land world surrounded by the encircling sea. The centre of the world is Jerusalem, the place where Christ walked on earth, thus placing the Christian vision at the heart of all understanding.

An even better picture of standard medieval geographic thought is available in the Psalter map, another thirteenth century work, which graphically represents the standard Ptolemaic argument for a land link between southern Africa and India. The Psalter Map records what one would expect to find in the ambiguous spaces of the Indies. Inset there are a series of 14 naked figures, one with a dog's head, others of people with no head but with their eyes and mouth on their torso, many recognizably consuming human limbs. These are the monstrous peoples of the Greco-Roman tradition which Christianity soon took over and made into its own.

Such speculations confirmed Columbus' confidence in his own argument that on 12 October, 1492 he had indeed arrived in the east, on the threshold of 'the Indies'. Both speculations marched straight off the page of medieval maps. If, instead of reading Columbus with a modern Mercator projection map in mind, one reads Columbus with the Psalter map in view he cannot any longer be thought mad or deluded. He emerges as a conventional European man of his times.

Thus, the personal or psychological profile of Christopher Columbus is less important than the cultural and ideological personality of European Christendom through which he operated. For Columbus, his inherited myths were the real charter that set historic events in motion, not merely so in terms of the geographic idea that there was a place out there to get to, but also in terms of the people one was likely to encounter once one arrived. Accompanying him was not merely a whole iconography, but also a mental geography, that included an anthropology of barbarism. The latter had its origins not in the medieval ages in Europe, but rather in the earlier culture of the Near East, particularly the part involving the Israelites, and the civilizations of Greek and Rome to which Europe became heir.

The widespread medieval belief in dog-headed people, amazons, and other monstrous races was part of an integrated set of ideas and a potent iconography of barbarism that sprang from classical sources. It was based on the retention and development of Greek and Roman knowledge and fused (as the Christian millennium advanced), with aspects of Christian ideology.

Frederick Turner writes that the original message of Christianity was that of the divinity that dwells within and that is present in all creation, and of how to live in accordance with this. Yet in the historical transformation of Christianity "the emphasis shifted from the message to the historical figure, who was now presented as having once intervened in the history of this world only to show it as the contemptible thing it truly was; who had assumed flesh only to show that it was possible to live beyond the body, to ruthlessly subordinate its desires to the utterly different needs of the spirit." This transformation is most obvious in the celebrated conversion of St. Paul, where the conversion is equated with a kind of on-going self-slaughter. No wonder St. Paul has often been referred to as the inventor of Christianity.

Here begins in New Testament scripture the fatal divorce between body and soul, between nature and religion, that has come to be seen as the very essence of the Christian faith. This development has had incalculable consequences for the history of the West and, through invasion and settlement, for the rest of the globe.

Turned away from nature, Christian history soon became a steadily lengthening chronicle of mass neurosis. The hatred for the body deepened, becoming most notable in the gory punishments inflicted by the mystics as they racked themselves on wheels.

By the end of the eleventh century, with the influence of St Augustine and his militant attitudes towards unbelievers, the violence had turned outward, first towards others within Christian society itself, then towards peoples beyond. The church had also by now begun to identify the heretical ones ('Saracens' or sects within) with all things natural, earthy, animal and primitive.

The Crusades truly commence the pattern of large-scale, international Christian violence against all unbelievers that bears its fruit in the ruins of Tenochtitlan. The First Crusade was preached by Pope Urban at Clermont at the end of November 1095.

The first major slaughter was effected in the spring of 1096. It was, however, not against the Muslims but against the Jewish communities at Worms, Mainz and Trier: the Jews were to be followed by Albigensians, 'Saracens', witches, Africans and finally, the primitives of the Americas.

The clearest illustration of the spiritual plight of the Western world before it reached out beyond itself into the wilderness is the Inquisition. This violence was visited against over another million people. By the sixteenth century and the Reformation, the full force of the thwarted desire had been reached and the enemies burned by the thousands. A bishop of Geneva, Turner informs us, burned five hundred in three months. A Bamberg bishop burned six hundred. A bishop of Wurzburg, nine hundred. In 1586 the spring was late: the Archbishop of Treves burned 118 women and two men in these fires of spring.

By the century of Columbus, European civilization was possessed of deep-set, long-established attitudes towards the wilderness and indeed all unimproved nature, toward those who lived in the wilderness, and toward the relationship of "civilization" to these.

The Indies, during Columbus' lifetime, would thus inevitablv become just a new battleground for a new Crusade. They would leave it littered with dead bodies. And not those of just human beings, but of other species as well.

Discovering Anew or Imposing the Old?

The moment he made land, Columbus began exercising the power of dominion that he had been granted by royal warrant and papal pronouncement. To locate the "new" land, he named it within European convention; his first landfall he called San Salvador, in honour of Christ the Saviour, even though he knew the people of the island called it Guanahami.

Most frequent are his references to the Holy Trinity (Trinidad), for whom he had a special reverence having dedicated his voyages to it in conventional medieval fashion. Other islands took the names of the Virgin: Santa Maria de Guadalupe, Santa Maria de Monserrate, Santa Maria La Antigua. The entire modern map of the Americas stands witness to the arrival of the European Christian vision to reorder and relocate its geography.

With his third voyage, Columbus was already convinced he was very near "the Earthly Paradise . . . where no man may go, save for by the grace of God." This conviction dawned on him when he chanced upon the four rivers that emptied into the Gulf of Paria.

Even on his first voyage, he found no dog-headed people nor any of the other monstrous races he expected to encounter. But to circumvent the religious doctrines and prohibitions that would have made it difficult for him to enslave the Arawak and the Taino, he reinvented the strangers, grafting on to them as it were fresh monstrous features. From the storehouse of the ideologies, imageries and expectations of medieval conventions describing the Arawak and Taino, Columbus invented people other than the Arawak and Taino he actually encountered. The church, after some initial reservations, seemed happy to accept the explanations.

It is usual to stress Columbus' sympathetic first accounts of the inhabitants of the Caribbean islands. When these are pitted, however, against the iconography of barbarism Columbus brought with him as part of his baggage, a different picture emerges. Thus he was lavish in his accounts of the tractability of the people he invented as Indians. But when the outrageous demands of the Spaniards caused friction among them and they revolted, he was equally swift to adduce further, entirely consistent evidence of heir barbarous condition. When these mythical Indians defied or opposed the invaders, they came to be seen as the fierce, wild Caribs, cannibals to the last man, woman and child. As we shall soon see, however, most other accounts repeated the lie. Even those reading the reports in Europe behaved little better than the Admiral. In most cases, the end result was a restoration and reaffirmation of ancient malformed images rather than their transcendence.

How then did one administer a new world and what was the status of the people it contained *vis-a-vis* Europeans? This question was earnestly debated in Spain by special councils or juntas called by the monarchs. Contending view-points were expressed by canonical and civil lawyers and by theologians to resolve the legal framework for the disposal of rights over land and people now brought under the control of Spain.

St. Thomas Aquinas had systematized the medieval understanding of Aristotle and given two general categories of Otherness to Europe: the vincibly ignorant, those who had heard the message of the Gospel and refused through their incorrigibility to accept its message. This category consisted of the Muslims, Jews and other Semites, and the others who had been within Europe's experience throughout its existence.

The second category were the invincibly ignorant, those who through no fault of their own had never properly encountered the message of the Gospel and hence could be evangelized and converted.

There was thus a gradation of Otherness in which adherence to Christianity and tractability to Christian instruction was made the distinguishing mark of what constituted fully humanised and civilized people. It was a quite explicit and persistent part of European consciousness that without Christianity not only was there no salvation but also no full civil life, since there was no space between the definition of the norms of behaviour of humanity in general and the norms of Christian behaviour.

The consistent tenor of the reports that came back from the New World depicted the social life of the Amerindian as the negative of European norms of civil life. These reports formed the substance of the legal argument about whether they could be enslaved. The reports were also adjudged against the concept of natural law, a law implicit in humanity by its common divine creation. To have social behaviour that was inimical to natural law was to define oneself forthwith as a barbarian. (This was a completely circular argument. The only way to be within the confines of natural law in the ultimate analysis was to be a Christian, since there was no conception of these laws that was not simultaneously a definition of Christian life.)

And then there were the reports about cannibalism. Cannibalism has been a standard trait of most Greek, Roman and medieval accounts concerning the nature of the barbarian. It was a condition to be expected along with the lack of civic attributes.

The most elaborate account of cannibalism is provided by Diego Alvares Chanca, the ship's doctor who accompanied Columbus on his second voyage. Chanca's tale of people herded ready for the pot, of women kept like battery hens to produce youngsters for the pot, of boys emasculated for fattening to make them plump and tender like capons was widely recycled. It was also a natural for illustration. Its imagery remained alive and potent in European discourse for centuries.

Such graphic images of cannibalism are an indivisible part of the early sources on the Americas. They were really meant to show that the peoples of the New World lived entirely contrary to natural law. These 'objective' tests confirmed the status of the Amerindians as barbarians and led the Europeans back to the argument that such people could be enslaved.

Jurists like Francisco de Vitoria (1492–1546) of the School of Salamanca, argued persistently against categorising the Amerindians as natural slaves. They were true humans, with reason, who were therefore in possession of *dominium* over their land and property and could only be enslaved according to the medieval conventions of being deemed inimical to Christ by resisting the preaching of the Gospel.

It is this strain of thought that led to the full development of the *Requerimiento*, a declaration the conquistadores were required to declaim before an uncomprehending people, announcing Spanish arrival and intention to preach the Gospels. If after it was read, there was the slightest sign of resistance, this would categorize the Amerindian as inimical to Christ and fit to be dispossessed of land and person.

De Vitoria had no problems with slavery as such. He expressed the European view of the matter: 'If they (the Africans) are treated humanely it is better for them to be slaves among Christians than free in their own lands, for it is the greatest good fortune to become a Christian.'

Civilizing to Enslave

Thus, the peoples of the New World were not natural slaves but natural children, heirs to true reason once they had been properly educated and grown up. Their cultural condition, based on their faulty education, made them incapable of fully rational behaviour and this warranted the Spanish Crown's right to hold them and their lands in tutelage, until they reached the age of reason. In other words, the Amerindians lived contrary to natural law, or they were opposed to Christianity when they resisted the conquistadores, or were not adults, but children, in permanent need of tutelage.

This anthropology of Otherness, the manner and methods of dealing with non-Europeans, soon became a new global convention that would envelop and change Europe's relations now with even those continents that had, unlike the Americas, been known within the medieval convention: Africa and Asia.

Howsoever crude it may sound, the uniform offer Europe made to the Other in the period of its great explosive movement around the globe was that the latter choose between either enslavement or conversion. Conversion was the tool for teaching the arts and usages of civilization.

The assimilation of the Other to the manners and mores of Europe was no instant transformation. It did not put the new Christians on a par with their masters. It involved changes in habits, dress, food, marriage customs, family connections, often abode, language and political affiliation, as the means of getting civilized. It was a process of transformation intimately connected with the debates on enslavement, as is revealed by the comment of Sir William Johnson, an English settler in North America.

Johnson explained that it was necessary to 'civilize the savages before they can be converted to Christianity and that in order to make them Christians, they must first be made Men.' The natural slave, and the natural child, were conditional men: they could not be left in their state of nature, acting contrary to natural law. That was an offence to the Christian conscience. Once that had been changed, they could be given, or would be ready to receive, the true benefit of civilization and its culmination, Christianity.

But conversion would also keep them second class citizens. Christianity remained a European cultural product, whose definition remained in the hands of the masters who perennially deferred the passing out examination.

Thus did the European Christian destroy whole ways of life in the name of civilization and improvement of the savage. It is ironic, indeed, that the improvement of the 'savage races' could only be carried out through nothing less than the deeper savagery of Christian civilization now infected with a relentlessness one only associates with a galloping cancer.

It is not difficult to understand why in the early nineteenth century a US Senator named Thomas Hart Benton saw no particular difficulty in resuming the vocabularies and design of Columbus: the children of Adam, proclaimed the Senator, were completing the circumambulation of the globe by marching across America from the east coast to the west upto the Pacific Ocean, "in sight of the eastern shore of that Asia in which their first parents were originally planted."

On the other side, the eastern coast of Asia, was the yellow race which "must receive an impression from the superior race whenever they come into contact." Thus America would regenerate the stationary and barbarous Chinese still in their childhood. Benton claimed that it was only the "white" that had received the "divine command to subdue and replenish the earth," no other race having busied themselves in the search for new lands. The American Senator went on to trace the movement of the whites from "western Asia", as they developed religion, art, science, destroying savagery and savages on the way and advancing civilization. About the disappearance of the Indians from the Atlantic coast, he noted that one could not murmur against what appeared to be the effect of "divine law".

Colonial expansion and missionary activity in Asia (India particularly) cannot be looked at apart from the expansion and doings of Europe from 1492 in the Americas. Naturally, the same attitudes prevailed, leading to policies that placed indigenous populations at a gross disadvantage. The Portuguese, Dutch, French, Danes, Dutch and the English might individually have had different roles to play, some more significant than others. However, the worldview behind what remained basically campaigns of conquest was overwhelmingly shared.

Change of Heart or Change of Strategy?

The difference in approach to the European conquest of India was largely due to the general perception that this was a more advanced country and would take time to politically subdue. One Englishman described himself before the Mughal Emperor "as the smallest particle of sand, John Russel, President of the East India Company with his forehead at command rubbed on the ground." After Albuquerque's disastrous attempt to challenge the Zamorin of Calicut, he had to be carried unconscious to his ship.

All this would dramatically change once total political control was indeed established. As in the case of China, which was seen in the eighteenth century to be more advanced than Europe, but which by the nineteenth century was seen to be abysmally primitive, India too became, after conquest, the recipient of denigrating stereotyping.

By 1800, Indian civilization itself was being described in the most obscene and contemptuous language, most notably by the likes of William Wilberforce and James Mill. Wilberforce termed the condition of the people of India as "wretched" and as "sunk in deep ignorance".

James Mill was more disdainful: "The inhabitants of Hindustan rank much lower in the scale of civilization than the nations of Europe", he wrote. "In truth, the Hindu like the eunuch, excels in the quality of a slave"; he was "disembling, treacherous, mendacious to an excess which surpasses even the usual measure of uncultivated society", was "cowardly and unfeeling", and, "in the physical sense, disgustingly unclean" in person and house. Also to soon become predominant was the idea of Indian culture being infantile and childish: similar to English descriptions of blacks in America or Africa or indigenous people in South America.

Karl Marx was not far behind in dismissing India's villages as "semi-barbarous and semi-civilized communities", which "restricted the human mind within the smallest possible compass, making it the unresisting tool of superstition" and where the peasants lived their "undignified, stagnant and vegetative life". He further argued that these little communities brought about "a brutalizing worship of nature exhibiting its degradation in the fact that man, the sovereign of nature, fell down on his knees in the adoration of Kanuman (*sic*), monkey, and Sabbala, cow."

All these new impressions laid the grounds for the introduction of the Indian educational system, raised after Lord Macaulay's famous 7th March, 1835 Education Minute, which laid down the policy for the use of English and the raising of a generation of clerks. Macaulay denigrated the entire corpus of Indian literature, saying it could be safely disposed of with no loss to humanity. It was a logical conclusion for people who now wished to replace the native character of the Indians by substituting predictable modes of thinking and feeling for the allegedly unpredictable native ones. Or for making the Indians men first before they could even become Christian.

The Columbus Project

This is what we call today the Columbus project: the wholesale insidious propagation of the values of Christianity emptied of any of the elements of Christian doctrine. It is into this grand scheme of education "with a firm Christian bias" that the missionaries charged when the imperial Indian government threw open the education field to the churches. The missions had always been interested in the institution of the school. Here it would be useful to provide some description, howsoever brief, of the association.

Unlike the North and South American experience, in which Christianity was closely associated with the debates on enslavement and extermination of unbelievers, and where settlers even saw divine sanction for the rapid elimination of the indigenous peoples, in India evangelization was to take a path largely autonomous of the colonial state except for a short intolerant while in the Roman Catholic enclave of Goa. The Anglican Church of England was only one of several missions that were established within the sub-continent including the Roman Catholics. More effort seems to have been spent in the years after the entry of Vasco da Gama by the denominations undermining each other's zones of influence than in converting the people of India.

How different the strategy of the Roman Catholics was in India from the one executed by the Spanish Catholics in South America is apparent from the attempts of the Jesuits to convert Emperor Akbar and, led by de Nobili, to convert leading caste elites in Madurai around 1606. De Nobili in fact separated himself from the Portuguese and the low-castes and adopted the manners, ways, language and dress of the higher castes. He was successful because the Hindus mistook him as the head of a new Hindu reforming sect.

The East India Company was being formed in England at the same time as de Nobili's efforts. Though it was soon clear that the goal of the company was the long term political domination of India, it seems to have had little interest in the evangelization of the Indian people. Only one baptism of an Indian by the Church of England is recorded for the entire seventeenth century.

It was the Danes who actually provided the necessary boost to the Protestant missions in India. Bartholomew Ziegenbalg, a German priest attached to the Danish Royal Mission, made the crucial decision that the New Testament must be translated. He also decided that if believers were to be able to read what was placed in their hands, *schools must be an indispensable adjunct of the church*. We have not, even in the twentieth century, moved much away from that German priest's shrewd strategy: today, the scriptures of Western culture, from technologies to theories of societal organization, come to us via the same school.

Or college. Worried that hitherto only the lower classes had been converted, Church leaders by the 1830s were convinced that the time had arrived for the Christian challenge to be presented once again to India's elite. This led to the opening of colleges in Calcutta and Bombay.

Through these means the Columbus project was soon incorporated by the Hindu community. The most striking consequence was what one may call the Christianization of Hinduism itself. Leaders like Ram Mohun Roy and Swami Vivekananda attempted to reorganize Hinduism to meet the challenge of Christianity: the form of the response was to model Hinduism on the same lines as Christianity, with its own sacred books, the *Vedas* and the *Gita*, missions schools, missionaries and so on, imitation being the sincerest form of flattery.

Thus, not for nothing has the result of the Indian educational system been any less severe than what the policies of Christianization/ enslavement had achieved in the Americas. There it led to the mass annihilation of millions and sent them six feet into the ground or into smoke. The Indian educational system has also succeeded is despatching a larger number of people in India into a similar kind of coma: their minds crippled, they are also in a sense quite dead, even though, unlike the Amerindians exterminated, they pretend to move about above the ground.

The Pope is not given to indulge in unmeditated exercises. His orations in honour of Columbus, in the company of King Juan Carlos of Spain, are entirely of a character with the nature of the western civilization he continues to represent.

Just as it is the prerogative of the victims to assess the impact of the discoveries, it is for the Christians to investigate how Christianity found itself comfortable with the political conquests and why it consented to be used for the purpose. This is indeed a useful question to ask today, when the same western civilization has also disposed of Christianity, after using it, in more ways than one and the discoveries (or conquests) have gone beyond the original message of Christianity regarding the divinity of all.

Acknowledgment

The paper draws much from Ziauddin Sardar, Merryl Wyn Davies, Ashis Nandy, Claude Alvares, *The Blinded Eye: 500 Years of Christopher Columbus*, (1993), Mapusa, The Other India Press.

REFERENCES

Lach, Donald, *Asia in the Making of Europe* (1965).

Nandy, Ashis, *The Intimate Enemy*, Delhi, Oxford University Press (1983).

Panikkar, K.M., *Asia and Western Dominance*, London, Allen & Unwin (1957).

Suarez, Thomas, *Behind the Veil*, World Scientific Publishing (1993).

Takaki, Ronald, *Iron Cages: Race and Class in 19th Century America*, London, Athlone Press (1979).

Turner, Frederick, *Beyond Geography: The Western Spirit Against the Wilderness*, The Viking Press. (1980).

2

THE CHRISTIAN MISSIONS IN THE AFTERMATH OF DISCOVERIES: Tools for shaping the Colonial Other

TEOTONIO R. DE SOUZA

Introduction

The Christian Church of India and elsewhere in the East commemorates this year the 450th anniversary of the arrival of the first Jesuit, St. Francis Xavier, in India. I thought it was an opportunity to place the missionary phenomenon represented by Francis Xavier in the context of the world-wide noises that are going on about the 500th anniversary of the so-called discovery of America by Columbus. I wish to share some of my convictions that have grown within me over the years of intellectual and experiential search for an understanding of the role and impact of the Christian tradition in which I was born, and of the Society of Jesus in which I have spent already a quarter century and perhaps the most active years of my life.

I wish to state that my historical assessment of the past events is not aimed at *blaming* the personalities and institutions involved or imputing *conscious* motivations to them, but rather at seeing them in the historical context in which they functioned and at understanding the trends and structures that we have been fortunate or unfortunate to inherit. In this process of understanding I cannot but share the hurt feelings of many of my countrymen and others in the Third World who feel helpless to reverse the effects and counter the deep-entrenched interests of the structures of world capitalism that were brought into existence by Europe with its expansion overseas.[1] My reflections include a couple of theoretical constructs which may require more detailed empirical research for confirmation, but they could be provisionally helpful to understand the missionary movements as part and parcel of the spirit that shaped Europe of the age of Discoveries. Hence my argument that they could not but be tools of expanding Europe and carriers of its values, marked essentially by a spirit of superiority, generally subtle, but at times open and arrogant.[2]

Christian Missions: Their Place in India

During a visit to Mahatma Gandhi in the last week of the year 1938, some American teachers asked him what would be the place of Christian missions in the new India that he was assisting to build. Gandhiji who saw his *Satyagraha* as an expression of the native Indian spirit, replied: "To show appreciation of what India is and is doing." He continued: "Up till now they have come as teachers and preachers with queer notions about India and India's great religions. We have been described as a nation of superstitious heathens, knowing nothing, denying God".[3] The father of the nation admitted that even the great Indian religions were imperfect like any other religions of the world, for having percolated through imperfect human agency. He welcomed the missionaries as fellow-helpers and fellow-seekers, but he warned them: "If you come as preachers of the 'true Gospel' to a people who are wandering in darkness, so far as I am concerned you can have no place. You may impose yourselves upon us".[4]

Gandhi was firmly convinced that Hinduism could be purified from within and without denationalisation and deculturation of the Indian people. He admitted that he owed his religious quest to his contact with Christians and Christianity, but he came to the conclusion that the doctrine of atonement as believed by some Christians at least was only a way of disowning responsibility for their continued transgressions and passing it on to the merciful redemption of Christ. He could not accept such a Christianity either as perfect, or as the greatest religion. Neither did he believe that the pious lives of Christians gave him anything that the lives of men of other faiths had failed to give him. He states: "Philosophically there was nothing extraordinary in Christian principles. From the point of view of sacrifice, it seemed to me that the Hindus greatly surpassed the Christians".[5]

We can see Gandhi in line with the other great social reformers produced by India, seeking to build up India's self-confidence, against a background of frustration and humiliation that foreign conquest and rule had produced in the course of previous eleven centuries or so. In the context of political and cultural siege the Hindu society had been eating itself and its inner contradictions had become more pointed and were only enhancing the process of self-defeat.[6] The westernised mission products were either too denationalised or too weak to withstand the superiors of their new dispensation to regenerate the Indian society and restore the nation to its dignity. He distinguished his own missionary work in India with that of the western Christian missionaries in a discussion with missionaries at Bangalore in 1927, stressing that the experience of God can only be in the context of the history and culture of every people. Gandhi also told them that Christians are preaching too much the Cross of Christ who died 2000 years ago, forgetting their duty to bear their own cross today: "While I am strengthening the faith of the people, you are undermining it."[7] Gandhi expressed on many occasions his unhappiness over the caricaturisation of Hinduism in Christian publications and other media. He saw it as a lack of Christian tolerance and their queer concept of truth over which they seemed to claim monopoly. He reacted to this by saying that the message of the Asian Christ was distorted by the West and was reduced to an imperial tool with the backing of the Roman Emperor, and the trend has continued.[8]

Jesus: A Monopoly Product of the West

In the context of slavery in Egypt and of captivity in Babylon and elsewhere the Jews had convinced themselves of their status as God's chosen people. The Christian inheritors of this "God's chosen" complex in western Europe, which was first made to feel politically and culturally inferior by the power and dazzle of the imperial court of Constantinople in the East, and then under centuries of Islamic siege, adapted the message of Christ to justify its crusades and much that was contradictory to the original message of the Gospel. It had Islamised itself unwittingly by adopting the *Jihad*. The Christian discourse of "Go and preach the Gospel to the ends of the earth" in the wake of the "discoveries" was only an extension of the crusades on a global scale. The colonialism that followed and the "world capitalism" to which it gave rise have thus remained intimately connected with an *unhealthy* globalisation of Christ.

I said "unhealthy" because Jesus was deprived from his

"incarnation" and was reduced instead to a "universal uniqueness". It was an engineered "incarnation" of the values, interests, and ways of life of the "missionary" church or churches of the West, representing the western society. It was not an incarnation that responded to the native understanding of God and its cry for life. In an open-ended Christology of the Apostolic times, or even the immediate post-Apostolic times, Jesus could freely assume a title or titles different from those borrowed from the West or needing its approval.[9] There have been some instances of historical exceptions known as Malabar Rites or Chinese Rites, but they were questioned and boldly suppressed in regions where the western colonial interests were entrenching themselves.

Though hardly anything systematic about the Local Church can be found in the texts of Vatican II,[10] which was dominated largely by West European concerns,[11] the Council did make some remarkably hopeful sounding statements in some of its documents. It was hoped that the spirit and openness of some participating groups would help to recognise the genuiness of the God-experiences of the Asian peoples (or other Third World peoples) and to accept their various names for them, rather than continue suspecting them and subjecting them to the test of the theological laboratories of the West. In practice, it has not been possible for the West-dominated Church to admit that there is no such thing as non-cultural expression of the Gospel, or that there is no such a thing as a transcultural quintessence of Catholicism.[12]

The traditional capitalist (*I am using the term as descriptive, rather than in its technical sense*) mentality of the Jews, which has become co-natural to the development of the western mind and its socio-political-economic structures, has sought to present Christ to the rest of the world, including Asia, as yet another monopoly good of its global market. As a result, their Christ remained to a great extent an intruder, not an Asian Christ as felt by Gandhiji and mentioned earlier. The churches preaching such a Christ have also remained largely churches *in* Asia, and have failed to be churches *of* Asia. Instead of joining the great religions of Asia as co-workers in the mission to the millions of poor, the missionary churches in Asia look upon these religions as rivals who threaten the "uniqueness" of their Christ-product. Such an approach implies a contradiction with their own central belief, namely that as long as these churches fail to die with Christ to their search for wealth and power, they are not likely to rise with him and communicate the life of the Spirit to the millions of Asian poor experiencing the forces of death in their daily lives. The foreign funding and the political power behind the western church structures have not succeeded after centuries to win over more than an insignificant percentage of the God-loving and deeply spiritual Asian masses.

A Short Interlude between Missions

The concept, and worse still, the reality of the universal and Catholic church is often in practice reduced to universality of juridical power which is visible in the way this power is used to chastise any questionings of its west-based authority or the authority of its native deputies and beneficiaries, serving consciously or unconsciously the interests of the western capitalist structures. There was a time when the cold war and the concomitant balance of forces permitted a semblance of a church that was beginning to live up once again to its prophetic origins and mission. The Vatican II (1963-65) and the general tone of the Church was one of strategic accommodation in the wake of decolonisation. However, the growing political instability and economic bankruptcy of the Third World countries, and the corresponding dominant position of the West as manifested in the proclamation of the New World Order are also beginning to be manifested in the orientations shaping the Church at the end of the millenium. The next General Congregation of the Society of Jesus fixed for early 1995 will be observed closely and is likely to be "guided" by the authorities to which that Religious Order has vowed unflinching obedience, to meet the expected goals of the New World Order with privatised spirituality of personal devotions and acts of charity gaining priority over effective response to the cries of the victims of structured injustice.

Seeking Sublimation Overseas?

The world outside Europe and America finds it hard to interpret the relation of the West to the East (and South) during the period which K.M. Panikkar has described as "Vasco da Gama epoch" in terms of anything but aggression. What would be barbarism in Europe was civilised or at least legitimate conduct in defence of metropolitan interests in the colonies. Terrorism and piracy in the seas was strongly objected to by Portugal in dealings with Spain, France, England or

Holland in the sixteenth and seventeenth centuries. However, it was heroism in the Indian Ocean against Islam or native countries bordering on it. The European involvement in peddling opium into China or in re-structurng Indian agricultural patterns to promote poppy-cultivation was no problem of conscience to imperial powers for long time. So was the case of enslavement for centuries. To quote Panikkar: "Till the end of European domination the fact that rights existed for Asians against Europeans was conceded only with considerable mental reservation. . . . this doctrine of *different rights* persisted to the very end and was a prime cause of Europe's ultimate failure in Asia."[13] It re-drew the boundaries of nations and churned the life-styles of peoples in the occupied lands. Traditional social and economic structures were adapted, modified or destroyed in order to make them contribute their share of the profits of the metropolitan interests.

The religious aggression was a part and parcel of the same game, and at least the knowledgeable and leading natives (here lies the rub of internal social contradictions that were exploited by the West to their benefit) did not see the Christian missionary work as a positive contribution, but rather as an unwarranted imposition from the outside, inseparably associated with the progress of the colonial powers.[14]

The spirit of "discoveries" of the sixteenth century had its counterpart in the passion for "exploration" of natural resources and exploitation of markets for industrial goods in the age of industrial revolution. Instead of coasting the continents, the movement was now for penetration of the continents. The earlier relations of partnership in trade with the "discovered" people (who were not already decimated or enslaved) was gradually giving way to relations of domination in trade, and control of internal administration.[15] Earlier trading companies became imperial powers with colonies or zones of economic interest all over the globe.

The Iberian religious zeal of the period of discoveries was followed in the 18th century England by the evangelicals, who took their places as the leaders of a "missionary movement", one side of which concentrated on the "heathen" at home and the other which concentrated on the "heathen" abroad.[16] This is a phenomenon which is linked up closely with the industrial revolution and modernization of the countries in Europe that began exporting missionaries. This applies also to the earlier period of the European expansion when the crisis of feudalism and the rise of states had weakened the traditional nobility, providing recruits, including the founder and some founding-members, to the Society of Jesus.[17] It is in this context that I wish to explain the missionary waves that came from the Protestant as well as Catholic churches, and a mushrooming of missionary societies and religious congregations in Europe and U.S.A. particularly from late eighteenth century.[18] Unlike the earlier missionary activities dominated by men, women appeared visibly on the scene as Protestant missionary wives or as Catholic nuns, and these gradually outnumbered men. The success was great among the socially and economically underprivileged, particularly as the traditional socio-economic systems collapsed under new economic policies introduced by the colonial powers leaving the traditional masses to fend for themselves without the traditional native security and protective links.[19]

Now my hypothesis regarding the above-mentioned missionary waves, including the predominance of women: It must be agreed that women are not just bearers of children, but are also important carriers of culture. The movements were a social response of the sections of the home society in the respective countries that were losing out in the race of development, or at least saw a threat to their traditional values. We need more studies of the missionary recruitment patterns in Europe to test this hypothesis. I believe that the values which these conservative-traditional sections of the society could not defend or promote in their own countries against the home "heathen", they sought to preserve and promote among the "heathen" elsewhere in the world. It suited the home governments to sponsor such missionary zeal to reduce their nuisance value and resistance to the development at home. At the same time the bourgeoining home industry could also appreciate the usefulness of these missionaries as the first marketing agents of their wares in the colonies! Professor Boxer, the veteran historian of the Portuguese empire has written in some place that Asia was a good place to send their illegitimate children or for "outdoor" relief that would not be tolerated in the home grounds.[20] The case of the missionaries was not very different, but they were usually more motivated to assist in the needs of the empire than the "degredados" (deported prisoners and criminals) whose only motivation was the hope of getting a reduction in their deportation period, and other victims of "reluctant" colonisation. Charles Marsh, who had been in the Admiralty Court in Madras for many years and was an opponent of Wilberforce at the time of the renewal of the Charter of the English East India Company in 1813, was an eloquent spokesman for those who regarded the missionaries as "vulgar fanatics" who had succeeded in converting only the dregs of the society.[21]

The missionaries were in some sense "social rejects" of their countries, but their ability to sublimate their situation gave them generally a positive and even privileged position in their metropolitan as well as colonial set-up. Psychologically that was perhaps what they were seeking against the background of the lost social status in the home society. In the colonies it was easy to impose their superiority on the native populations. And as generally more educated and more socially-concerned agents of the colonial-imperial society, the missionaries became more effective tools for shaping the native populations and transmitting to them the Western cultural values through their Gospel package. The published correspondece of the Jesuits in the Portuguese *Estado da India* since their arrival in mid-16th century provides ample illustrations of this attitude. The letters of St. Francis Xavier,[22] and the decrees of the Church Provincial Councils[23] held in Goa from time to time from 1567 corroborate the active missionary role in alienating the native populations from their traditional cultural roots.[24] Just one little case to illustrate. It may amuse today to read the account of a Jesuit writing from Goa in 1567 describing a group of newly baptised in the village Telaulim of Goa. He was tired of dressing them and cutting their *xendys* until "they looked like people in whom the Holy Spirit could dwell" (*ja pareciam gente em que morava o Espirito Santo*)![25]

Missionary Deculturation

My second hypothesis for explaining the missionary imposition of their values calls for the consideration of the provenance of the missionaries. With the exception of those coming from the Italian city states which were cosmopolitan and where the nation-state did not develop till as late as mid-nineteenth century, elsewhere in Europe the process of the formation of nation-states was more advanced, though at different pace in different parts of Europe. West Europe had a longer common history of cultural and political growth marked by Greco-Roman and Carolingian legacy of the Holy Roman Empire.[26] The missionaries from these regions of Western Europe were as a result more conscious of their cultural superiority and less accomodating, while the Italians as represented by Ricci, De Nobili, Beschi were capable of going beyond the efforts of learning the native languages to appreciating the local cultures more positively. With these exceptions, the common run of the missionaries, including the Jesuits, saw no elements in the native culture that they could emulate, and much less consider as superior to their own culture. The native religious practices are almost always described as worship of the devil. The language used for other native customs is also usually offensive.[27]

It is often said that the missionaries were the ones who made the earliest and most effective contribution to many native languages by compiling dictionaries and composing grammars. This was not an expression of their appreciation of the language or culture. The mastery of the languages was a necessary tool for domination, specially at times when the colonial hold over the native populations was still uncertain. A clear proof of this is the dwindling interest in learning the native languages by the same religious orders who showed great interest in the earlier period by mid-18th century when the colonial control was firmly in place and the time had come to force the natives to forget their languages and learn the languages of the colonial powers. This change of attitude was already noticed in Goa from 1684.[28]

Concluding Remarks

Roland Allen, an Anglican missionary in China for many years, wrote his reflections in 1927 and they created a sensation in his Church quarters at that time. He came to the conclusion that true missionary work could be only the work of the Spirit. These reflections appeared in a book entitled *The Spontaneous Expansion of the Church* in which he questions the traditional control exercised by the West-based Church structures on the churches around the world as hardly a work of the Spirit distinct from the spirit of the West.[29]

The early Christianity experienced a "spontaneous expansion" nurtured by the irresistible attraction of the Christian life as described in the *Acts of the Apostles* of the New Testament. The spontaneous expansion is not controlled by human structures, like all great things of God that are beyond our control and "ordered" approach. The expansion of Christianity that accompanied and followed the "Discoveries" has been hardly allowed to get out of control and order as conceived in the West and regulated from the West till this day!

Instead of drawing my conclusions I wish to refer to yet another more recent and posthumous publication of someone whose dedication to the indigenous Christianity in India is beyond easy questioning. It is Cardinal Parecattil's *Syro-Malabar Liturgy as I see It* (Ernakulam, 1987). The Cardinal does not mince words when he refers to the manipulations in the *modus operandi* of the Vatican in the liturgical affairs of the Church of Kerala. He does not see Rome playing the role of an honest broker among the divergent trends in the pre-colonial Church of Kerala.[30]

NOTES AND REFERENCES

1. I. Wailerstein, *The Modern World-System*, 2 vols., Florida, Academic Press, 1974-80. Provides a good understanding of the crisis of feudalism in Europe on the eve of the Discoveries, manifested by frequent peasant revolts all over Europe. The stagnant technology of the time did not permit any further expansion of agricultural land or agricultural production. The world-system introduced by discoveries permitted appropriation of surplus through a world-market mechanism through the assistance of State machineries. The territorial expansion of Europe was theoretically a key pre-requisite to a solution for the "crisis of feudalism". Without it, Europe could well have collapsed into relative anarchy and further contraction.
2. I had an opportunity to place my hypothetical explanations before a group of historians, anthropologists and theologians at the South Asia Institute of the University of Heidelberg during a visit there as a guest-lecturer in September 1992. Cf. Also my paper entitled "Christianisation and Cultural Conflicts in Goa, 16th-19th Centuries", presented at the Congress on "Evangelisation and Meeting of Cultures" (Lisbon, May 2-5, 1992).
3. M. K. Gandhi, *Christian Missions: Their Place in India*, Ahmedabad, Navajivan Press, 1941, p. 288; M. K. Gandhi, *An Autobiography*, Ahmedabad, Navajivan Press, 1940, p. 480 and *passim*: Gandhi was disgusted with the cruelty, hypocrisy and dirt in the temples and places of pilgrimages he visited.
4. *Ibid.*, pp. 288-89; M.K. Gandhi, *An Autobiography or The Story of My Experiments with Truth*, Ahmedabad, Navajivan Press, 1940, 322-24: Gandhi describes how he learnt by heart 13 chapters of *Bhagvadgita* while brushing his teeth for 15 minutes every day in South Africa. *Gita* became for him his "infallible guide of conduct" and "dictionary of daily reference". Gandhi compared his learning from Gita with the Sermon of the Mount and could appreciate the latter. However, he confesses being bored with the Old Testament (*Ibid.*, pp. 91-92).
5. M. K. Gandhi, *Christian Missions: Their Place in India*, Ahmedabad, Navajivan Press, 1941, p. 25.
6. J. Nehru, *The Discovery of India*, London, Meridian Books Limited, 1960, pp. 337 ff. Describes Tagore and Gandhi as the two outstanding and dominating figures in the first half of the 20th century, who forced the people in some measure out of their narrow grooves of throught and made them think of

broader issues affecting humanity. Both had a world outlook, and were at the same time wholly Indian.

7. Gandhi, *Christian Missions: Their Place in India*, pp. 158-60.
8. *Ibid.*, p. 152.
9. George Soares-Prabhu, "The Jesus of Faith: A Christological Contribution to an Ecumenical Third World Spirituality" (Conference at the Third General Assembly of EATWOT, Nairobi, Jan. 5-16, 1992). Provides a critical discussion of the theme along with a useful introduction to relevant bibliography.
10. *The Documents of Vatican II*, ed. Walter M. Abbott, New York, Geoffrey Chapman Book, 1966.
11. Joseph A. Komonchak, "The Local Realization of the Church", *The Reception of Vatican II*, ed. Giuseppe Alberigo et al., Washington D.C., The Catholic University Press, 1987, pp. 77-90.
12. Komonchak, *Ibid.*
13. K.M. Panikkar, *Asia and Western Dominance*, London, George Allen & Unwin, 1953, p. 43
14. Stephen Neill, *op. cit.*, p. 252: This great age of missionary societies saw the rise of the *English Baptists* (1792), *London Missionary Society* (1795), the Anglican *Church Missionary Society* (1799), the *British and Foreign Bible Society* (1804), the American Congregational *American Board of Commissioners for Foreign Missions* (1810), the *American Baptist Missionary Board*, the German *Berlin Society*, the Swiss *Basel Mission* (1815). Denmark, France *(Missions Etrangeres)*, Sweden, Norway also followed with their societies.
15. B.B. Kling and M.N. Pearson, *The Age of Partnership: Europeans in Asia before Dominion*, Honolulu, The University Press of Hawaii, 1979, p.2.
16. P.S.E. Carson, *Soldiers of Christ: Evangelicals and India, 1704-1833* (Unpublished Dissertation for Ph.D. in History, King's College, London), p. 12.
17. G. Schurhammer, *Francis Xavier: His life, His times*, I, Rome, 1973, pp. 64-69, 156-8.
18. Stephen Neill, *A History of Christian Missions*, Middlesex; Penguin Books, 1964, pp. 249 ff.
19. Duncan B. Forrester, "The Depressed Classes and Conversion to Christianity, 1860-1960", *Religion in South Asia*, ed. G.A. Oddie, pp. 65-93.
20. C.R. Boxer, *Portuguese India in the Mid-Seventeenth Century*, Delhi, OUP, 1980, pp. 11, 39.
21. P.S.E. Carson, *op. cit.*, pp. 136-7. Marsh argued that if "every inspired cobbler, or fanatical tailor, who feels an inward call, has a kind of apostolic right to assist in the spiritual siege" there would be disastrous consequences for the British rule in India.

    The draft clause for inclusion in the Charter provided that the Board of Control should be "authorised and required to grant, from time to time, licenses to fit and proper persons to proceed and reside in India for the purpose of communicating to the inhabitants of that country the blessings of religious instruction and moral improvement" (p. 128).

    This analysis of the missionaries cannot be generalised to include some missionary societies like the Basel Mission, and a few other German and Danish groups, which came from better-off social groups. But this is explained by the nature of industrialisation in these societies, and their lack of serious colonial interests.

22. *Epistolae S. Francisci Xaverii aliaque eius scripta*, 2 vols., ed. G. Schurhammer and J. Wicki, Rome, 1944-5. He wrote both to Ignatius of Loyola as well as to Fr. Simon Rodrigues in Portugal, asking for zealous Jesuits to be sent to India, even if they were not intellectually much trained. He said that there is no need of very intellectual Jesuits for India, because "los infieles destas partes es gente muy barbara e ignorante" (II, 37).
23. Cunha Rivara, *Archivo Portuguez-Oriental*, IV, Nova Goa, 1862 (AES Reprint, New Delhi, 1992).
24. There is much published material in this connection. One may usefully refer to: *Jesuit Presence in Indian History*, ed. A. Amaladass, Anand: Gujarat Sahitya Prakash, 1988; *Jesuits in India: In historical perspective*, ed. Teotonio de Souza and Charles Borges, Macau, ICM, 1992; C. R. Boxer, *The Church Militant and Iberian Expansion, 1440-1770*, Baltimore, 1978; J. Correia-Afonso, *Jesuit Letters and Indian History*, London, OUP, 1955; A.M. Mundadan, *Sixteenth Century Traditions of St. Thomas Christians*, Bangalore, Dharmaram College, 1970; F. Houtart, *Genesis and Institutionalization of the Indian Catholicism*, Louvain-la-Neuve, 1981.
25. *Documenta Indica*, VII, ed. J. Wicki, Rome, 1962, p. 301. It was the practice to give western-style white dresses to the persons to be baptised. We are told that in the beginning some people used to turn up again for baptism in order to get another set of dress. *Xendy* was a tuft of hair grown traditionally by Hindu men on the crown of their heads, while shaving the rest of the head. *Cf.* Teotonio R. de Souza, "Xenddi Tax: A phase in the history of Luso-Hindu relations in Goa (1704-1841 A.D.)", *Studies in the Foreign Relations of India* (Sherwani Felicitation Volume), ed. P.M. Joshi and M.A. Nayeem, Hyderabad, 1975.
26. Martim de Albuquerque, *Estudos de Cultura Portuguesa*, I, Lisboa, Imprensa Nacional, 1983, pp. 163 ff.
27. *Epistolae S. Francisci Xaverii,* I, p. 165. One can find umpteen instances of such derrogatory expressions in the correspondence published in the *Documenta Indica,* 18 vols. ed. J. Wicki, Rome, 1948-88. *Cf.* also Francisco de Souza, *Oriente Conquistado a Jesus Cristo,* Porto, 1978; C.R. Boxer, *Race Relations in the Portuguese colonial empire 1415-1825,* Connecticut, Greenwood Press, 1963.
28. M. Almeida, "Jesuit Contribution to Indian Languages", *Jesuits in India : In historical perspective*, ed. Teotonio R. de Souza and Charles J. Borges, Macau, 1992, pp. 197-208; Teotonio R. de Souza, "The Portuguese in Asia and their Church Patronage", *Western Colonialism in Asia and Christianity,* ed. M.D. David, Bombay, Himalaya Publ. House, 1987, pp. 11-29; Charles J. Borges, "Foreign Jesuits and Native Resistance in Goa, 1542-1759", *Essays in Goan History*, Ed. Teotonio R. de Souza, Delhi, Concept Publ., 1989, pp. 69-80.
29. Roland Allen, *The Spontaneous Expansion of the Church,* Michigan, Grand Rapids Book, 1971.
30. Card. Parecattil, *Syro-Malabar Liturgy as I see It,* Ernakulam, 1987, pp. 61, 81 : "I pleaded that it is meaningless to attach more importance to the views of a two member committee in Rome than to those of a twenty member commission here. . . . They cited canon 195 of *Cleri sanctitati* the code of law, art. 5 and 6 referring to oriental rites and pointed out to me that it was within the competence of the Holy See to control and correct the liturgy".

3

THE DISCOVERERS VERSUS THE DISCOVERED:

Psychological Perspectives on Portuguese-Goan Prejudices in the 16th-18th Centuries

ANTHONY DA SILVA

While in some quarters the 500th anniversary of the "discovery" of the Indies may be legitimately celebrated as an event of triumph and glory, we, in India, cannot ignore the work of several Indo-Portuguese scholars who have documented carefully and amply the prejudices and oppression suffered by the "discovered".

The present paper will focus on the period of the Portuguese discovery and subsequent conquest and occupation of the Island of Goa from the 16th century. It will argue that right from the outset the entire enterprise called "discovery" could never have augured well for the discovered peoples. The discovered were doomed to be "objects" of this discovery and as such to be targets of prejudice of the powerful discoverers. After all, the kudos for these maritime enterprise always went to the Portuguese discoverers. They were feted, celebrated and rewarded by their Royalty while the discovered peoples were reduced forcibly to the status of passive bystanders in a drama of their subjugation in their own land!

The paper will seek to highlight the psychology of the discoverer as well as the discovered. It is hoped that such an analysis will enable the reader to understand the dynamics of the interaction that prevailed then between the Portuguese and the Goans. Furthermore, it will draw out the implications for the present times of this sixteenth century encounter between two cultures, Portuguese and Indian.

The paper is not meant as an indictment of the present-day Portuguese people. The Portuguese of bygone centuries were a product of their cultural times. The benefit of hindsight, however, should enable us not only to be aware of our history but to strengthen our resolve to avoid repeating the mistakes of history. It is in this spirit that the following analysis is being presented.

I. The Psychology of the Portuguese Discoverers

Firstly, one has to bear in mind that the discoverers set out from Portugal with very clear goals and a method to achieve these. Their twin goals were trade and the spread of Christianity or as some have put it more simply, "spices and souls"! Secondly, they were committed to their mission in spite of the heavy cost in terms of sufferings, sickness and even death. Psychologically, this is indicative of the very high level of motivation and the need for achievement present in these men. In a way they were extraordinary men. Thirdly, the Portuguese overgeneralized this excellence to mean frequently a cultural and religious superiority *vis-a-vis* the local people they encountered during their voyages.

I think this pervasive feeling of superiority holds the key to understanding the psychological dynamics of prejudices and other oppressive behaviour of the Portuguese who interacted with the local Goans in three different but sometimes overlapping roles: as conquerors, as traders and as Christianisers. I will analyse these roles indicating how each of these was permeated by an inherent sense of superiority. Given such a pervasive attitude one can understand why the local people were doomed from the outset of the "discoveries" and become victims of prejudice and discrimination.

(a) *The Portuguese as Conquerors*

The 16th century Portuguese conquerors were total masters of the lands and peoples they conquered. They dealt with the local people from a position of absolute supremacy both militarily and politically. For practical purpose their word was law. On the other hand, the conquered people were only burdened with duties, the principal one being one of servile obedience.

The psychology of the Portuguese conquerors was naturally that of victors. Thanks to their military victories over the local people they projected an image that implied "our victory proves our superiority over you". This air of superiority, unfortunately, did not restrict itself to military matters only, but was asserted in all spheres of the lives of the conquered peoples.

As conquerors, the Portuguese always safeguarded their own interests and the goals of their conquest. This meant very often trampling on local sensibilities and age old cultural traditions. It is reported that when Alvares Cabral's expedition suffered many casualties in the early 16th century he avenged this loss by "putting to death 600 innocent boatmen who had nothing to do with the riot and for two days bombarded the town".[1] Such inhuman actions were carefully tailored to terrorise the local people and reinforce the conquerors' image of control and superiority.

Further, in contrast to the Muslim conquerors of India, the Portuguese never seriously considered making India their home. Hence they did not care to assimilate the Indian culture, language or customs. In fact, they always remained foreigners. Their cultural distance from the greater majority of the local people served to nurture carefully the superior image they sought to project. In addition, they sought to re-create the image of Goa in the fashion of a European city complete with a kind of Baroque architecture, western clothes and the Portuguese language. Home for them was always Portugal whereas Goa remained merely a lucrative trading post for the Portuguese empire.

(b) *The Portuguese as Traders*

Military superiority gave the Portuguese an upper hand in dealing with the local traders. The former were in a position to dictate the terms of trade. In fact, in the Sixteenth century, the Portuguese were known as the "lords of commerce and navigation".[2]

It seems the early Portuguese in Goa were clearly very preoccupied about getting wealthy and making the most of their trade status. A letter from Viceroy Albuquerque to his king Dom Manuel gives us an inkling into this mentality: "I do not believe that in all Christendom there will be so rich a King as your Highness, and therefore, do I urge you, Senhor, to strenuously support this affair of India with men and arms, and strengthen your hold in her, and securely establish your dealings and your factories; and wrest the wealth of India and business form the hands of the Moors".[3]

The above quotation also indicates the intensity of the resolve of the Portuguese to pursue wealth at whatever cost and to use their military superiority to reach that goal. There seems no indication that the feelings of the local trading population were respected or the consequences of such rapacious trade assessed in terms of its impact on the local situation. Naturally, such an attitude served to reinforce the inherent attitude of superiority of the Portuguese traders *vis-a-vis* their local counterparts.

(c) *The Portuguese as Christianisers*

The dictum *cujus regio eius religio* became the hallmark of Portuguese policy in Goa. This gave momentum to the Christianization of Goa sometimes in total disregard of the local religion and traditions.

The Portuguese were convinced that they were on a divinely inspired mission. In a letter to the Zamorin of Calicut, King Emmanuel expressly mentions this conviction: ". . . because it is well to be believed that Our Lord did not permit this marvellous achievement – our navigation – merely as a means for temporal relations and temporal advantages between you and us, but also for the spiritual advantage of souls and their salvation. . . ."[4] Not infrequently, therefore the Portuguese King and the ecclesiastical authorities joined hands to bring enormous pressure on the locals to convert to Christianity. Irrespective of the controversy whether actual physical force was used in the process, there is ample documentation to show that a lot of psychological pressure was exerted and economic incentives offered to convert.[5]

Punitive laws, like the destruction of temples and idols, the indoctrination of orphans, the confiscation of Hindu lands, etc. are indicative of the conviction of the Portuguese that the Hindu religion was inferior to Christianity and that it needed to be eradicated, if possible, from the Portuguese territories. Further evidence of a similar mentality is the manner in which the Portuguese used pejorative labels to refer to the Hindus, e.g. heathen, infidels, pagans. Hence the only way out of this prejudiced situation for large sections of Hindus was to deny their religion and convert to Christianity.[6] The notorious Goa Inquisition (see Shirodkar's article in this volume) remains a glaring example of excessive paranoia of the Portuguese which in turn led them to persecute the non-Christian locals.

Ironically, there was even a lot of prejudice and discrimination practised by the Portuguese Christians against the local Goan Christians after their conversion.[7] In spite of the fact that Christianity preached a doctrine of equality and brotherhood, some of the Portuguese missionaries did not hesitate to keep themselves apart from the local Christians as well as the local priests. In fact, the locals were not considered "worthy" of the Catholic priesthood by some Portuguese.[8] Later, when some locals were permitted to be ordained to the priesthood they were discriminated against by being assigned marginal positions and that too in poorer parishes.

II. The Psychology of the "Discovered"

The psychology of the discovered is typically the reverse of the psychology of the discoverers. Whereas it was pointed out that the superiority feeling of the discoverers was an important underlaying attitude in all their dealings with the locals, likewise a deep inferiority feeling accompained by fear was a pervasive attitude among the discovered. It was an adaptive response to the Portuguese rulers; a response generated by a need for survival under a hostile, foreign power. It was not an inherent personality trait of the Goan people as was sometimes alleged by the Portuguese in their assessment of the locals.[9]

Following the model of analysis in the previous section, the psychology of the discovered will be presented along three respondent roles the locals were forced into. These roles were that of a conquered people, a captive trading people, and a Christianized people.

(a) *The Goans, a Conquered People*

Psychologically, some of the experiences that are most debilitating to the collective identity of a people are those of defeat, conquest and humiliation. The history of colonisation has always been one of violence, and dehumanisation. However, benign and noble the colonisers have claimed themselves to be, the very act of colonization is brutal and destructive. The deep psychic wounds it causes to the identity of a people remain raw and unhealed for centuries. The present day convulsions of violence between Hindus and Muslims in India is a case in point. Almost ten centuries later, we are not able to lay to rest the feelings of mutual hatred and suspicion that were a by product of the invasion of India by the Mughals. The experience of the colonised peoples of Goa must not have been different at the time.

Since the colonised had to learn to live according to the rules drawn up by the Portuguese colonisers, they had of necessity to develop psychological coping mechanisms. The more common coping mechanism was that of submissiveness. This enabled the local population to avoid conflicts and tensions with the Portuguese. Such an environment of "peace" also helped the local population to pursue their daily lives without serious disruptions. In addition, the feelings and the image of superiority projected by the colonisers triggered a pattern of servile behaviours in the local people. It seems the mere projection of a superior image by the colonisers became a reality for the colonised. In other words, the perception of the colonised got so distorted that they accepted reality the way the colonizers defined it. That it took the Goans over 400 years to finally overthrow the yoke of colonialism is indicative of how deeply entrenched this servile, inferior mentality had become.

An accompanying emotion that became most dominant in the wounded psyche of the colonised was fear. It emanated from a basic biological need, namely, the need to survive. The absolute power of the coloniser, whose single word could spell death and destruction hung like a Damoclean sword over the colonised. Being aware of this dynamic, the colonisers did not shy away from using all sorts of terror tactics to keep their populations in line. One can well imagine the kind of psychological damage this must have done to a people who lived under such continuous stress and constraints for decades and centuries. A constant feeling of insecurity, lack of self-esteem and a general climate of lack of freedom are some of the psychological realities that went into the building of a colonised consciousness among the Goan people.

(b) *The Goans, a Captive Trading People*

To begin with, any trade carried on from an unequal status puts such a person at a distinct disadvantage in commercial transactions. Such was the case of the Goan traders who had to frequently carry on their business under colonial constraints.

In addition to the colonial constraints were also tensions between

Christian and Hindu Goans who had trade links with the Portuguese. Although many laws favoured the Christians economically, the Hindus seem to be have been preferred as trading partners. The Viceroy in 1738 states in a letter, "In matters of commerce the Christians cannot have the same means as the Hindus, since the main commerce of this land is wholly dominated by the Hindus".[10] No doubt such a situation must have caused the Christian traders to feel insecure and inferior in their transactions both with the Portuguese as well as the local Hindus.

(c) *The Goans, a Christianized People*

Although becoming Christians brought benefits on several fronts from the Portuguese, nevertheless, equality between the Goans and the Portuguese remained elusive. In fact, the Portuguese were concerned lest, thanks to Christianity, such equality be demanded by the locals. Hence a reminder from the king in 1718 to the Viceroy, "Greatest care should be taken to see that the Canarins (Indian Christians) were not given preference over or equalised with the Portuguese in any manner as this is necessary in the interests of my service and authority and respect of the nation".[11] It seems that almost 200 years after the Christianising of Goa, the locals continued to experience prejudice and discrimination. The image of superiority projected by the Portuguese seems to have been accepted submissively by the local Christians. With a few exceptions (Bishop Mateus de Castro and some other Goan Christians) we do not hear of protests and demands for justice and equality.

Interestingly, although the Goan Christians would not quarrel about their status with the Portuguese, they were not averse to maintaining caste distinctions among themselves. They had separate *Confrarias* (Church confraternities) in order to perpetuate the caste hierarchy. In some situations there were ongoing dissensions between the Brahmin and Chardo Christians about their pre-eminence in Church circles. It almost would seem that the aggression that was repressed in encounters with the Portuguese was more freely expressed against fellow locals. In a way this suited the Portuguese very well. Their own superior status *vis-a-vis* the Goan Christians was undisputed. On the other hand the inter-caste squabbles would leave the locals very little ego strength or self-esteem to challenge the status of the Portuguese.

In spite of the status discrimination between the Goan Christians and the Portuguese, the Portuguese tried to make sure that the Goan Christians would remain culturally closer to them than the Hindus. Given the passive and submissive psychology adopted by the local Christians, it was not too difficult for the missionaries to get them to break away from from several socio-cultural practices that pre-dated their conversion. As Mascarenhas states in her article, "After conversion Goan Christians were expected to make a clean break with their Hindus past. Not only were the personal names changed, but food habits, social customs, and even dress had to conform to the way of living of European Christians".[12]

The fact that such drastic social changes could be pursued with impunity is indicative of the fear that must have gripped the new Christians. In fact, with the Goan Inquisition breathing down their necks, the Goan Christians could not have been left with too many alternatives. With their former identity annihilated and the new identity in its infantile stage, the Goan Christians must have experienced severe feeling of self-rejection as well as rejection from their erstwhile Hindu community. To be robbed of one's culture and traditions and forced to adopt new and strange cultural ways is the ultimate assault on one's psyche and identity. It is, therefore, not surprising that some of Goan converts would revert clandestinely to their former socio-religious customs only to be terrorised by Church authorities. One can surmise that thousands must have come out of this conversion experience with deeply wounded psyches and a host of associated personality problems.

III. Some Psychological Consequences of the Encounter

Having examined the underlying psychological dynamics of this historical encounter between two cultures, I would like to reflect on some of its consequences. It is hoped that these will make us sensitive to similar encounters between cultures in our country and worldwide, today.

1. The analysis indicates that an encounter based on an unequal status is almost certainly doomed to cause tensions, social disruptions and even violence. Should one of the cultures in an encounter consider itself somehow superior, its whole relationship tends to get vitiated by prejudices and an air of arrogance. May

be that is why, in the history of colonialism, the larger masses of the colonised people perceived the colonisers in the most negative light. This has often surprised colonisers who have mistakenly perceived themselves as doing good and bringing "civilisation" to the colonised. So, even if good was intended it was mostly perceived as a sinister design by the colonised.

2. Simply annihilating socio-cultural traditions or showing callous regard for another culture, however alien, is the best prescription for sowing seeds of long-term hatred and violence against the "discoverer" or more aptly the "intruder". Forcibly eradicating local religio-cultural values and traditions and supplanting them with foreign ones is tantamount to an assault on the very lifeline that psychologically sustains a society. Such a "new" society will always remain psychologically weak because it is not fully rooted in the local soil. It is merely a "carbon copy", replica of the colonisers. Consequently it is neither held in esteem by the parent society from which it had to break away nor by the new society to which it seeks affiliation. Such I believe has been the sorry plight of the Goan Christian community in India.
3. The Portuguese discoverers in their zeal to propagate what they believed was the only and true religion had shut themselves from the outset from any possible dialogue or appreciation for what they had discovered. They, in a way, became the victims of their own mind-set which led them to believe that they were superior in every aspect of life and had nothing to learn from the discovered peoples. In our times now, such tunnel-like vision is likely to alienate one from a world so culturally rich and complex. This was an error of the discoverers that we are challenged to guard against today. Tolerance and respect are the factors that enable cultures to interact and discoverers and discovered to work in partnership.
4. With the virus of communal violence gnawing at the very soul of our nation during these times, the above analysis focuses on the need to constantly evaluate one's attitudes toward one's own and others' religion. Since cultures are closely associated with religions, religious prejudices and bigotry tend to get perpetuated under the guise of upholding cultural values. Multi-religious India presents us with the unique opportunity to break out of our own small worlds and truly discover other religions and cultures. The alternative could be self-destructive, where

consciously or unconsciously we become agents of communal violence and bigotry.

NOTES AND REFERENCES

1. D'Souza, B.G., *Goan Society in Transition*, Bombay, 1975, p. 86.
2. Souza, T.R. de, *Medieval Goa*, Concept Publishing, New Delhi, 1979, p. 24.
3. Wolpert, Stanley, *A New History of India*, Oxford University Press, New York, 1982, p. 137.
4. de Melo, Carlos M., *The Recruitment and Formation of the Native Clergy in India*, Lisbon, 1955, p. 11.
5. Priolkar, A.K., *The Goa Inquisition*, Bombay, 1961.
6. *Ibid.*, p. 114ff.
7. *Ibid.*, pp. 143-144.
8. Mascarenhas, Mira, "The Church in the Eighteenth Century" in *Essays in Goan History*, ed. by Teotonio R. de Souza, New Delhi, 1989, pp. 83-84.
9. de Melo, Carlos, *op.cit.*, pp. 244-245.
10. Priolkar, A.K., *op cit.*, p. 139.
11. *Ibid.*, p. 143.
12. Mascarenhas, M. "The Church in the Eighteenth Century" in *Essays in Goan History*, p. 84.

4

DISCOVER TO CONQUER:
Towards a Sociology of Conversion

WILLIAM R. DA SILVA and ROWENA ROBINSON

Medieval Mind in Discovery and Conquest

This paper, firstly, places conversion within the historical context of European discoveries and missionary activity in Asia and also in Africa and America. In the following section of the paper, an attempt is made to define conversion as a sociological concept. Conversion of religious systems is delimited as the object of our analysis and the term is distinguished from concepts similar to it, such as proselytism. The last section focuses on mechanisms of conversion through an analysis of the specific historical case of the Portuguese conquest of Goa.

It is appropriate to begin by locating the subject that we have chosen for our discussion, conversion, within the context of the theme of this seminar – Discoveries, Missionary Expansion and Asian Cultures. In doing so, we find that the formulation of our thesis on conversion leads us to initiate an understanding of at least two more significant terms that emerge in the field of discourse: discovery and conquest.

In the discovery and conquest of American, African and also, Asian cultures could be seen the confrontation of the world of the European, the conqueror, the missionary with the world of the conquered, the missionary field, the 'other' of historical and anthropological discourse. The world in which the European was steeped in when he set out on the sea-routes that led to the discovery of these other cultures was a feudal world in which the dominant meaning-framework was provided by religion, Christianity. Religion constructs man's place in the universe and his relationship to nature and society in terms of a divine or supra-social reality. In this period, religion was the dominant force and politics, kinship and economics found their place in relation to it. The linkage between politics and religion may be brought out by the ready slogan – 'the search for Christians and Spices'. Spices, here, or pepper may be taken as a term representative of the entire nexus of political and economic linkages, ties and alliances made by the Europeans with merchants and local rulers. As we have already noted, the search for spices and the opening up of new routes led to the discovery of new, hitherto unknown cultures. These 'others' had, necessarily, to be understood in order to be coopted within trade dealings and political ventures. This understanding, inevitably, took place in accordance with models provided by the dominant symbolic framework which was that rendered by Christianity. Christian Europe's own historical experience had given it a model of dealing with the 'other'. Emperor Constantine had transformed the cross into a militant, conquering symbol and the potential of this symbol was most forcefully realized in the battles of the Crusades, those relentless wars waged against the enemies of Christianity, the 'unbelievers', the Moors. Again, Europe had an internal experience of conversion. Early Christianity emerged from Judaism and Roman paganism, creating allies by conversion in order to generate a community. In this early phase, Christianity emerged as a sect breaking with an established religious tradition, Judaism. Persuasive methods and preaching were, thus, used to create allies. The later experience of the spread of Christianity shows that while it did not altogether reject the methods of persuasion and preaching, it was transformed by the new symbol of the militant cross. We know that the conversion of Europe was part of this experience of the spread of Christianity. The Roman Empire became Christian, officially, in the 4th century and the pages of history, thereafter, record the battles for the conversion of Europe with figures such as Charlemagne emerging as emperors who conquered with the cross. In this phase of Christianity and that viewed in the Crusades, the dominant image that emerges is that of 'Christ the Conqueror'.

Early discoverers, the Portuguese used the word 'conquista' to describe the nature of their overseas undertakings. Their struggle against the Moors, their main commercial rivals, was conducted in the name of religion. Defining themselves as believers in the one true God, the Portuguese could mark themselves off from the Indians, as well, who were pagans and idolators. In other words, in the age of discoveries, the European answer to the question of how to deal with the unknown 'other', the newly found cultures of Africa, America and, in particular, Asia which is of specific concern to us here was 'conquer and convert'. In the final part of this paper, we will analyse one specific instance of the working out of this spirit of conquest – the conversion of Goa by the Portuguese. In the following section, we shall try to develop a sociological understanding of the term conversion.

Understanding conversion

In defining conversion sociologically, we face something of the problem that Durkheim had in isolating suicide as a social fact on account of the emotionalism that surrounds the issue. In the course of fieldwork enquiry, it has been found that the violence that accompanied the conversion of Goa is viewed as an "unfortunate occurrence" which is now buried in the past and should not now be raised again for fear of rousing emotions. Such an attitude inhibits free inquiry into the subject. In this paper, we shall attempt a rationalized discussion of the phenomenon of conversion.

In initiating that discussion, let us first come to terms with the variety of contexts in which the word conversion finds usage. In chemistry or physics, it refers to the change of a particular composition or form of energy into another form. We speak of the conversion of weights and measures, the conversion of currency, the conversion of matters from one form to another. In all these usages, the term implies a turning, a change in an element from what it was into something else. In this paper we shall isolate for analysis the phenomenon of religious conversion. Religious conversion shall be defined as a change from one belief system to another.

Having selected religious conversion as the subject of our sociological inquiry, let us attempt to understand what Durkheim meant when he defined 'generality' as an essential component of a social fact. In the common understanding, conversion is usually associated only with religions such as Christianity and Islam that are known to have a history of engagement in bloody battles of religion. These religions are seen to possess an inherent tendency towards conversion: their leaders and prophets called upon their followers to make converts. A necessary step towards the sociological understanding of conversion will have been taken when we realize that conversion is a more general phenomenon. Other religions besides Christianity and Islam converted. Buddhism arose in 500 B.C. in the

North Gangetic valley when groups of wandering monks were formed by conversion from the existing Hindu groups. The formation of Hindu sects involves an act of conversion. Even the *shuddhi* movement started by the Arya Samajis in various parts of the country to re-convert groups who had broken away is a converting movement. The Hindu who has broken away and joined Christianity or some faith is converted back by aligning him with a specific group, making him Arya Samaji, not merely leaving him with an uncertain adherence to an amorphous set of beliefs lumped together as Hinduism. Thus, conversion is a general phenomenon rather than one unique to a particular religious tradition. Establishing the generality of conversion permits us to pose questions regarding the causes, consequences and mechanisms that this sociological phenomenon adopts in a specific historical instance.

Having touched upon the sociological issue of generality, let us distinguish our definition of conversion from terms that are often viewed as similar to it. Conversion and proselytism are two terms that are often used indistinguishably by writers. For example, in his book on the Goa Inquisition, Priolkar uses the two terms interchangeably. They do have something in common, in that they both imply a change from one belief system to another. However, we may make here a fine distinction between them. The term proselytism will refer to the impact made by the leader of a converting group upon his immediate family, his disciples, the small group which surrounds him, believes in him and surrenders to his teachings. Conversion, on the other hand, will refer to the changes that occurs when the agents of conversion use certain mechanisms such as preaching, exhortation or extraordinary acts to change the belief system of the people to the one he espouses. It is this phenomenon that we are dealing with here.

Let us now clarify what is specifically sociological about our approach. When we confront the issue of conversion, we find, always, the presence of two groups each with its own belief system – the converting group and the group to be converted. When an entire social group changes its religion, voluntaristic explanations of the phenomenon prove inadequate, because this societal transformation requires a sociological understanding of the conditions under which it emerged. Further, that sociological explanation will not focus only on the religious aspect but will attempt to place religion in the total life of the group. We must, therefore, ascertain when a group becomes available for conversion and, also, what kind of groups set out to convert.

We had said earlier that religion provides societies with a meaning-framework in terms of which their relationships to the universe, to nature and their social relationships are constructed. Thus, a change in religion or beliefs involves a change in the entire social life of the group and the manner in which it organizes and reproduces its means of production and itself around those means. Durkheim demonstrated the change in the system of symbols and bonds of solidarity holding people together that is involved in the shift from a simple society based on kinship and age hierarchy to a complex one with a more complicated system of the division of labour. In other words, the moment for change is ripe when the old religious system is no longer able to render meaningful a new social situation. This may happen as in the case of certain tribes in India, their kinship-based system already weakened by a new feudal element, who adopt the Christianity brought by foreign missionaries under colonialism. It may be brought about by an external converting agent as in the case above or in the case of the Portuguese conquest of Goa. Or it may be a result of breaking away from within as in the case of the European middle classes who, emancipating themselves from feudal relationships and the grip of feudal Catholicism, found in Protestantism the appropriate expression of their new social impulses. The same occurred with the Buddha, whose message was first heard by the groups who found themselves disprivileged in the prevailing Hindu caste hierarchy.

We can now go on to ask: What societies set out to convert. Among precapitalist social formations, we may distinguish the lineage-based tribal societies, tributary societies where each caste or community retains its autonomy while paying a tribute to a central leader and feudal society where the surplus is appropriated by a privileged class of persons under a central ruler. Capitalist society does not appear to require religion in order to construct its relations of production symbolically. In the colonized societies, capitalist forces merely use the already existing traditional structures to skim off a share of the profits though they may operate in ways that tend to destroy these structures as well. Religion, however, plays no more than a 'civilizing' role, providing some social and cultural services. Among precapitalist societies, too, the kinship-based tribal societies do not set out to convert; rather incorporate strangers in terms of kinship constructions. A tributary society permits the autonomy of various groups with their own religion and practices. In feudal society, however, religion defines the symbolic field. Political cohesiveness is a function of incorporation into the religious body. This is clearly demonstrated in the Portuguese conversion of Goa.

In the last paragraphs we have attempted to understand the social conditions under which entire social groups change their religion. Two areas remain unexamined. Firstly, we must ask under what conditions violence becomes a means of conversion. Secondly, we would like to address ourselves to the ideological basis of conversion which we had touched upon earlier when speaking of Europe's confrontation with the 'other'.

Let us take up the first question. We had mentioned earlier how the early Christian 'sect' arose from within the existing Roman-Jewish society, teaching and appealing to disprivileged groups. Buddhism, too, we noted, arose in the Ganges valley making many converts among the non-Brahmins, in the Vedic-centred society of the time. These conversions were, at least in the early period non-violent. Preaching and persuasive means have already been cited as the methods used. The early Buddhists did not advocate violence themselves, but were subject to attack by the Brahmins who saw them as a threat to their own power and labelled them as heretics. In its early period, Islam preached tolerance and non-violence, but with the acquisition of power took to a different path. We saw how the cross, transformed into a militant symbol, accompanied Europe in its long history of religious conquest. It may be possible, then, to argue that the formation of a sect involves a small group breaking off from a larger one and having to establish itself in a largely hostile environment. At this time, a discourse of a particular kind is adopted which is that which speaks of tolerance and peace. With the acquisition of power, a group becomes a dominant force and often chooses violence as a means to gain its aims. This may be historically established and the 'ethnic purges' we witness occuring in the course of history may also be understood from this perspective.

Before we analyse the mechanisms of conversion used by the Portuguese in Goa, let us focus on the ideological stance of a religion that sets out to convert. Conversion requires the identification of the self in terms of religion. The 'other', therefore, is conceptualised as perverted in relation to the self, the enemies' of one's religion, the pagans, the heretices, the 'unbelievers'. It is this conceptualisation that leads to the emergence of a legitimating ideology that justifies the destruction of the other in order to render it more like the self. Throughout history, we have seen the construction of labels such as – Christian and Pagan, Christian and Moor, Muslim and Infidel and, even, Aryan and Dasa. Regarding the 'other' group as a perversion of the self necessitates its constant purging in order to render it purer. We have already pointed out how this ideology informed feudal Portugal's encounter with the 'other'. In fact, throughout its history in Goa, the Church, established by the Portuguese, has found occasion to decry the 'pagan' and 'irreverent' customs of the land such as celebrating feasts with fireworks, visiting the 'dishtikaan' to remove evil spirits or celebrating the carnival. All complex religious systems appear to entail this dualistic vision of the world which engenders conversion except, perhaps, tribal religions which do not convert but seem to incorporate the 'other' in kinship terms. In the following section, we examine some of the methods used by the Portuguese in their conversion of Goa.

Conversions by Feudal Portugal

Missionary activity under the Portuguese functioned within the system of the Padroado and was closely linked with the establishment of Portuguese military and political rule in an area. The Portuguese king functioned as the Grand Master of the Order of Christ and a series of papal bulls granted him the authority to conquer, convert and administer pagan territories, thus, investing Portuguese conquest with divine significance. The Portuguese went out as traders but required for the protection of their trade interests, the establishment of permanent support structures overseas for their fleets and men. This involved political rule and the need to gain the support of the local population. Since the Portuguese defined themselves, primarily, in religious terms, their mechanism for ensuring local support and incorporating the locals in their political body was conversion to their own religion, Catholicism. Thus, conversion had its social function in creating allies. From the first, therefore, the Portuguese granted a series of privileges to those who converted and denied them to those who did not, thus, assimilating the converts into their own population and separating them from the Hindus.

The Portuguese took over their initial territories in Goa from the Muslims to whom the local population were to pay a tribute for protection. Village life and organization was, however, largely untouched by the central rulers. The villages were organized around the cultivation of land and the recourse to Hindu dieties ensured a symbolic mastery over the forces of nature. Each village had its *rakhno,* the village deity. Nevertheless, each lineage also had its kul-deva and a variety of other deities could be invoked when occasion arose. Kinship was binding force of the lineages and clans but external relations between various lineages within the village were organized by hierarchies of caste. Each caste had its specific occupation – the mahar, the chamar, the carpenter, the blacksmith, the fisherman and others. Their occupations ensured them a share in the produce of the land but ranged them along a hierarchy of purity and impurity. The fear of pollution by the lower castes ensured that interdining and intermarriages were not permissible. Services could be exchanged at certain levels but not food or women.

The Portuguese used many measures to align the local population on their side. One of the methods was the taking over of orphans. Girls below the age of 12 and boys under 14 whose fathers were dead had to be entrusted to the care of Christian guardians. These orphans who received a Christian upbringing and Portuguese education were easily incorporated in the service of the Portuguese. The privileges granted by the Portuguese brought about other mass conversions. More pertinently, however, the system of disprivileges was important here. The Portuguese prevented any non-Catholic religious places from existing in their territory. The systematic destruction of temples in the areas under their rule, polluting temple wells, breaking temple images ('idols') and preventing Hindu forms of celebration were another means used to block the continuation of Hindu worship and, hence, make available social groups (often entire villages) who turned to Catholicism in order to reconstruct their socio-symbolic life organized around village life and centred in the new place of worship. We have only to look at the conversion of Divar, Chorão or Moira to confirm this.

Food for Conversion

A third means used by the Portuguese was one which they rendered people outcastes in relation to their own society, thus, making them turn to Catholicism. The need to be brief has restrained us from expanding upon each method of conversion. However, the use of the symbolism of food as a means of outcasting the Hindu from his own society is quite interesting and we shall, therefore, look at it a little more closely.

We may recount the story first. Two Hindu women were going to the city in the isle of Goa to buy rice. One of them had brought along her son who grew tired with the walk. His mother asked her companion if she would sit with him while she went ahead to get rice for them both. The woman who remained had few scruples. She went up to the door of the house where they were seated and asked the lady who answered whether she wished to buy the child, settling the price with her. The lady of the house who was the sister of one of the Jesuits, asked if she had no compassion in selling her in this manner. At this, the woman got worried and saying that she would return to collect the agreed amount, left. The woman of the house asked the child if he desired to become a Christian. He said yes and in order to confirm it, she gave him a piece of beef to eat which meat is hated by the Hindus who lose their caste if they eat it. The boy's mother returned to find neither her son nor her companion. She heard her son's voice from inside the house and understood what had happened. She went to Fr. d'Almeida in tears and told him that she wanted to become a Christian because her son had eaten beef and already become one. (J.Wicki,IV: 345-6)

For the Portuguese the sharing of food, as of the Eucharist, was a means of incorporating persons into the body of Christ. They clearly understood, however, that eating food with 'outsiders' defiled the Hindu. As Provincial Quadros wrote to the King of Portugal (D'Costa, 1965: 87-88): " . . . among other ceremonies which the devil taught this people, there is one according to which they can in no way either eat in our company or of our food. For if they eat anything we give them, they immediately lose their Hindu nature, so that eating from our hand is with them what the sin against the Holy Ghost or final impenitence is with us. For those who eat from our hand cannot be Hindus any more nor mix with Hindus nor Hindus with them".

The Portuguese, thus, incorporated the Hindus by first rendering them outcastes, excluding them from their caste and their law. The woman requested conversion not from a desire to share with her son in the brotherhood of Christ but from the feeling that if her son has lost his caste she may as well convert with him since there is nothing left for her.

Our analysis has shown that the Portuguese mechanism of conversion utilized the symbols of the culture available to them, the culture which they wished to replace. The attempt to understand these mechanisms of symbolic transformation sociologically enables us to get away from vague accounts of the 'force', 'compulsion' or 'threats' used to make converts. And, further, it becomes possible for us to place the specific historical instance of the Portuguese conquest of Goa within the context of a sociology of conversion, the steps towards the establishment of which have been initiated with this paper.

REFERENCES

Baden-Powell, B.H., "The Villages of Goa in the Early Sixteenth century", *Journal of the Royal Asiatic Society of Great Britain and Ireland*, 1900, pp. 261-91.

Boxer, C.R., *The Portuguese Seaborne Empire, 1415-1825*, Penguin, Middlesex, 1973.

Correia-Afonso, J., ed. *Indo-Portuguese History: Sources and Problems*, Oxford University Press, Bombay, 1981.

Danvers, F. C., *The Portuguese in India*, 2 vols., London, 1894.

D'Costa, A., *The Christinization of the Goa Islands*, Bombay, 1965.

De Souza, T.R., ed. *Medieval Goa: A Socio-Economic History*, Concept Publishing Company, New Delhi, 1979.

Durkheim, E., *Elementary Forms of the Religious Life*, London, 1976.

Gazetteer of India — Union Territory of Goa, Daman and Diu, District Gazetteer Part I — Goa, Panaji, 1979.

Houtart, F., and G. Lemercinier, *Genesis and Institutionalization of the Indian Catholicism*, Universite Catholique de Louvain, 1981.

Pearson, M.N., *The Portuguese in India*, Cambridge University Press, 1987.

Priolkar, A.K., *The Goa Inquisition*, Bombay, 1961.

Whiteway, R.S., *The Rise of Portuguese Power in India, 1497-1550*, London, 1899.

Wicki, J., *Documenta Indica*, Vols. 1-4, Rome, 1940-1962.

5

THE GENESIS OF PORTUGUESE DISCOVERIES AND THEIR INFLUENCE ON INDIAN CULTURE

BAILON DE SÁ

Varying Views

The Portuguese discoveries in the East had a specific purpose in the material and spiritual order. Hence, it would be enlightening to study the background that led to them. One could ask whether the Portuguese discoveries were the result of mere cosmographical curiosity or were motivated by economic necessity or missionary zeal, or whether there was the 'politics of secrecy' behind it all? They did however, all contribute in a greater or lesser degree.

Nautical science in Portugal, towards the end of the fifteen century was dominated by the great figures of Duarte Pacheco and Prince Henry the Navigator. Pacheco was deeply interested in cosmography, while Henry was the *homo economicus*. The former had calculated the value of a terrestial degree to be about 170 kilometres, while Christopher Columbus found it to have the value of 84 kilometres. This disparity led the latter to believe that the Lesser Antilles was a part of India. King John II basing himself on Bartolomeu Dias who had proved that the Atlantic was joined to the Indian Ocean over the Cape of Good Hope, and had indicated the route to India, declined, without giving any reasons, to finance Columbus for a nautical exploration to India. Here begins the politics of secrecy. Prince Henry, on the other hand, was a practical man and used the knowledge garnered by the Portuguese cosmographers for his politics of expansion.

Jaime Cortesão while summing up the achievements of prince Henry believes that through him and for the first time the thought of the exploration of the planet became the plan of a nation. He infused it with method and it took the shape of an organic and scientific character. The winds and ocean currents were studied. The caravel was created. Fresh efforts were made in the navigational art to observe through astronomical means the latitudes of the earth. Cartography was modernised. But above all he lit up in Portugal the spirit of discovery, transmitting to a whole people his own fire. He concentrated in his hands the strength of the whole Christianity, to mould a new man, eager for the universe. The greatest merit of the Prince lay in having shaped this new man, the man of the Renaissance"[1]

The rivalry between the Catholic kings (Aragon and Castille) and Portugal over thē discoveries that promised them wealth and a better living, snarled up their relations. The Portuguese, thanks to the calculations of Pacheco and the discovery of Dias, had the card up their sleeves, while the Spanish had only the faulty computations of Columbus based on the ptolomaic astronomy. To settle the issue they drew up the treaty of Alcacovas in 1479. This put an end to the dispute over the Canary Islands between Portugal and the King of Castille. The treaty settled that the king of Portugal should own Guinea and the Cape Bojadar, *usque ad Indos* (till the land of the Indians) with all the adjacent seas and the coasts discovered and to be discovered, as also the islands of Madeira, Azores, Flores, Cabo Verde and the kingdom of Fez. To the king of Castille and his successors were given the Canary Islands and Granada.

However, the dispute over the proper demarcation of the meridian that would divide the route to India continued. To put an end to this the treaty of Tordesilhas was drawn up in 1494, stipulating that a line be drawn from pole to pole at a distance of 370 leagues (a league is about 3 miles) west of Cape Verde and all that was discovered or would be discovered to the east of this line would belong to Portugal, and to the west of the line to Castille. However, it had a time and space frame, as it could happen that the ships of the Catholic kings would discover islands and other lands within the agreed limit. All such lands discovered by the Spanish ships within the first 250 leagues of the 370 to the west of Cape Verde would belong to Portugal, but all those that would be found within the stipulated time and of the 120 remaining leagues would belong to Spain.

John II, the real instigator of the Portuguese maritime adventure, had in mind at the time of signing the treaty the monopoly of the commercial traffic of the East, in particular the spice trade. It is not difficult to imagine that the king would have thought of the division of the opposite hemisphere, which from his knowledge of the Arab charts brought by Pero de Covilhã, contained the Moluccas and other islands in the Indian Ocean which were known to have rare and expensive spices.

At the celebration of the treaty, the kings of Spain and of Portugal were very satisfied with themselves. Why? The former because they were convinced that they were now in possession of the shortest route to India, while the latter were sure that they would very soon complete the real discovery. On Vasco da Gama's return in 1498 from India, the Spanish kings realised that they had been duped!

Complicated as were the conditions embodied in the treaty, much more were the reasons that lay at the basis of the Portuguese expansion. They were the geographical situation of the territory, imbalance between the demographic evolution and internal resources, maritime experience of those who lived in the littoral, the existence of advanced nautical science, the rise of the middle-class and the growing need of wheat and gold, class ideology (mercantile spirit of the middle-class, cavalier spirit of the nobility, adventurous spirit of the people, the cruzading spirit of the clergy and of the kings) and personal influence particularly of Prince Henry the Navigator.[2]

Modern Portuguese historians like Antonio Sergio, Jaime Cortesão and Magalhães Godinho, have each their own opinion. Sérgio gives greater prominence to what he considers one of the causes of Portuguese expansion, namely, the crisis of subsistence in Portugal in the fifteenth century, the crisis for which the granary of Morocco furnished immediate solution. Simultaneous with this regional crisis, there was the European crisis, European economy threatened by the Turkish triumphs in the Levant, in which the Muslims would replace a civilisation accommodatingly mercantile by one that was belligerent, perhaps intolerably belligerent, thus upsetting the balance and breaking commercial contacts with India. He stresses the fact that in the fifteenth century, Portugal was in the hands of the commercial and maritime middle-class. To the Portuguese the instability of the commercial economy in Europe was the most sensitive aspect of its relations with India. Influenced by Oliveira Martins, Sérgio was carried away by the former's linearly economic interpretation and discarded the aspect of religious fervour that was one of the stimuli for the expansionist activity of the Portuguese in Africa and the East.

Cortesão on the other hand, found it difficult to dissociate, in his attempt to explain the Portuguese expansion, the economic motive, from the religious. If the maritime and mercantile aspect that the European economy including the Portuguese took, forced Europe to confront the other civilization, maritime and mercantile like that of the Arabs, who were since long intent on the exploration of the same gold and the same oriental spices now sought after by the Europeans, it also favoured the conflict between the two civilizations thanks to the theological hatred that divided the Christian from the Muslim. Among the Christians the group which was militantly expansionist was the Franciscan.[3]

Godinho, however, notes that Cortesão has changed his interpretation of Portuguese expansion and emphasizes the religious factor as the real stimulus of the discoveries. For him the 'decisive diagnosis of the cause' has three aspects – sociological, physiological and logical. The convergence of the needs of the territorial expansion of the nobility, and of the conquests of markets of the middle-class, concurrently with the search for cereals, cloth, gold, chillies, slaves from Guinea, spices, precious stones, rare and aromatic timbers from India, and the strategic position of Morocco. To the Order of Christ belongs the initiative of Portuguses discoveries, not due to religious fervour (excepting in the case of Prince Henry) but primarily to materialistic aims.[4]

Mixed Motivations

Another motive that instigated the expansion was the quest for Prester John. The aim of king John II was both religious and commercial. It would beat the Muslims from behind and obtain the powerful support of Prester John. He could thus divert to Lisbon the commercial current from which the Turks and the Venetians made their fortune. The strategy was two-pronged: to contact Prester John by land and by sea, the latter being less chancy.[5] He abandoned the coastal navigation and utilized the regular winds and sea-currents. This led to the rounding of the Cape of Good Hope by Dias and the opening up the sea-route to India.

One cannot overlook, as Prof. Boxer reminds us, the relative internal and political stability in Portugal, while other countries like Spain and Western Europe were embroiled in internecine quarrels and were settling their problems. He believed that the four main motives which inspired the Portuguese leaders were the crusading zeal against Muslims, the desire for Guinea gold, the quest for Prester John, and the search for spices.[6] The motives that led the Portuguese to conquer Ceuta have usually been explained as being aimed at striking the Muslims and breaking the stronghold that commanded the trade route. Yet an alternative explanation could be that it was inspired by economic and strategic motives. The Portuguese were desperately in need of cereals and they thought that Ceuta would provide their need while unaware that the Muslims imported them from elsewhere.

Though 1415, the year Ceuta was conquered, is considered the year the maritime Portuguese expansion began, yet seafaring explorations had been on before that date, yet after 1415 marine activities assumed real significance in Portuguese history. H.G. Wells mentions that all over Europe in the fifteenth century merchants and sailors were speculating about new ways to the East. The Portuguese, unaware that Pharaoh Necho had solved the problem ages ago, were asking whether it was not possible to go round to India by the coast of Africa. Their ships followed (1446) in the course that Hanno took to Cape Verde. They put out to sea to the west and found the Canary Isles, Madeira and the Azores. That was a fairly long stride across the Atlantic. In these maritime adventures in the eastern Atlantic and on the west African coast the Portuguese were preceded in the thirteenth, fourteenth, and early fifteenth centuries by Normans, Catalonians, and Genoese. But in the fourteenth and fifteenth centuries their activities rose to pre-eminence, and it is they, at any rate, who fixed and established discoveries that hitherto had been mere vague and incidental visits. They were the pioneers of nautical astronomy. The Portuguese were already working their way to the east before the Spanish went west.[7]

For Cortesão the word *descobrimento* (discovery) contained all the reasons that led to the Portuguese expansion in the fifteenth century. He believes that *discovery* is linked with the concept of the revealed secret. What Vasco da Gama did was to discover the great secret of the efforts of prince Henry and of King John II. The secret that involved astronomical science and one of its most significant results, namely, the verification of approximate value of the degree, the secret that increased the co-ordinates and distorted the contour of southern Africa, the secret that hid even from the chroniclers the two joint voyages of Bartolomeu Dias and Pero de Convilhã, the secret that was the key of the treaty of Tordesilhas and which hushed up entirely the exploration of the Mozambique Canal in 1495 and the experimental voyages in southern Atlantic, a secret finally revealed in 1498. The world learnt with surprise of the great objective of more than half a century of sailings. The significance of *discovery* was at last revealed in its plenitude.[8]

On 20th May 1498, the day Vasco da Gama reached Calicut, was the day when two civilizations met, one ancient, the other Christian and comparatively new, the one peaceful and content with itself, and the other fired with a consuming zeal for proselytization. Three armadas came in 1503 one of which was captained by Afonso de Albuquerque. He was to follow in 1509 D. Francisco de Almeida, the first Viceroy of India, and one who followed a strictly commercial policy.

With Albuquerque began the first real encounter between the two cultures, though he was mainly interested in the material aspect of conquests. He had very clear ideas of his mission in the East. Briefly, they were to destory the Muslim power and lay lasting foundations of a strong empire. He gave immediate proof of the first objective. On 25th November, 1510 he ordered all Muslims who were found inside the city to be killed. Subsequently he set about building fortresses in Panjim, Banastarim, Chorão and Divar. He found Goa an excellent *point d'appui* to keep the Indian potentates in check as also to protect Portuguese navigation and dominate the sea routes between India and the straits of the Persian Gulf and the Red Sea. When he died at the age of 53 he had laid the foundations of the Portuguese empire on a solid basis. Of his achievements one could say briefly that he set about organising the municipal government on the lines of that of Lisbon, established legislation and tribunals of justice, revived commerce, preserved the system of *communidades*, lightened the imposition of heavy taxes, built a mint, was tolerant towards religious beliefs, banned *sati*, and encouraged marriages between the Europeans and local women.[9] Preoccupied as he was with organizing and establishing the empire, he had hardly time to interact, or even care, for Indian culture. His was the attitude of the conquistador.

A Clash of Cultures

Since Indian culture is intimately linked to religious thought, the only impact that Portuguese discoverers could make on it would be by its encounter with the religious culture. This would immediately imply the methods of missionary conversion and the intervention of the Portuguese civil authorities in the local social life.

While on the above theme, the present Dominican master-general, Fr. Timothy Radcliffe writes that the fundamental blindness that marked the evangelization of the Americas continues to afflict the church today. Even the best of the missionaries shared the mentality of the conquistadores. They automatically accepted assumptions about the superiority of western culture.[10] Learning from evangelization history, Cardinal Lavigerie, founder of the White Fathers, asked his men to let Africans be themselves. They were to use the local languages, were to record the indigenous languages, make grammars and dictionaries and even collect oral traditions for catechetical purposes, before they were adulterated by European influence.[11]

Vasco da Gama on his first voyage to India was accompanied by six priests, who made no conversions, and the only success was that Vasco da Gama could carry some merchandise back with him. In 1500, Pedro Alvares Cabral and the missionaries with him made some conversions among the inhabitants of Angediva. Three years later three armadas arrived, one of which was captained by Afonso de Albuquerque.

The new converts they obtained were mainly household slaves, outcastes and poor. There were exceptions and the mass conversion of the Parava pearl fisherfolk subsequently gave lasting results. But it was the Society of Jesus in its role as the spearhead of the Church Militant, which made the struggle for souls as intensive and wide-ranging as the competition for spices. The Jesuits set and maintained much higher standards than did their predecessors, and the remarkable development of the Portuguese missions between 1550 and 1750 was mainly their work, which frequently elicited glowing tributes from otherwise hostile Protestants.[12]

But it was not exactly so. They used the carrot-and-stick methods in which the stick predominated. The Tridentine Council had expressly stated that conversions must never be made by force for nobody came to Christ by faith unless he was drawn by the Heavenly Father. The missionary policy departed considerably from the decisions of the Council.[13]

Subsequent events made a mockery of this. Conversions were not individual. They were either in groups or village-wise. Refusal meant destruction of their temple. At the height of the fanatic fury all the Hindu temples in Ilhas, Bardez and Salcete were razed to the ground. Some of the higher castes agreed to be converted in order to preserve their ancestral property, while the lower castes found an emancipation from the tyranny they were subjected to by the higher castes. The Muslims did not fare better. In fact the old hatred manifested itself more virulently. Copies of the *Koran* were destroyed and the Muslims were not allowed to utter the name of their Prophet. On the site of the destroyed temples and mosques, churches were built. These were maintained by the income possessed by the mosques and the temples. Public celebrations of non-Christian marriages were banned and inter-faith conversions were likewise forbidden, excepting conversion to Christianity. The Portuguese were under the impression that the Brahmins were the real obstacle to conversions of other Hindus because of the influence they exercised on the lower strata of their society. Francis Xavier himself found them a stumbling block. In an interesting discussion he had with this class in Cape Comorin, he wrote that despite convincing them of the truth of the Christian religion, they refused to be baptised because they wondered how they would live if deprived of alms they usually got at the temples. But in Goa many of the higher castes preferred to abandon their possessions and flee to the neighbouring territories rather than submit to the missionaries. In their blind fanaticism the missionaries did not pause to study the ethos of the Hindus.

Religious Aggression

But the religious aggression of Goa had gone too far. As it has often happened in the history of nations, there comes a stage in such development when a certain psychological blindness sets in. The Portuguese onslaught was arrested because at that time the moral and economic decadence of Goa was already patent. Viceroys and bishops quarrelled, the population led an idle life without resources and wasted time on vice and bad habits, the judiciary was weak and corrupt, Portugal struggled with its internal and external problems. The empire was rapidly declining, the Dutch had taken Moluccas and Sumatra. Persia, with the help of the English had taken possession of Ormuz.[14]

The great empire had now begun its descent. Towards the latter part of the sixteenth century, despite the initial efforts of Albuquerque to have the Portuguese populate Goa, there were very few who had managed to stay on. Goa had become a very unhealthy place to live in, due to the primitive sanitary conditions of the city. All that the Portuguese craved for was a life of luxury and sensuality which was one of the factors that shaped their disaster. Xavier on his last visit to Goa in 1542, in his capacity as the Fr. Provincial of India, reformed the Seminary of St. Paul by dismissing those novices who were unfit for religious profession and punished the Fr. Rector. He was unhappy with the small number of converts in Malabar, and with the lack of enthusiasm in his missionaries. In his great zeal he resorted to secular power to aid the religious. In 1548 he wrote to one of his companions in Kochi mentioning that the only effective way to spread religion in India was for the king to trust only those who exerted themselves for the spread of the faith.[15]

Xavier did not live to see the indiscretion and brutality of the way in which conversions were carried out nor of the rigours of the Inquisition. His exasperation of the slowness of growth of his missionary endeavours, is reminiscent of St. Dominic (1170-1221), when he faced a similar situation while dealing with heretics. It would be wrong to condemn these two great saints for the methods they advocated. They were both products of a society that considered such acts as a matter of course.

The Church today has moved a long way from the Tridentine structure. The Ecumenical Council convened by John XXIII in 1962, tried to prevent, among other things, disturbing the life of communities, overthrowing traditional wisdom and endangering the character proper to each people.[16] The new missiology that flows from it tries to inculturate the elements of the new culture it encounters, into Christian culture. Neither Dominic nor Xavier did this but followed compulsively the temper of their times. They could not contradict each other. If Francis was not in such a great hurry, he and his Portuguese overlords missed a golden opportunity to point out the evil of the prevailing caste system which still prevails among the Christians in Goa and certain parts of Malabar. We would probably have a situation like that of the Rawat Christians in Rajasthan where the two faiths, Christianity and Hinduism, have worked out a *modus vivendi*.

The real terror, however, was the introduction of the Inquisition. It was left to the Marquis of Pombal to remedy the situation. He had a remarkable grasp of the conditions prevailing in Goa. In 1774 he issued his *Instructions* to the Governor D. Jose Pedro da Camara and to the Archbishop D. Francisco de Assuncão e Britto in which he abolished the Inquisition and ordered means to be used to remove caste divisions. He wrote to the Archbishop telling him to offer posts in the parish, and in public life to the natives of the land.[17] This was indeed hard for the Portuguese clergy and officals to accept.

One of the most odious orders of the Inquisition was regarding local customs and habits. The *tulsi* plant, the *dhoti*, the *choli* were forbidden for Christian use under severe penalties. However, what outdid all the ridiculous methods at civilizing the Goan was the order issued on 27th June, 1684 by Viceroy Francisco de Tavora regarding Konkani. The order forbade its use and ordered school teachers, priests and their parishoners, to learn Portuguese within three years. Earlier the Franciscans had half-heartedly used Konkani for their work. But 23rd March, 1567, Pope Pius V declared that no religious should occupy the post of parish priest unless he was conversant with the language of the place.[18] This papal brief served as a boost, and for the next hundred years or so Konkani flourished under the Franciscans and the Jesuits.

It was left to Cunha Rivara, the chief secretary of the Government of Goa, and a great lover of Konkani, to write prophetically in 1865, in his *Historical Essay on Konkani Language*, a stirring appeal to the Goan youth to restore Konkani to its rightful place. Since then Konkani has risen like a phoenix from its ashes.

Concluding Remarks

Though in the historical time-frame the great discoveries of the Portuguese turned into an ephemeral sideline, thanks to their shortsightedness, their impact on Indian culture continues to echo, amidst much that is negative, some of the positive influence they left behind.

The genesis of the expansion cannot be traced to a single factor but rather to a plurality of motives. While for king John II, territorial conquest and the resulting commercial advantages were uppermost in his mind, for Prince Henry, the prime mover of it all, the spirit of the Crusade and politico-strategic considerations were all-important. But behind it all were the politics of secrecy. What Portuguese historians like to call 'civilizing action', consisted in the establishment of the printing press through which men like Cunha Rivara, wrote not only about Konkani but also spread much knowledge about the geography of the conquered territories whereby the Renaissance in Europe profited immensely.

On the religious front the wildcat missionary efforts left much to be desired. Though one would feel compelled to condemn conversion by force and material enticements, yet there were conversions through genuine conviction. That could perhaps explain the great missionary accomplishments of Goan priests not only in Goa but in other Portuguese conquests. Faith is a fragile virtue and it rebounds to the credit of the Goan clergy that they endured the scandalous discrimination of the Portuguese hierarchy until Pombal with his sense of justice relieved them of their subjection. It was short-lived though, because old prejudices die hard.

In fine, what is the upshot of all this long cultural encounter? It has produced a Goan who is open and receptive to western influence and culture, yet with roots firmly in the soil. The Goan of the thirties till the fifties was already stirred seeking the source of his heritage. It would be a pity if this symbiotic culture disappeared with time, but since genetically the hybrid is, as a rule, more resistant than its parents, Goan culture had every probability of forming an integral part of Indian culture, and will therefore endure through the usual vagaries of historical cultures.

NOTES AND REFERENCES

1. *Os Descobrimentos Portugueses*, Vol. II, Lisbon, 1980, pp. 639-40.
2. J. H., Saraiva, *História Concisa de Portugal*, Publicações Europa-America, 1979, p. 129.
3. Gilbert Freyre, *Aventura e Rotina*, Lisbon, 1952, p. 192
4. *Ibid.*, p. 194.
5. Albert-Alain Bourdon, *História de Portugal*, Coimbra, 1973, pp. 65-66.
6. *The Portuguese Seaborne Empire*, London, 1969, p. 18.
7. *The Outline of History*, London, 1925, p. 491.
8. Cortesão, *op. cit.*, Vol. 4, 1981, p. 917.
9. G. Saldanha, *Historia de Goa*, Vol. 1, New Delhi, Asian Educational Services, 1990, p. 43.
10. *The Examiner* (Bombay), Vol. 143, (n. 36, 1992), p. 8.
11. *The Tablet* (London), Vol. 246, (n. 7933, 1992), p. 1039.
12. Boxer, *op. cit.*, p. 66.
13. *Ibid.*, p. 67.
14. Rui Gomes Pereira, *Hindu Temples and Deities*, Panjim, 1978, p. 12.
15. T. B. Cunha, *Goa's Freedom Struggle*, Bombay, New Age Press, 1961, pp. 74-75.
16. Vatican II (*Gaudium et Spes*), 1981, p. 960.
17. Cunha, *op. cit.*, pp. 74-75.
18. Antonio Pereira, *The Makers of Konkani Literature*, Pilar, 1982, p. 11.

SECTION II

6

EVANGELISATION AND ITS HARSH REALITIES IN PORTUGUESE INDIA

P.P. SHIRODKAR

The missionaries on board the armada of Pedro Alvares Cabral landed at Anjediva on 22nd August, 1500 and converted 23 islanders by force. However, after converting them, they did not stay there for long and left the converts to their own fate. With time, colonisation and evangelisation became inseparable. Those who resisted conversion were branded 'pagans and unfaithful' with the colonisers giving themselves the right to civilize others. The methods of conversion had been wrong leading to misery for the people, large-scale migrations, and the separation of families within themselves, all problems never before witnessed by the people.

There were complaints to the crown as early as 1523 that no justice existed in the land. At Kochi, it was said, the parish priest had allowed persons to marry many times over on their producing false certificates.[1] Fr. Sebastião Dias, vicar at Quilon, a good gunsmith, had taken part in the war against the queen of Quilon. She had owed the Portuguese pepper, and in the resulting siege of the fortress in 1520, Dias had killed many. Frei Vicente de Laguna informed the crown that about eight priests in Goa indulged in bribery. He urged the king to invite only such priests who had an attachment to the great cause at heart, for too many useless priests deserved to be sent back.[2]

Missionaries not only made converts but saw to it that temples and shrines once destroyed remained un-rebuilt. Brahmins who insulted Christians were punished for doing so. Converts had to work hard, and parents of these had to hand over their inheritance in favour of them.[3] Yet even the new converts were treated with such contempt that the clergy-administration combine prevented them from occupying the posts of judges, town councillors and municipal clerks.[4]

Like all powerful delusions, the missionaries in collusion with the viceroys and the crown believed that in order to advance the faith they had to destroy the faiths of others, a point contrary to the teachings of Jesus. The fact of few conversions led them to resort to the 'rigour of mercy' in 1541 during which they destroyed temples and attached its lands to the churches, and to the college of St. Paul's to meet the expenses of the Confraternity of the Holy Faith.[5] On the sites of the former temples they built churches and chapels to help the 'pagans' maintain their attachment to their former places of worship. Yet this sense of attachment has not been erased totally from the minds of generations of former devotees. The Hindus faced this darkest phase of Portuguese colonialism and religious persecution with great fortitude for which there is no parallel in India.

The Inquisition was established in Portugal the year the 'rigor of mercy' came to Goa. Vicar-general Miguel Vaz had written to the king in Portugal in 1543 from Goa about its need in Goa too.[6] Three years later, a similar request was made by Francis Xavier to the crown in view of the many Muslims around, and due to the scatter of the Christian flock.[7]

When Lourenço Pires, Portuguese ambassador at Rome heard of the excesses of the Inquisition in Goa, he expressed to the crown in Lisbon his displeasure warning that this zeal for religion would be of disservice to God and to the kingdom. The Inquisition was hell for the victims and struck the death-knell for the Portuguese empire in the East.[8]

Today it is inconceivable how Xavier, later to be canonised as saint could have made such an inhuman proposal which resulted in the sufferings and cruel deaths of many. The victims remain termed 'evil' while those who meted out the punishments to them or who suffered in the backlash of popular feelings, are honoured.

What then, is the remedy for correcting the major flaws in church history? Should present-day historians turn a blind eye to these facts in history and dismiss them away as merely wounds and scars of the past ? Yet, the criminal acts of the Inquisition which surpassed those of the Nazis in horror deserve better scrutiny and investigation. Until then, this inglorious chapter in history will remain an eyesore for generations to come.

Prior to the Inquisition, Miguel Vaz while in Évora had drawn up plans which were later sent to the crown in November 1545 for implementation. Hindus in Goa were to be deprived of all human rights, idolatry was to be outlawed, temples to be destroyed, idols in no form to be made, Hindu festivals to remain uncelebrated, Brahmin preachers to be debarred from the island, and personnel from St. Paul's authorised to search houses of suspect Brahmins and others. King John did agree to these measures as is evident in his letter of 8th March 1546.[9]

This action too was a classic example of hypocrisy since icons were revered in churches all over Europe. Similarly, feasts dedicated to saints have been celebrated with much pomp and revelry in contrast to the celebrations in India. Yet the idea had been to force Hindus to convert to Christianity.[10]

John III had allowed Miguel Vaz to destroy all the idols on the mainland and to replace them with crosses at which sites the converts could be taught. Yet was not this an idolatry of a different sort? Hindu painters were not to be allowed to paint sacred images in churches for fear they would be tempted to prepare their own idols with their new earnings.[11]

A systematic attempt was thus made to kill local talent and to deprive those adamant in their old faith of their livelihood. The new converts enjoyed exemptions from dues, and could hold offices as they had in the past. This was perhaps one of the first attempts made by the missionaries with the consent of the crown and the governors to divide the people, a discrimination which unfortunately has survived for centuries on. The seeds of discrimination sowed then have grown to such an extent that one can detect the remnants of them in the fabric of Goan society even now.

In a letter to the crown, a Azu Naique from Bassein cautioned about dividing the communities for it was they who increased the capital of the state, paid rents, and defended the territories. There ought to be one law for all, he pleaded. His views were never considered, for the crown most easily believed the church and governors on these matters.[12]

Converts were made to check on the movements of those who had not as yet converted. The surveillance was stricter on days like *Ganesh Chaturthi* or *Diwali*, with punishments for those who broke the law.[13] All this and more did not prevent the Hindus from observing their traditions and a fresh resolution against them was passed in

1568.[14] A judge was appointed to deal with all matters, civil and criminal, arising from the conversion drive.[15]

The crown cautioned the missionaries about giving to themselves superior powers over the Hindus which did not rightly belong to them.[16] In the seventeenth century, it called for some relaxation in the drive, and fearful lest the situation get out of hand, allowed Hindus, much to the annoyance of the missionaries, to celebrate their marriages in Goa itself. They earlier had to flee to the neighbouring territories to do so.[17]

The dark spots in missionary activity were their involvement in diplomacy and in espionage on behalf of the State. The count of Linhares had been informed by the Jesuit Paulo Reimão from Surat about enemy plans in 1622-23. He revealed English-Spanish plans against the Estado da India, and that eight British ships anchored off the port of Surat had taken part in the conquest of Hormuz. Linhares pledged to defend the State at all cost.[18]

Conclusion

Though in the years following the conquest of Goa in 1510, the church in Goa had no major role in regulating the social, economic and administrative life of the people, yet later in the eighteenth century she did succeed in curbing traditional social life. She had a hand in the infamous edict of 14 April 1736 which sought to preserve and exalt the faith and rid it of any 'impurities'.[19]

The tables were turned on the missionaries in the nineteenth century. A 17 February, 1804 report of the Augustinians to the crown mentions the hard times they were in with no houses of their own and their mission in Bengal in shambles due to 'the barbarities of the enemies in the name of God'. He urged the king to turn his pious eyes to this pass.

NOTES AND REFERENCES

1. Antonio da Silva Rego, *Documentação para a História das Missões do Padroado Português do Oriente* (Henceforth *Documentação*), II, Lisbon, 1949, p. 19.
2. *Ibid.*, pp. 11, 192, 230-231.
3. *Capitulo Oyto de Estatutos da Confraria da Converção a Fé*, 25th July 1541, Goa; *Documentação*, III, p. 6
4. Heliodoro de Cunha Rivara, *Arquivo Portuguêz Oriental*. Fasc. 2.

5. *Documentação*, II, p. 14.
6. *Ibid.*, pp. 338-39.
7. *Documentação*, III, p. 351.
8. A. K. Priolkar, *The Goa Inquisition*, p. 25.
9. Priolkar, *op. cit.*, pp. 73-5. See also Josef Wicki (ed.), *Documenta Indica*, I, Rome, 1948, pp. 66-72; *Documentação*, III, pp. 203-208, 316
10. *Documentação*, III, p. 63.
11. *Ibid.*, III, pp. 261, 223-24.
12. *Documentação*, IV, pp. 450-55, 507-509.
13. Historical Archives of Goa (HAG), *Relação de Goa* (1548-1692), I, fls. 41v-42v.
14. HAG, *Livro do Pai dos Cristãos*, fl. 35v.
15. HAG, *Monções do Reino* (MR), n. 47, fl. 218.
16. Antonio de Noronha, *Os Indus de Goa e a Republica Portuguesa*, Panjim, 1922, p. 65.
17. Cunha Rivara, *Arquivo Portuguêz Oriental*, Fasc. 6, Reprint, New Delhi, 1992, pp. 1235-6. HAG, *Relação de Goa*, L. Verde — 1o, *Registos e Assentos*, fls. 124-135.
18. HAG, *Ordens Régias*, n. 2, fls. 31-32.
19. HAG, MR, n. 106, fl. 118.

7

DISCOVERIES AND MARTYRS OF MISSIONARY EXPANSION IN THE EAST

JOSEPH DE BARROS

Not a Pretended Zeal

With the discovery of the sea-route to India by Vasco da Gama in 1498, a social, political, cultural and missionary contact sponsored by Portugal was established. Da Gama's fleet comprised of four vessels well-equipped with men and material. This discovery-cum-missionary expedition arrived at Malabar on 20th May, 1498 in quest of Christians and spices.

The first known expedition, undertaken by prince Henry's navigators, was to the Canary Islands in the Atlantic in 1415. In 1418, the Portuguese discovered an island which they named Porto Santo (Holy Harbour) as a symbol of their missionary expansion. The following year they discovered the uninhabited Madeira, and carried there Catholic migrants from the Algarve. Such was their missionary zeal that they named the first boy and girl born on the island Adam and Eve![1]

The idea of missionary expansion is clear in the way king Manuel I addressed da Gama at the start of his maiden voyage of discovery of the Indies while handing over to him the Flag of the Order of Christ: "*Leva neste pendão a honra do meu reino. Vai planta-lo em terra da India e protege-o com a cruz da tua espada. Traze-me novas da terra que se esconde há tanto na penumbra dos séculos. Realiza-me este sonho.*" (Carry with this flag the honour of my country. Go and implant it on the Indian soil and protect it with the cross of your sword. Bring me the news of that land which is hidden for so long in the shadow of the centuries. Make this dream come true).[2]

Missionary expansion was not unknown in times prior to the discoveries, but it gained special significance in the context of Portuguese discoveries. It is psychologically relevant to note that the ships carrying da Gama and his sailors, had at the top of their masts, white sails with crosses and that da Gama himself carried a flag with a cross of the Order of Christ and a letter of His Majesty Manuel to his counterpart at Calicut, written in Portuguese and in Arabic.[3]

The letter stated among other things that king Manuel was dispatching along with the fleet, Catholic priests well-versed in Christian doctrine, to undertake their missionary expansion through indoctrination and conversions, of the local inhabitants. It also referred to the fact that the services of these missionaries who were expert in Christian doctrine, preaching and teaching could be availed of by the Zamorin,[4] in order to discover the mysteries of the Catholic faith. So the plan of missionary expansion with the support of the discoverers was quite obvious.

Conquering for God?

To implement the plan of missionary expansion, the fleet under da Gama carried several priests too. Among these were Fr. João Figueira, preacher and administrator of the holy sacraments. There was another missionary under the category of "capelão" (chaplain), Pedro de Covilham. About their missionary expansion and martyrdom, Antonio Bragança Pereira writes, "Some missionaries were martyrs like the Trinitarian Pedro de Covilhã who was the first Portuguese priest to enter India".[5] As the forerunner of Portuguese missionary expansion in the East his martyrdom is mentioned by Faria e Souza in his *Asia Portuguesa* ("Besides the chaplains of the armada, Vasco da Gama took as confessor, the missionary friar Pedro de Cobillones, a religious of the Order of Holy Trinity who was the first priest who celebrated the mass on the altar and risked his life for the sake of the faith in the East").[6] He was the first Catholic priest of Portuguese origin to say mass. According to Faria e Souza, there were eight missionaries who were the Portuguese pioneers of religious expansion in India.

The urge and drive for missionary expansion is quite discernible in almost all the Portuguese overseas discoveries. For instance, when da Gama's expedition touched the east coast of Africa on 25th December, 1497, the nativity of Jesus Christ, they baptised the land they touched as *Terra de Natal*,[7] and celebrated Christmas along with the local inhabitants, on whom the Catholic liturgy had its due impact. According to Damião de Gois, the people of the locality were quite friendly to the new ideas and ideals and hence it was regarded as *Terra de Boa Gente* (Land of Good People). A similar place was called Bay of St. Helena as they had arrived there on her feast day, 4th November. The urge for missionary expansion is also visible in the crosses (padrões) which the Portuguese erected wherever they went, and in the religious hymns which they sang when they sighted new lands.

Recognizing the great zeal of the Portuguese for missionary expansion, Pope Julius III in his bull *Non Dubitamus* remarks, "The unknown world was in great part made known (by Portugal) and what is more it was conquered for God by the Christian truth", and Pope Leo XIII felt that the Portuguese flag was hoisted everywhere under the patronage of the cross so that the Portuguese discoveries could be regarded as that of the Catholic religion. Similar feelings were also expressed by Pope Pius XI who believed that the Church could not forget what Portugal had done in the expansion of the faith and the ways that it had opened across the ocean for the propagation of faith, missions and civilization.[8]

To encourage the missionary expansion in the East, king Manuel decided to establish religious centres for the propagation of Catholicism and for missionary expansion. At his request Pope Alexander VI in his Bull *Exponis Nobis* (26th March, 1500) gave the king the privilege to found twelve convents and missionary centres in the discovered lands. Thus, convents, churches, chapels and missionary centres came up where missionaries toiled and shed their blood and the mission fields flourished abundantly. Thus according to cardinal Gilroy, Goa became a focal point and a glorious centre of the missionary expansion in the Indies.

This vast panoramic view of missionary expansion leads us to state that although the Portuguese discoveries and conquests are practically forgotten, the Catholic faith implanted by missionary sacrifices, sweat and blood have expanded and flourished throughout India and the East.

According to the author of *Memória Histórico-Eclesiastica*, Amaro Pinto Lobo, Angediva was the starting point of the missionary expansion in the East and the cradle of the Goa archdiocese. Unfortunately this cradle which ought to have been considered as a historico-religious seed has been gifted recently as a base to Indian navy.[9]

Seventeen priests came along with the Portuguese discoverer

Pedro Alvares Cabral to India and started in right earnest their activities, which were quite successful. Of these, eight were Franciscans, and the rest secular priests, all headed by the Franciscan Henrique de Coimbra, missionary advisor and royal confessor. Their drive was so successful that they converted many inhabitants of Angediva which was then a pioneering missionary base. The other members of the group were Frs. Gaspar de Gama, Francisco da Cruz, Simão de Guimarães, Luis de Salvador, Masseu, Pedro Nelo and João de Vitoria. Of these three died at Calicut on 16th November 1500, and four on 3rd April, 1520, all as martyrs, not before converting many at Kochi, Calicut and Cananore.

Amaro Pinto Lobo writes, "They disembarked on this small island and tried to find out the mood of its inhabitants towards the new religion and explaining its mystery to those who were well-disposed, baptised them. They also celebrated many masses and sang devotional hymns which resulted in more conversions to the new faith." The converts were solemnly and publicly baptised with great pomp.[10]

Afonso de Albuquerque too during his voyage to India was accompanied by three Dominicans led by Fr. Domingos de Souza. On their arrival, they built a fort at Kochi, named it Santiago, erected a church in honour of St. Bartholomeu and laid its foundation on 26 September, 1503. The inaugural sung high mass was attended by king Iterama Martinguel Trivmumparti.[11] Such was the psychological impact of the liturgical function that the king of Kochi even thought of converting to Catholicism along with his royal household. This church was probably the first one to be erected in Kochi.

During the takeover struggle of Goa, the missionaries joined in, with the Dominican João do Rosario carrying the cross aloft in the forward ranks. The church of St. Catherine was built under instructions from Albuquerque after the conquest and Fr. do Rosario looked after it. In 1513, the church of Our Lady of the Mount was built. The mortal remains of Albuquerque lay buried in it till they were transferred to Portugal in 1565.

Paying with Blood

Missionary expansion was not an easy affair. There were many hurdles on the way. The drive to introduce a new faith among the people was looked on with suspicion by a section of the local population from Cuncolim, and five Jesuits (Rudolf Acquaviva, Alphonsus Pacheco, Pedro Berno, Antonio Francisco and Francisco Aranha) were put to death at Toliebhat along with their seventeen companions (Gonçalo Rodrigues, a Portuguese living at Rachol, Afonso da Costa, Goan from Margão, Francisco Rodrigues from Loutolim, Paulo da Costa from Rachol, Gonçalo Rodrigues, a Portuguese and Dominic Aguiar, a local boy from Cuncolim). Today a chapel stands as a silent witness to the martyrdom. The corpses of the five Jesuits were dragged and thrown into a ditch and covered with twigs and leaves. They were recovered after about three days and taken to Rachol to be buried.

We read in the *Memória* that in 1563 a twelve year old boy, hailing from Goa was murdered by a Muslim fanatic in north Bombay for refusing to leave the Catholic faith. In 1564, Bro. Pedro Alcaçova from Rachol was stoned to death. On 16th March, 1581, two Goan friars, Simão das Montanhas and Francisco Calassa, were done to death at Solor. In 1594 a Franciscan Manuel Pereira from Goa was killed at Kandy in Ceylon.

In 1598, a Goan from Chimbel, Lourenço Gonçalves, sacristan in a church at Solor was killed. On 16 August, 1631, Fr. Giberto, a Goan, was murdered at the altar, and several other Goans and Africans too, at Mombasa under orders from Sultan Yussuf. As the area was under the ecclesiastical jurisdiction of the archdiocese of Goa, the case papers were sent to Rome in 1636, but nothing has been heard of ever since.

All these and others plunged into the mission knowing well enough the sacrifices involved. One recalls the Embaixada Martir which sailed from Macau to Nagasaki in 1640. It carried missionaries to Japan. But, orthodoxism, obscurantism and a fanatic hatred of the Catholic faith, culminated in the death of four missionaries and their fifty seven helpers. These deaths were neither economically nor politically motivated but they had their roots in religious antagonism and in a reluctance to accept a foreign faith. It was a gruesome massacre and almost unparalleled in the history of missionary expansion.[12]

Yet another martyr of missionary expansion in the East was the noble and gentle Fr. João de Brito, *caballero andante del Cristianismo*. Born in Portugal on 1st March, 1647, he sailed on 15th March 1673 and reached Goa in September. Known in the Portuguese court as "petite apostle" (*o apostolinho*), he used to often say, "I long more for the heavens than the earth, and the forests of Madurai more than the royal palace of Portugal". He dressed in saffron robes, wore *padukas*, ate vegetarian meals, and found himself at ease among the common masses. He converted no less than 2,070 Indians in 75 days, and created an alarm among the non-Christians who jailed him, tortured him and finally killed him at Madurai on 4th February, 1693.[13]

The Portuguese Left, their God Remains

This is the great galaxy of Catholic martyrs who sacrificed their lives for the sake of missionary expansion, and enabled the Catholic faith to gain a firm foothold in the East, while the once-mighty Portuguese empire witnessed its sunset.[14]

NOTES AND REFERENCES

1. Charles R. Boxer, *The Portuguese Seaborne Empire,* London : Hurchinson, 1969, p. 27.
2. Jeremias X. de Carvalho, *Precursores do Cristianismo no Oriente,* Bastora, 1980, p. 7.
3. Damião de Gois, *Cronica do Felecissimo Rei Dom Manoel,* Pt. 1, Coimbra, Imprensa da Univ., 1926, p. 92.
4. Daniel Boorstin, *The Portuguese Discoverers,* Lisbon, 1987, p. 27.
5. "Historia Religiosa de Goa," in *Oriente Portugues,* nn. 2-3, Bastora, 1936, p. 31.
6. Vol. 1, Porto, Livraria Civilização, 1945, p. 102.
7. Gois, *op. cit.*, p. 71.
8. Carvalho, *op. cit.* p. 3.
9. p. 12.
10. p. 20; Cristovam de Nazare, *Mitras Lusitanas no Oriente*, I, Panjim, 1887, p. 10.
11. Amaro Pinto Lobo, p. 22.
12. Benjamin Videira Pires, *Embaixada Martir*, Macau, p. 5.
13. Jayme Rangel, *São João de Brito*, Bastora, 1954, p. 18.
14. Gabriel de Saldanha, *Historia de Goa*, I, Goa, 1925, p. 33.

8

THE PROSELYTISATION AND PURIFICATION MOVEMENT IN GOA AND KONKAN

A.R. KULKARNI

Book Religions in India

The problem of proselytisation followed by the movement of purification, covering a period of four hundred years of Indian history, was essentially a conflict between a book religion on the one hand, and a religion based on tradition, customs, practices, and worship of a multiplicity of deities by different types of people brought under the umbrella of one religion called Hinduism, on the other. When India was invaded and occupied first by the Muslims in the early medieval phase of its history and later by the Europeans, in spite of their efforts to convert this sub-continent to their own religions, they could not succeed, and both these religions remained a minority in this country. With the decline of their political power, their control over religion declined likewise, and the conversion movement came to an end. Some of those who were converted, particularly to Christianity, could not forget their old moorings and came back to their original fold en masse, retaining their old castes, names, customs, practices, etc.

The early settlers in India came with a few spiritual concepts which were developed in the process of their settlement in this land. They worshipped nature either to avoid its wrath or seek its mercy. However, the case of Muslim or Christian invaders of India was a different one as they had already a well-developed religious system. What they needed (the Turks or Afghans for instance), was a permanent home where they could establish themselves politically and spread their religion among the residents of their newly-conquered territories with a view to securing support from the local population for their political power. The Portuguese, on the other hand, were the least interested in making their new conquest a permanent home, but were interested in spreading their religion in occupied territories without severing their links with their homeland.

The different attitudes of these two foreign invaders in the medieval period were mainly responsible for developing different types of religious policies towards the people of the newly conquered areas. The Muslims learnt Hindu scriptures, translated them into the vernacular languages with a view to merging themselves with the way of life of the native people, without compromising much on their own religion. Conversion to Islam, therefore, became merely a political issue, rather than a religious one for the Muslim rulers of medieval times.

The Christian rulers, however, with the support of a well-organized missionary system, particularly as was the case of the Portuguese, were bent on proselytizing the natives en masse, and exploited their superstitious or wrong notions about the loss of purity on some flimsy grounds or other. With the Portuguese, conversion was a religious issue, and political power, was the major tool in turning the Hindu land into a Christian one.[1] As Prof. Boxer has rightly said "the Portuguese overseas empire was a military and maritime enterprise cast in an ecclesiastical mould".

Inquisition and Forced Conversions

This essay seeks to survey the problem of conversion to Christianity and the movement of purification that followed on the west coast, particularly in Goa and its surrounding Marathi-speaking areas. In fact to reach the masses, the Christians – saints and missionaries – produced a vast amount of popular literature in Marathi to promote the policy of proselytization of the Portuguese rule.

Christianity reached the shores of India much before the advent of the Portuguese, but the history of Christianity in Goa begins with its conquest by Afonso de Albuquerque in 1510. The job of spreading Christianity was assigned to different religious orders in the early years. For instance, Ilhas was assigned to the Dominicans, Bardez to the Franciscans, and Salcete to the Jesuits. Francis Xavier reached

Goa in 1542, with the object of spreading the Christian faith. He involved himself in serving the sick in the hospital, the poor and downtrodden, and in improving the character of the prisoners.[2]

Later, he started actively participating in the work of conversion. It was at his instance that the Goa Inquisition was set up to try the cases of violation of the Portuguese Act of 1547 imposing restrictions on non-Christians. The Jesuits always claimed that they did not inflict their religion on unwilling people, but only on those who had sought it on their own. The Jesuits in fact, were more powerful in Goa than the Portuguese officials. It was said that the viceroys come and go, but the Paulist (*Padree*) is always there. They had acquired property, particularly in Sashti, and often quarrelled among themselves over the property claims. The Inquisition was closed for a short period in 1774, but was revived between 1779 and 1812.[3]

The methods adopted by the Jesuits made some people leave Goa and seek asylum in the Maratha country. One of the documents from the Konkan mentions that in order to increase the Christian population in Konkan, the Portuguese forcibly converted Marathas which resulted in en masse migrations. We need not enter into the controversy whether the Jesuits used force or not, though one is inclined to agree with Dr. Noronha's opinion that "almost none was converted from conviction."[4]

The Viceroy in 1667 issued an order that all except the Roman Catholics were to be deported from Goa. The threat of a large-scale massacre of the Hindus was feared as a consequence. Shivaji, the Maratha king, in retaliation detained four missionaries from Bardez and asked them to embrace Hinduism, but when they refused to do so, they were killed. The Portuguese Viceroy withdrew his order of deportation as a result.[5]

The Talkonkan area was saved from the designs of the missionaries by the gallant efforts of the Angres, the Admirals of the Marathas.[6] But the situation in North Konkan, particularly in Vasai was different. The Deshmukhs of Vasai deserted the place and reported to the king that the Portuguese had destroyed the temples, the holy places and had suppressed the Maharashtra *Dharma* (the Maratha way of life) by converting Hindus to Christianity.[7]

The French traveller Dellon's account of the Inquisition, himself a victim of it for three years, was considered fabricated till another French traveller Abbe Carre, who met him in Goa, confirmed it. The Inquisition can be compared with the Revolutionary Tribunal set up in France during the Revolution of 1789 or with its Reign of Terror and the guillotining of anti-revolutionaries. It was an ecclesiastical tribunal set-up to suppress heresy and punish Christian heretics. But in the course of time Hindus and other non-Christians were also accused of obstructing conversion and were brought before the Inquisition for punishment.[8]

The Portuguese had enacted a number of anti-Hindu laws, all with a view to coerce Hindus into Christianity. These laws included banishment from the territory, the banning of performances of Hindu religious rites and ceremonies, and the prohibition of religious activities by Hindu priests. Measures were adopted to deprive them of their means of subsistence, of their rights and privileges in village communities.[9] Shivaji, it appears, had raised the issue of forcible conversion and confiscation of the properties of the orphans with the Portuguese government in 1675.[10] Even the Factory Records confirm the imposition of Christianity on the orphans by the Jesuits. The Portuguese officers at times resented such moves of the Jesuits. The Captain-General of Vasai had ordered the Jesuits to return the confiscated property to the orphans.[11]

Teotonio R. de Souza in his *Medieval Goa* mentions that the methods adopted disrupted several social bonds and traditional attachments which had kept the village communities together. On the basis of state documents and ecclesiastical records, he aptly remarks that the missionary harassment was the hallmark of Luso-Hindu relations during the 16th and 17th centuries in Goa.[12] The first ecclesiastical council of 1567 was a systematic and relentless war against Hindu religious and social practices. In 1704, a law made Hindus pay an annual contribution, a heavy capitation tax like the *jiziya* of the Mughals. The *xenddi* tax, which was imposed on the Hindus, according to de Souza, was the last flicker of proselytism.[13]

Iconoclastic Zealotry

The first target fo the Jesuits were the temples, which always reminded the Hindus of their religion. The temple was the centre of all political, cultural and economic activities of village communities. The Christians adopted measures which disrupted several social bonds and traditional attachments which held the rural population together. The Portuguese banned all public celebrations of the Hindus, and even forced them to wear a dress which could distinguish them from converts.

According to a government statement, there were 126 temples, 106 Christian churches and 4 mosques in Goa. But according to a private source there were 157 temples, both big and small in Goa.[14]

The Jesuits had realised that their aim of the Christianisation of Goa could be realised only if they could reach the masses through the vernaculars like Marathi or Kannada and their respective dialects. Fr. Thomas Stephens (1549-1619), an English Jesuit who came to Goa in 1579, wrote his *Christ-Purana* in 1616, a poetic work bigger in size than the first Marathi poetic work *Jnaneshwari*, a commentary on the *Bhagvad Gita*, composed in the last decades of the 13th century. Stephens had earlier written a Marathi grammar. His works were meant from spreading Christianity among the natives.

The books of the Christian missionaries in the 16th and 17th centuries were aimed at persuading the Hindus to abandon their false gods. They refuted Hindu beliefs with great vehemence and ridiculed their deities, like Vishnu, Mahesh, and Ganesh, and the accounts connected with them. The Portuguese in the wake of their religious fanaticism pulled down temples, burnt or confiscated religious literature, and created a vacuum in the spiritual life of the community. It was perhaps to fill this vacuum that the missionaries wrote books in Marathi on Christianity. A.K. Priolkar writes, "on the one hand, this literature aimed at a popular presentation of doctrines of Christian religion mainly through accounts of the life and work of its founder and other saints, and at providing manuals to serve as aids for the daily practice of the new faith; on the other hand it aimed at weaning away the converts from their old faith by attacking and ridiculing forcefully the tenets of Hindu religion and the gods of Hindu pantheon".[15]

When John Wilson, the well-known missionary published his *First Exposure*, he declared that if anybody dared challenge his views or rather criticism of Hinduism, he was prepared to enter into a debate with him. The main contention was that whosoever would try to establish the superiority of the Hindu religion would in the process expose more and more of its falsehood and supersititions; and those who would follow the debate between Brahmanas and the missionaries would find in the long run the hollowness of Hinduism and would, by the grace of God, accept Christianity as a last resort. It is true that some prominent Brahman families from Ahmednagar like Modak, Kelkar, Tilak, etc. did accept Christianity, but Vishnubawa Brahmachari, a Hindu missionary replied to all the points raised by John Wilson, and thereby checked the tide of conversion.[16]

Historical Background of Purification

It seems that purification or reconversion to the original faith of the converts did not pose any serious problems in the 16th and 17th centuries, when the movement of proselytization was at its height. The Portuguese tried to spread Christianity, sometimes, with the sword. Theodore Greesinger, a historian of Christianity, writes, "It so happened that the native priests, the Brahmins, had not the least difficulty in bringing the people back again to the religion, in which they had been born and bred".[17]

The Hindus were highly superstitious and the missionaries did not fail to exploit these weaknesses. They believed that even drinking water or eating bread offered by a Christian led to their acceptance of the new religion. It was, therefore, easier to take back such people en masse, by simply sprinkling sacred water or perhaps by their sipping a few drops of cow urine. History is full of instances of en masse purifications from Muslims or Christian religions. The Brahmins of the 16th to 17th centuries had devised various simple methods of reconversion. For instance, on the birthday of Krishna (*Gokulashtmi*), the converts on bathing in the sea, or being sprinkled with holy water of the *Ganga*, had all their sins, including the conversion rite, washed away, and could then be readmitted to their original faith. The Brahmins made them believe that the procedure suggested by them had the sanction of the scriptures.

The Christian missionaries retaliated by erecting crosses at various places on the sea-shore. The Brahmins countered by avoiding such places and arranging the mass-bathing ceremonies at other places. They discovered an old lake at Vasai and the bathing ceremony was done there secretly. In Goa too there was a *Madhav Teertha* – a lake, used for similar purposes.[18]

The four major agencies authorised to purify persons were the (1) Brahma-Sabha or the assembly of Brahmins held at holy places like Karhad, Mahuli, Wai Karveer, Paithan, Nasik; (2) The *Jatt-Sabha* or the caste-council; (3) The King and his Prime Minister, the Peshwa; and (4) The *Maths* or monasteries of Shankaracharya at Sankeshwar and Kolhapur. Shivaji had created the post of Panditrao, the ecclestical affairs minister whose main job was to help all these agencies in their job of repurification of converts.[19]

Yet another institution (*Gota* and *Deshak*) may be considered with regard to the ceremony of purification. According to the medieval practice, the sanction of *Gotsabha* comprising the *Watandars* and *Deshaks* of the village as well as of the *Pargana,* was necessary for *Gotai*, i.e. acceptance of the converted person into his *Gota.* The purified person had to be acceptable to all. At such a public meeting, the fees prescribed for purification were collected and a document under government seal attesting to this was issued to the person concerned.[20]

There are a number of official documents pertaining to conversion by force and readmission to the original fold, with details of the policies adopted by both the parties. The general procedure was the consulting of the *Brahma Sabha*, the state officials, for perscribing the mode of penances [illegible] llowed according to scriptures and the award of final documents, certifying the purification. Shivaji secured many outlying parts of the Portuguese territory between 1665-1670, and asked the Brahmins to purify the Christian converts in those areas and bring them to Hinduism. Many of these converts probably regained their places and they are now lost among the masses of Hindus.[21]

After the capture of Vasai fort from the Portuguese in 1739, the Hindus of Bhandari, Kriyapal and Mogate castes, who were forcibly converted to Christianity while they were in service of the fort, were readmitted to the Hindu fold against a small fee of Rs. 25, in the early decades of the 19th century. (BISM, Shaka 1837; D.B. Parasnis: *Peshwe Daftaratil Sanada Patratil Mahiti).*

The Maratha power became extinct in 1818, and the East India Company took over the territories of the Peshwas. The cholera epidemic of 1828, frightened some low caste converts like the Orap, the Agri, the Bhandari in the Vasai region, and they suddenly decided to go back to their old religion to escape the wrath of the goddess. They were readmitted to Hinduism without any inhibitions, and Shankaracharya approved this decision by accepting alms at the hands of the re-admitted people. However, the Brahmins of Vasai refused to perform the religious rites of the new castes, perhaps due to the fear of their masters belonging to the four *varnas* of Hinduism. Nityanand Saraswati, the Shankaracharya, in his *Ajnapatra* (order) asked the Brahmins of Vasai, to accept the re-admitted people and to render all religious services to them as the Peshwa, after consulting the scriptures and the procedures laid down for purifiction, readmitted them to Hinduism.[22]

Swami Vivekanand, the advocate of Hinduism in the international forum, justified the purification of the Brahmins all over the country. He suggested that the purified people would go back to their original castes; and those who were non-Hindus, now coming to Hinduism, could form a new caste of their own.[23]

However, the problem of purification became complicated gradually due to the stubborn opposition from the orthodox Pune Brahmins. There was a marked difference in the attitudes towards change between the Bombay and the Pune Brahmins. The former, influenced by western ideas, were for the removal of the evils that had crept into society, reform of all customs, traditions, and superstitions acting as hurdles to human progress. The latter had not forgotten even in the 19th century that they were political masters of the country and preferred revolution to reform. For instance, the movement of widow marriages which was mooted by the Bombay pandits, was opposed tooth and nail by the orthodox of Pune. The Brahmins of Pune, having lost their political power in the recent past were perhaps not willing to surrender their control over religion in the 19th century.

One can recall the case of purification of Shripat Sheshadri, sponsored by Bal Gangadhar Jambhekar (1810-1846), the editor of the first Marathi periodical, the *Darpan.* He was assistant professor in mathematics at Elphinstone College, Bombay and the inspector of education with the government of Bombay. He was a constructive reformer. When Shripati's father approached Jambhekar to secure the release of his son from the custody of the Christians, he worked hard, at the cost of his health, and loss of money to get him back to the fold. At his behest, Jagannath Shankershet, agreed to bear the travel cost of Shripati, who was to visit Kashi, as a part of the programme of penances. But the orthodox Brahmins argued that as the boy had deviated from the Hindu religious practices, and had violated the customs and traditions, he was as good as dead to them. If such a spoilt child was to be absorbed, it would lead to the total destruction of Hinduism sooner or later.

Jhambhekar, on the other hand argued that if the challenge of the missionaries was not boldly faced, and the aggression was not checked in time, it would weaken the Hindu religion. When the Shankaracharya upheld the purification of Shripati, there should have been no further difficulty. But the Bombay pandits, supported by the Prabhus-Shrimant Dadaji Dhakaji opposed the move. Jambhekar was threatened with ostracism. It was rumoured that the missionaries of Bombay had bribed the Brahmin pandits to vote against taking Shripati back into the Hindu fold.[24]

Vishnu Bhikaji Gokhale (1823-71), popularly known as Vishnu Bawa Brahmachari, a contemporary of Jambhekar, made a virulent attack through his writings and public speeches on the practices of Christian missionaries. The ways and means adopted by the Bombay missionaries were more subtle and sophisticated than the atrocities of the Jesuits of Goa in 16th and 17th centuries. They could win over the ignorant and poor by service, or by helping them in need, or by providing them facilities for education. They would influence the intellectuals by arguments. Many Brahmin families like the Karmarkars, Modaks, Tilaks, Kelkars, Sheshadris, the intellectuals in society, were won over by arguments and debates. Brahmachari believed that the British aggression was more dangerous and ruinous to Hinduism than that of the Muslims. His fight with the missionaries for close to fifteen years, certainly checked the propaganda and the spread of Christianity in the Maratha country. His Saturday lectures in schools and residential *wadas* were well attended by large crowds that bought the one *anna* tickets. As these places could not accommodate the growing crowds, and as the lower castes were not admitted to such places, Brahmachari started lecturing at the Chowpatty beach. These public meetings were attended by Muslims, Christians and Parsis for his interpretation of the *Bible*. He presented his progressives ideas without fear or favour. His major work *Vedokta Dharma Prakash* epitomises his ideas on various aspects of religious and social life.[25]

Mass Reversions to Hinduism in Goa

The *Shri Dasbodha,* the mouthpiece of the Brahmacharyashram of Masur, Satara, which launched the movement of purification in Goa, in the early decades of this century, has a day-to-day account (1930). During this period there was hardly any opposition from the Portuguese Government, which had become a Republic now. But the vested interests, the Jesuits, harassed the volunteers of the ashram and made their life miserable according to the accounts of this movement depicted in the periodical of the ashram.

The leader of this movement was Vinayak Maharaj Masurkar's disciple Anand Murti, who launched it at Chimbel in April 1927. It is estimated that nearly 3,300 *gavadas*, for whom the movement was initially started, were readmitted en masse, in a very short period. The *gavadas* spread over Chimbel, Karmali, Tagaon, Kurk, Kalapur, were Christians in name only as they did not observe or know any Christian practices expect those of baptism, wedding and funeral. They attended the church services for these three rituals only. In practice, however, they were Hindus, having their same dress, diet, and customs. The *gavada* community of about 20,000 or more, was a major group of the Goan population which was purified in this century.[26]

Reconversion and Social Relations

Cases of reconversion and their absorption in the former communities, the attitude of the Got or Jati Sabha and the state or village councils towards such reconverts, are interesting from the point of view of social relations. In most of the cases, we find adjustments, generally through the agency of the state, were made for fostering harmony and a spirit of fellow-feeling and love for others in the society.

A long stay in an alien territory raised suspicions about the religious status of a person. On returing from Portuguese territories after a while, he would be suspected of being a convert to Christianity, and all social relations, particularly eating with him, would be banned for him. But on agreeing to fulfil all conditions of the *Got,* and on the intervention of the chief of that region with a request to the *Gota* to accept him, the *Gota* would consent. The procedure of acceptance in the *Gota* was usually a simple one. The person requesting the *Gota* for admission was presented before it and on compassionate or other grounds, he was admitted to the caste by allowing him to dine with the fellow members of the caste. The cost of the feast, of course, was borne by the person himself.[27]

The converted members of a caste called Pathare Panch Kalse of Chaul, started pressing their *Got Sabha* for readmission to their caste. But the *Gota* refused to accept them in view of the probable social and economic problems such readmissions were likely to create in the harmony of the *Gota.* But Shivaji had told the Hindus of this state to accept the converts without subjecting them to any difficulties should they express a wish to return. The senior members of *Gota,* however, argued that had it been in the case of first converts things would have been simple, but as several generations of families of the Pathare Panch Kalse had been created, all types of mixed marriages, *anuloma* and *pratiloma* may have taken place with their names changed in the process. It would be a disgrace to the pure community to establish cordial social relations with such people. The members did, however, leave the matter to the good offices of the king, who respected the views of the elders and did not press for their admission. These converts have been referred to as *Katikoma* (belonging to an unknown caste).

As Shivaji did not press the *Gota* to accept the so-called *Katikoma*, the converts did not leave the matter there. When a new king came to the throne, probably Sambhaji, a similar appeal was made and a positive order from him was obtained. A feast was arranged for the members of the caste and they were absolved of their sins and declared Hindus. But before the king could put his final stamp on this decision, the leaders who were not in favour of it requested the government to ask all the members of the *Kotikoma,* including the pregnant women to go to Kashi and to bring a decree from the pandits there, permitting them to join the original caste. The matter was thus postponed.[28] This clearly shows how the castes were reluctant to readmit a person to his/her original fold. The caste-rules were made very rigid in such cases, with a view to preserving purity of the caste and better social relations among its members.

The *Deval Smriti* composed in the 8th century, sanctioned reconversion of those who had not spent more than 20 years in the new religion. Of course, when the *Smriti* was compiled, the problem of conversion was not a serious one, and the authors must have considered 20 years time limit as adequate. This *Smriti* also laid down that a woman of any *varna* becoming pregnant willingly or unwillingly from a *Mlencha*, could be purified after undergoing certain penances.[29] The lacuna of time-limit in the *Deval Smriti*, however, was removed by *Agni Purana.* According to this *Purana,* a person of any *varna,* who was in the company of the *mlenchas* or robbers, or one who had to take prohibited eatables while travelling through forest, could be purified after the performance of certain rituals.[30]

However, in spite of these sanctions of the scriptures, the caste continued to be rigid and sometimes refused to carry the order of the state. These rules became more rigid in the 18th century than in the earlier period.

Tradition, which also determines social relations needs to be studied while considering the problem of conversion and purification.

They die hard. The change of faith often does not prevent the converts from observing the traditions and religious practices of the family. They respect the family traditions to win the sympathies of people, or to avert the probable wrath of the family gods of their former religion.

The rise and spread of Christianity in Maharashtra made the problem of social relations much more complicated. According to an account given in the *Konkanakhyan*, a Sardesai who failed in driving the Muslims known as *Nayale* or *Navayats* (of the Arabic origin) out of Goa, invited the Portuguese from Cochin to help the local people in expelling the Muslims from Goa. Being pleased with the natural beauty of Goa, the Portuguese accepted the invitation, brought their naval force from Portugal and drove the Muslims away from the island. George Moraes in his *History of Christianity in India* writes that the Portuguese enterprise in general was a crusade against Islam, an act of defiance of Europe against the Muslim menace and that they 'neutralized the victories of triumphant Islam in the west by the annihilation of its sea power and the establishment of the Portuguese hegemony in the eastern waters'. Albuquerque, the first Portuguese Governor in Goa, tried a novel method of colonization through racial or mixed marriages between the Portuguese and the good-looking Muslim captive and converted women. He purchased these women from their masters and gave them in marriage to anyone who wished to have them as wives, along with a dowry of 18,000 *reis* from the royal treasury.[31]

The relations between the Christians and non-Christians in the Portuguese territories were not cordial. But the gradual suspension and final abolition of the Inquisition in the 18th century, and the existence of a large number of Hindus in Goa, indicate that the rulers realised that a ruthless policy of conversion embittering social relations would not help them in justifying their rule in Goa, which was ultimatley to depend on the will of the people.

Conversion-Reconversion Today

The conflict between the Christians and the converts has assumed political colours these days. Balasaheb Gaikwad, an advocate, a convert to Christianity from his original *mahar* caste, accuses the Christian priests and nuns of Ahmednagar in his *Christi Mahar.* A wholesale reconversion under the auspices of Balasaheb Thakare of the Shiv Sena was announced, but except for Gaikwad, nobody got himself converted to Hinduism.[32] It was planned perhaps with an eye on the concessions which they hoped to get by going back to their Hindu caste, promised them by the Mandal Commission Report. The Shiv Sena had an eye on the coming elections. But the experiment of en masse conversion failed miserably. Even the Vishwa Hindu Parishad, an organization interested in purification, did not support this move of Gaikwad. The other political parties too did not show any interest in this movement. On the contrary, they praised the good work of the missionaries in this district. This indicates that purification or reconversion is not a burning issue in this last decade of the 20th century, as it was in the earlier decades.

NOTES AND REFERENCES

1. A.R. Kulkarni, "Social Relations in the Maratha Country in the Medieval Period", *Proceedings of 32nd Session of Indian History Congress,* Jabalpur, 1970, pp. 231-268. See this for further details.
2. A.K. Priolkar, *Goa Re-discovered,* Bombay, 1967, pp. 35-36; *Gomantakacha Aajacha va Kalacha Itihas* (Marathi), Bombay, 1954, pp. 102-103.
3. A.K. Priolkar, *Goa Inquisition,* Bombay, 1967, p. 53.
4. Priolkar, *Goa Rediscovered*, p. 36.
5. Priolkar, *Patra Sar Samgraha, (PSS)* Vol. I, Pune, 1930, Letter No. 1186, p. 331.
6. S.V. Avalaskar, (ed.), *Angrekalin Ashtagar,* Pune, 1947, Letter No. 12.
7. V.S. Bendre, (ed.), *Maharashtretihasachi Sadhane* Vol. II, Bombay, 1966 pp. 364-365.
8. Priolkar, *Goa Inquisition,* pp. 42 & 159.
9. *Ibid.,* pp. 114-149.
10. *Ibid.,* pp. 128-129.
11. Priolkar, *PSS*, vol. II, Letter No. 1798.
12. *Essays in Goan History*, Teotonio R. de Souza (Ed.), Delhi, Concept Publishing Co., 1979, pp. 91-97.
13. "Xenddi Tax — A Phase in the History of Luso-Hindu Relations in Goa" in *Studies in the Foreign Relations of India,* P.M. Joshi and H.K. Sherwani (Eds.), Hyderabad, 1970, pp. 447-463.
14. George M. Moraes, *A History of Christianity in India, A.D. 52-1542,* Bombay, 1964, pp. 121, 154, 155 and 162; Pissurlencar, P.S.S., *Portuguese Marathe Sambhandha,* (Marathi), Pune, 1967, p. 58.
15. Priolkar, *Goa Rediscovered*, p. 78.
16. John, Wilson, *A Second Exposure of Hindu Religion in reply to Narayanrao of Satara including strictures on the Vedanta; Dusare Hindu Dharma Prasidhikaran* (Marathi translation), Bombay, 1835.
17. S.D. Kshirasagar, *Gomantak Shuddhicha Itihas* (Marathi), Bombay, 1930, Part I, p. 71, footnote.
18. *Ibid.*, pp. 70-71.

19. *Ibid.*, p. 72.
20. S.N. Joshi, in *Bharat Itihas Samshodhak Mandal Journal* (BISM), Vols. 1-2 Shaka, 1849.
21. Kshirasagar, *op. cit.*, pp. 72-75.
22. *Ibid.*, pp. 80-81.
23. Prabhudha Bharat, April, 1899.
24. Y.D. Phadke, *Social Reformers of Maharashtra*, Delhi, 1975, pp. 1-4.
25. G.B. Sardar, *Maharashtrache Upekshit Mankari* (Marathi), Pune, 1941, ch. 3.
26. Kshirasagar, *op. cit.*, (Marathi), Part II, Chapter IV, pp. 1-60.
27. R.V. Oturkar, (ed.) *Peshwekalin Samagik ani Arthik Patravyavahar*, Pune, 1950, p. 112.
28. S.V. Avalaskar, (ed.), *Angrekalin Patravyavahar*, Pune, 1948, pp. 40-41.
29. A.S. Altekar, *Sardesai Smarak Grantha*, Bombay, 1938, pp. 91-96.
30. Kulkarni, *op. cit.*, p. 252.
31. *Ibid.*, pp. 253-254.
32. *Times of India*, 17th November, 1992, p. 6.

9

MISSIONARY TEACHINGS AND SOCIAL REFORMERS IN 19th CENTURY INDIA

ADI H. DOCTOR

The aim of this brief essay is to examine missionary teaching and strategies adopted to undermine Hinduism in 19th century India, their impact on leading reformers like Raja Rammohun Roy and Jotirao Phulè and to conclude with indicating why the missionary strategy misfired.

Missionary Strategy to Undermine Hinduism

The Scottish and American missionaries adopted various strategies to undermine Hindu religious beliefs during the early and mid-nineteenth century. In Bengal, for instance, Alexander Duff adopted the strategy of direct assault on the central stronghold of Hindu society, the intellectuals, especially the Brahmins. It was Duff's conviction that western education in arts and natural sciences, accompanied by the teachings of Christian scriptures was enough to make the intelligentsia abandon heathen ways. According to Duff, social progress and the progress of scientific understanding were inseparably linked or connected with Christian religious truth. This view of course came to be subsequently abandoned when Darwin's theory of evolution came to pose a challenge to Christian ideas of creation. However, in Bengal from 1793 to 1836 missionary education held fast to the belief that western learning would naturally create the desire for the Christian truth on which it was built and hence the emphasis stayed on assaulting Hinduism at the intellectual level. In Maharashtra, likewise, the Protestant missionaries concentrated not only on direct evangelism but also founded numerous small vernacular schools. While missionaries like John Wilson (of Bombay's Wilson College fame) and James and Murray Mitchell worked at Bombay and Pune; Stephen Hislop (of Hislop College fame) worked at Nagpur; and Robert Nisbet at Nasik and Ahmednagar.

The early missionary endeavour was not only confined to starting educational institutions, but the assault on Hinduism was conducted at other fora too. Thus the arrival of John Wilson in Bombay saw the era of open public debate between missionaries and the defenders of Hinduism. Pandit Lakshman Shastri in 1830 and Morobhat Dandekar in 1831 came forward to debate with Wilson the merits of Hinduism. Both parties to the debate published their versions. Wilson's arguments were published in two texts, "Exposure of Hindu Religion" and "Second Exposure of Hindu Religion", which were also translated into Marathi and Bengali and reportedly sold very well. In addition to publishing various books and tracts, the Maharashtra-based missionaries brought out a most successful Anglo-Marathi newspaper, *Dnyanodaya* (during 1850-1860) which ran numerous articles and letters discussing the weakness of Hindusism.

What were the principal arguments marshalled by the missionaries against Hinduism in these various publications? These are summed-up below.

In the first place, the missionaries sought to expose the claim that Hinduism was divine. John Muir published three volumes of original Sanskrit texts with commentary to show that the origins of Hinduism could be historically analysed and there was nothing divine here. The purpose of publishing these texts, he wrote in the introduction to the third volume, "is to assist the researches of those Hindus who may desire to investigate critically the more important points in the civil and religious history of their nation". The thrust of the volume was to show that central Asia was the home of a common Aryan civilization (Persian, Greek, Roman and Indian), from where some Aryan tribes invaded India through the North-West passes, subjugating the native people called *Dasyus*, who differed from the Aryans in colour, language, religion and customs. In short, the so-called Aryan gods of the *Puranas* were actually Aryan warriors and conquerors and not divinity descended on Indian soil to fight the demons (called *Dasyus*).

To further disprove any claim to divinity, John Wilson in his "Exposure of the Hindu Religion" showed how Hindu gods could be cruel, capricious and unjust and how such gods could not, therefore, provide spiritual guidance for worldly conduct.

The missionary strategy was to publish religious texts (like *Rig Veda*) in translations in Marathi and Bengali to show that what the Brahmins had all along claimed to be divine revelation and eternal wisdom was plain nature worship (verses in praise of nature and natural phenomena). This strategy seems to have succeeded because many converts and radicals, on the first reading of the Marathi translations of the Vedas, claimed it came to them as "an anti-climax". Babaji Padmanji, a Christian covert, who published the book *What is in the Vedas* (1880) openly stated that their actual contents came as a great disappointment to him.

The newspaper *Dnyanodaya* in numerous articles sought to show that Hindus did not have a distinct idea of a unique creator, that some Hindu ideas of the divine were pantheistic, while others were polytheistic. Again, while sometimes the divine nature was presented as without qualities, at times the qualities ascribed to the divine were "of the most offensive kind".

Dnyanodaya also ran numerous articles to show that what the Brahmins described as divine and magic, was natural phenomenon that could be scientifically explained. Thus it explained the movements of planets as part of a natural order, involving no divine or magical powers. The *Dnyanodaya* issue of 1st March, 1886 ridiculed such notions of Hindu cosmology and creation, as earth is sustained on the head of an immense serpent and surrounded by seven immense seas of salt-water, sugarcane juice, etc., as "massive ignorance". Likewise, it attacked the ideas of ritual impurity as non-scientific. There is nothing inherent in any man (Shudra included) or for that matter in any food which polluted the high castes. In fact the idea of ritual impurity was unholy and ungodly since God made all men spiritually equal and gave the whole natural world to all men for their support and enjoyment. The paper also highlighted the terrible consequences of a variety of senseless and cruel religious practices like hook-swinging in the service of god Khandoba, religious prostitution and the obscenities of Holi celebrations, arguing that a holy and pure God could never be pleased by such practices.

If the first prong of the missionary strategy was to expose the hollow claim to divinity made on behalf of Hinduism by the Brahmins; the second prong was to attack the Brahmins's own claims to high status. Robert Nesbit wrote a pamphlet entitled "The Brahmins' Claims" (1834) comparing the statements in the *Shastras* regarding brahminic superiority and privileges with their real human weaknesses. He subtly suggested that the Brahmins had themselves written the sacred books to ensure a privileged position for themselves and this had gone unchallenged for centuries thanks to general Hindu ignorance.

The third prong of the missionary strategy was to deny and attack the caste system. Missionary teaching, first of all rejected the metaphysical basis of caste, stating that birth in a caste cannot be the result of past karma or deeds since God gave man only one life to live and ultimate salvation depended on how it was lived. Secondly, the missionary argument ran, caste being an ascriptive value system it cannot be the product of divine intention since God made men equal and intended to reward them only on the basis of individual effort and virtue. Therefore no particular merit attached to the accident of birth in a caste. *Dnyanodaya* frequently stressed the social benefits that would follow from the rejection of ascriptive values. A point often repeated by the paper was that the difference between the Hindu and western societies was because the West did not have a caste system. An article in the issue of 15th November 1848 gave a long list of examples of eminent people in Europe and USA who had risen to greatness from very humble origins to the great advantage of the community.

Finally the missionary rejoinder to those who argued that each society should keep to its own traditional religion for that provided the path to spiritual fulfilment most suited to its conditions and needs, was given by Murray Mitchell thus, "It is inconceivable that God should reveal one system in Asia, and other systems, contradictory to the former in Europe and Africa".

Missionary Impact on Indian Social Reformers

The missionary impact was pronouncedly felt on Hindu intellectuals and reformers in Bengal and Maharashtra since it was here that the missionaries had concentrated their activities in the early and mid-nineteenth century. I shall illustrate the missionary impact and the Hindu intellectual's response with reference to two great reformers Raja Rammohun Roy from Bengal and Jotirao Phule from Maharashtra.

Raja Rammohun Roy had been hailed as the father of the Indian Renaissance and modernization. His contact with missionaries began from 1805 (when he became the private secretary of John Digby).

Roy not only acquired fluency in English, but also learnt Hebrew, Greek and Latin in order to gain access to the original sources of Christianity. This enabled him to stand his ground against cruder missionary propaganda. Roy is perhaps the best example of how the Hindu intellectual not only learnt well from the missionaries, but also tried to turn the tables on them by preaching to them the true religion of *Advaita*.

In his book *The Precepts of Jesus* (1820), which he wrote as a reply to the Christian missionaries, Roy states the strong points of Christianity as he perceived them. In the introduction to the book he observes, "I found the doctrines of Christ more conducive to moral principles and better adopted for the use of rational beings than any other which have come to my knowledge".

But, having said this, he also goes on to highlight the unacceptable in Christianity which he describes as no different from Hindu mythology and superstition. Thus, he lampooned the doctrine of Trinity in a satirical piece he published in 1823 entitled "A Dialogue between a Missionary and Three Chinese Converts", arguing that if God is unitary and one, how can we speak of the Father, the Son and the Holy Ghost. In the Precepts he ridiculed the missionaries for wanting people to accept Christ's miracles. He once wrote to the Rev. Henry Ware of Cambridge (USA), "the doctrines that the missionaries preach are less conformable with reason than those professed by Muslims and in several points are as equally absurd as the popular Hindu creed". In another letter to Rev. R. Tytler, he wrote, "If Jesus could be divine, so could Ram". Nor was Roy impressed by the missionary argument that Christ died for atonement of men's sins. According to Roy the only way to atone for sin was sincere repentance and solemn meditation; another cannot atone for one's sins, nor can they be wiped out by bribes and sacrifices.

Thus Roy who began by praising Christianity for its social values ended up isolating the doctrine from its followers. The impact of missionary thought/teaching nevertheless made him reinterpret Hinduism and "purify" it. He distinguished between the true Hindu religion of Advaita (ethical monism) and the practices of popular Hinduism which were the proper subject of religious and social reform viz. suttee, idolatry, imposition of caste disabilities, etc. His attack on idolatry, and Brahmin priesthood as greedy and ignorant, his preaching the Vedas by translating them into the vernacular and his relentless tirade against idolatry and numerous Hindu superstitions show the heavy Christian influence on him. In fact Roy confesses that he perceived himself as another Luther. In his own words, "Having read about the rise and progress of Christianity in apostolic times and its corruption in succeeding ages and then of the Christian reformation which shook the foundations of these corruptions. . . . I began to think that something similar might have taken place in India and similar result might follow here from a reformation of popular idolatry".

In contrast to Roy, Jotirao Phule was far less erudite and hailed from the low caste of *malis*. He took over many missionary arguments wholesale and employed them with devastating effect to portray the Brahmin as the real villain of the piece, responsible for the conspiracy to keep the low castes suppressed and oppressed.

Phule acknowledged his debt to the missionaries in many direct and indirect ways. In his play *Traitya Ratna* (The Third Eye), written in 1855, he narrates the story of how a missionary helped open the eyes of a poor peasant couple to the inhuman exploitation by the Brahmin in the name of religion. The story revolves round how a Brahmin priest frightens a peasant woman, telling her that an unfortunate conjunction of the zodiac would destroy the child she is carrying unless she propitiated god Maruti and feasted all the village Brahmins. The poor, debt-ridden peasant couple are about to go into further debt when they meet a missionary who shows how the priest is fooling them in the name of *karma, dharma* and *varna*. And Phule tells us that thanks to the missionary "The Third Eye" of the couple opened and they now realized the diabolical Brahmin conspiracy.

Then in his famous work *Gulamgiri* (Slavery), Phule openly thanks the missionaries and the British for making the low castes realize that as human beings they too are worthy of all human rights. The aim of the Satyashodak Samaj founded in 1873 was in fact to make amends for the neglect of natural rights of men, especially of the Shudras, and establish a new moral community based on natural rights of men as opposed to the brahminical society based on graded privileges of castes.

The missionaries had in subtle ways hinted at a Brahmin conspiracy. Phule took up the missionary hints to openly accuse them with deliberately having invented mythology and the caste system to keep the low castes in perpetual slavery, by claiming divine sanction for various brahminical privileges. Building on the arguments contained in John Muir's volumes, and often repeated by *Dnyanodaya* in his various issues, viz., the origin of the caste system dates from the Brahmin (Aryan) conquest of India, Phule claimed that because the Mahars and Mangs, the true and original natives of the land, had put up the toughest resistance to the Aryan invaders, the latter had sought to completely subdue them by isolating them in the caste system as the Shudra varna whose very presence and touch polluted.

Again thanks to the missionaries, Phule argues that salvation lies not in respecting and following caste taboos and practices prescribed by the Brahmins, still less by giving gifts to them, but in leading a good and virtuous life. Here, in a sense, Phule turns tables on the missionaries arguing that if God is holy and believes in moral governance, he needs no intermediary like priests to help laymen approach him. The end result of the missionary effort was thus not what the missionaries had expected: a natural and grateful conversion to Christianity.

Phule learnt from the missionary strategy the vital importance of school education in shaping young minds. His lasting contribution to the uplift of the low castes infact lay in the starting of numerous schools for girls and for Mahars and Mangs. It is unlikely that liberal Brahmin reformers like Chiplunkar or Deshmukh would have ever opened such schools for the low castes.

How telling was the impact of missionary and English education on young minds can be gauged from the letter written to the newspaper *Prabhakar* (edited by leading reformers Jambhekar and Bhau Mahajan) cautioning Hindus from sending their children to learn English in mission schools because those taught English by the missionaries soon became disillusioned with their own religion and looked upon Christianity as providing a better account of the relations between God and man.

Missionary thought and teaching also compelled the British India government to take a firmer stand on the issue of the human rights of lower castes. In 1851, when the Board of Education, decided against admitting Mahar boys to government schools under Brahmin pressure, the *Dnyanodaya* protested bitterly against "this deference to a set of rules that took no account of individual qualities".

Why the Missionary Strategy Misfired

The early missionaries like Duff and Wilson had expected that western education along with the teaching of the Christian scriptures

(Christian scriptures were compulsorily taught in all mission schools even to non-Christians) would eventually make for extensive conversions of the educated. If in spite of their best endeavours this did not exactly take place, the reasons are two.

Firstly, reformers like Raja Rammohun Roy (and this is true of all the high caste liberal reformers who followed, Ranade, Gokhale) accepted most of the missionary criticism of popular Hinduism but counter-argued that true Hindu dharma taught *Advaita*, the idea of an impersonal absolute contained in the Upanishads. Roy, for instance, reinterpreted Hinduism as "ethical monism" which he considered superior to the monotheism of Christianity. (Monism considers everything as part of God/Brahma; whereas monotheism believes in only one God who exists separately from man and nature). Some have even claimed that Roy succeeded in converting Scottish missionaries to Unitarianism.

Secondly, it must not be forgotten that Hindu intellectuals came under the powerful impact of not only missionary teaching but also of Western Enlightenment thought, the rationalist thought of eighteenth century Europe and the USA, as symbolised in the writings of Voltaire, Thomas Paine and others. Deist ideas, rejection of religious hierarchies, re-examination of claims of revealed religion, concern for natural and political rights of individuals, were all taught to English-educated Indians by free thinking Europeans who were often teachers in government schools. Religious radicals in England denied that any of the world's religions was a direct divine revelation. They also exposed how large parts of the *Bible* (the Old Testament in particular) were inconsistent with human reason and with the idea of absolute purity and universality of the creator. The religious radicals in England argued that man with the help of reason could arrive at the true knowledge of his spiritual duty to worship his creator and love his neighbour.

European radicals provided the western-educated Hindu reformers with material they used not only to attack Hindu superstition, but also what they called 'Christian superstition'. Raja Rammohun Roy, for instance, argued that conversion to Christianity was no real alternative since Christianity suffered from exactly the same inconsistencies as Hinduism. They therefore advocated an impersonal and universal creator and emphasised man's moral and spiritual duties. The attack by European radicals on the inconsistencies and immorality to be found in the *Bible* convinced Hindu reformers that they must advance the cause of secular knowledge and material progress along with a belief in a universal creator. Phule, for one, was profoundly impressed by Paine's doctrine of natural rights which existed as moral imperatives even if society and religion at any given time did not recognise them. His main charge against Hinduism (in *Gulamgiri*) was that in the name of religion it had not only sought to bestow privileges on the Brahmins but had also trampled on the natural rights of all other men.

Almost all the Hindu intellectuals responded to the missionary teaching/thought, not by seeking conversion to Christianity, but calling for religious reform within the community. Leading reformers of the period, men like Krishna Shastri Chiplunkar and Gopal Deshmukh urged young Hindus to take to western education and especially to the study of western secular and scientific subjects "which could purify their moral standards". Even an orthodox priest like Shastri Sathe of Pune opined that the best way to repond to the missionary and western challenge was by becoming civic-conscious and "actively civic-minded".

The missionaries may not have succeeded in their evangelical objectives to the extent they had expected, but it must be admitted that they generated a most healthy moral debate among Hindu intellectuals of the nineteenth century, a debate which was to usher in major reforms and transform Hindu society beyond recognition.

REFERENCES

Keer, D. and S.G. Malshe, (eds.), *The Collected Works of Mahatma Phule*, (Marathi), Bombay, MSSLC, 1969.

Keer, Dhananjay, *Mahatma Jotirao Phule: Father of Indian Social Revolution*.

Kotnala, M.C., *Rammohun Roy and the Indian Awakening*, New Delhi, 1975. Ch. 4 on Roy and Christianity.

Masselos, J.C., *Towards Nationalism: Group Affiliation and Politics of Public Associations in 19th Century Western India*, Bombay, 1975.

O'Hanlon, Rosalind, *Caste, Conflict and Ideology, Mahatma Jotirao Phule: The Low Caste Protest in 19th Century Western India*, Cambridge, 1985.

Omvedt, Gail, *Cultural Revolt in a Colonial Society: Non-Brahmin Movement in Western India 1873-1930*, Bombay, 1976.

Singh, Iqbal, *Rammohan Roy - A Biographical Enquiry into the Making of Modern India*, Vols. 1-3, Bombay, 1987.

Tucker, Richard, "The Early Setting of the non-Brahmin Movement in Maharashtra" in *The Indian Historical Review*, 7 (no. 1-2, July 1980-January 1981).

Webster, John C.B., *The Christian Community and Change in the 19th Century India*, Delhi, 1976.

10

EDUCATION AND MISSION: The School as an Agent of Evangelization in India

RUDOLF C. HEREDIA

I. Introduction

The close association between religion and education has been a common phenomenon in all societies, up until the predominance of secularization in modern ones. Indeed, as long as the religious world-view dominated the "fiduciary system", to use a Parsonian category,[1] education had to be a subordinate agency of socialization under the umbrella of the religious one. The corresponding affinity between these two sub-systems of society, and even the dependence of the educational one on the religious is not surprising. The earliest teachers in society were first the medicine-men, shamans and bhagats, later these become more formalized with brahmins and bhikkus, monks and maulvis; and eventually they are institutionalized in ashrams and monasteries.

It is only later, as learning becomes more secular, that education can break out from under the religious umbrella. Today even religiously affiliated educational institutions are more concerned with the secular than the sacred, and serve communitarian objectives rather than theological purposes. But this is a comparatively recent phenomenon. Little wonder then, that "the school has been the principal agent of evangelism in the modern missionary movement"[2] that began with the colonial expansion of the west, and ended with its decline.

The penetration was gradual and drawn over four centuries. but

Asia was better able than Africa or Latin America to absorb its impact without surrendering as completely. The scale of these societies, the complexity of their civilizations, the rigidity of their hierarchy rendered them far more resilient, but not quite unaffected either.[3]

This essay treats not only of Christian education within the missionary enterprise, but extends itself to the socio-political impact beyond as well. The first is discussed within the ecclesial context of conversion and evangelization, and it is crucial in order to understand the inspiration and gradual evolution of missionary institutions. The second is framed by a more secular discussion, and is important because of the pioneering role the missions had in bringing western education to India and the consequent effect this had on Indian society. It concludes to the need for a socio-political analysis of and a contextualized theology of secular action for Christian education, if the liberating potential of its ideals and purposes is to be realized.

The continuing commitment of the church's resources to education is today far less than it once was, in proportion to the overall outlay by the government. Certainly the influence of Christian institutions is no longer the dominant one in education any more, but neither is it insignificant.

As can be expected, the religious concerns of the missionaries were first articulated within a theological discourse. But education must also be understood within a more secular one. The dominance of the first has too easily led to a neglect of the second, because traditional theological issues are too often insensitive or impertinent to the socio-political concerns of our changing times. And even as old controversies are laid to rest by an on-going working consensus, new ones arise, and the discourse in which they are located already delimits the kinds of conclusions that can be reached.

Now it was at the religious level that the issues were debated at first and this continued to be the dominant discourse up until the decline of the west's missionary venture at the end of the colonial period, when changing socio-political conditions precipitated a different set of concerns and a correspondingly different theology. The debate among the missionaries, is well recorded, specially among the Protestants, and equally well articulated too. But as we shall see it does not provide an adequate understanding of the decisions and events over time, and certainly not a comprehensive one. Socio-economic exigencies, even though often not explicitly articulated in the debate, do get expressed in political decisions which may well be only tangentially connected with religious or theological issues.

It is our contention here that the neglect of the socio-political context of Christian education has not helped us to understand or orient it to some of the most relevant and noble objectives the church has opted for. But before we can address ourselves to this issue, we will first make a brief historical sketch of mission education in India, in the context of the wider educational system that emerged over this period, to serve as the backdrop for the discussion of the issues to follow.

II.1 An Historical Sketch

The history of the Christian mission in the east since the 16th century is intimately bound up with the colonial expansion of the west. The gospel came in the ships of the conquistadors whose purpose was to conquer and convert. Inevitably this fusion of the sacred and the secular led to a confusion of the religious and political, the entanglement of the ecclesial and the economic. Until the very end of the colonial period, Christian education was very much part of the missionary enterprise and could not but be involved in the same controversy and confusion. The tendency was to confound the two distinct discourses and coopt the secular one into the religious.

There have been three main agencies for the spread of western education in India: the Christian missions, the governmental, and private Indian ones. Obviously different agencies would have different goals for their educational involvement. The usual way of conceptualising these has been to polarise them within a dualistic framework: "Government versus private, indigenous versus western and imperialist versus nationalist", etc.[4] Again most modern histories of education in India follow a periodisation that was first used by Nurullah and Naik.[5] But our concern here is more limited. It is mainly with the Christian educational agencies, in the context of the others in order to situate historically the issues to be discussed later.

II.2 The Catholic Missions

The Portuguese were the first to bring western education to India establishing schools in their settlements at Goa, Daman, Diu, Cochin and on the Hooghly.[6] Already in 1543, on January 25, the feast of the conversion of St. Paul, the Jesuits opened a college named after the saint in Goa.[7] It was originally begun "to promote the training of priests",[8] but its scope was very soon extended as in most Jesuit institutions of the time, to other students as well. The French too had begun elementary schools at Pondicherry, Mahe, Chandernagore, and Yaman.[9]

These schools were generally in the vernacular, at least at the elementary level, and for religious instruction.[10] However, in 1684, in order to strengthen Portugal's hold on Goa, Konkani was banned by viceregal decree on June 27th, and parish priests and school masters were instructed to teach only in the colonial language, so "that in time it may become the common language for all, making thereafter no use of the mother-tongue".[11]

Gradually the local *pathshalas* were replaced by parish schools throughout the colonial territories and "churches replaced temples as centers of learning in the wake of conversion to Christianity. Church schools were maintained at the cost of the village communities which paid the school master for teaching the sons of the ganvkars".[12]

Further north, "the early history of education in Bombay is chiefly a record of Christian Missionary enterprise".[13] The Portuguese "Franciscans were not only the first missionaries, but also the first school masters".[14] In fact, a month after taking over Bombay island from the Portuguese, Humphrey Cooke wrote to London on 3rd March, 1665: "The general language is Portuguese, so that it will be necessary the statutes and laws be translated into that language".[15] The British eventually changed this. Fearful of the influence of the Portuguese friars, they expelled the Franciscans on 13th May, 1720. They were then replaced by Italian Carmelites.

This began the gradual decline of Catholic education in Bombay. By "1770 the former parish schools were no longer functioning, illiteracy, which had practically vanished, now reared its head again . . . from 1770 to 1850, not a single Carmelite school was started in Bombay".[16]

In 1850 a Protestant account in a local publication described "the Bombay Papists" thus: "With two or three exceptions, the respectable portion of European community and of this creed appear to be ashamed of it and do not even acknowledge it".[17] This opinion is corroborated from within by a certain Doctor Dallas speaking in St. Xavier's College hall in 1876: "When I arrived in Bombay in the early fifties, I found the condition of the Catholics especially as regards education so miserable, and their social position so low and contemptible, that I felt almost ashamed to profess my religion; compared with Protestant institutions, ours were the merest corner-schools, or rather, there were no institutions worthy of the name school".[18]

In was only in 1869, that the founding of St. Xavier's College by the Jesuits marked "the emergence of the Catholic community from obscurity into the public eye".[19] Beyond Portuguese territory as well, it was the "Roman Catholic missionaries who took the lead in establishing elementary and secondary schools in Madras and Bengal".[20] However, "Catholic Missions did not do effective work during the period from 1720 to 1850".[21] The suppression of the Society of Jesus in the Portuguese colonies about this time and later in the Roman Church as well in 1773, certainly had a disastrous effect on the missions the world over, and in India quite definitely.

However, with the restoration of the Society in 1814, and the return of the Jesuits to India a revival in Catholic education began, especially with regard to higher education.[22] Some of the colleges that marked this turning point in Catholic education in the 19th century were: St. Joseph's College, founded at Negapatnam in 1844 and moved to Tiruchirapalli in 1882, St. Xavier's College, Calcutta (1862), St. Xavier's College, Bombay (1869), St. Aloysius College, Mangalore (1880), St. Joseph's College, Darjeeling (1888).[23] In the post-independence period Catholic colleges have rapidly increased from 30 in 1944 to 38 in 1948 and to 76 in 1967.[24]

Yet there still remains the urgent "need to do something about the poor level of higher education among the Christian community. For a community that has practically the highest level of literacy in the country, the percentage of University educated Christians is disproportionately low".[25] Today Catholic education is so much sought after that now "there is always the temptation to forget one's roots – e.g., Christian institutions which began as orphanages, today appear as high class boarding schools, so restrictive in admissions that there is no place for the poor in the inn".[26]

The accusation of elitism, academic or otherwise, may be somewhat of an unfair over-generalization. But the widespread perception of these institutions having an "almost exclusive concern with the social elite and the intellectual elite"[27] is not entirely without a basis.

Already from its beginnings in India four kinds of institutions can be distinguished in Catholic education:[28] (1) Elementary grammar schools attached to churches and mission stations. (2) Orphanages and other like institutions, for Indian children in which besides elementary instructions, agricultural and industrial work was provided. (3) Seminaries and religious houses, for theological instruction and training candidates for priesthood. (4) Jesuit, and later other colleges for higher studies.

Basically it is still these four kinds of institutions which account for the largest part of formal Catholic education, and the typology does help us to derive some provisional but pertinent conclusions. The brief historical outline above was meant to be selectively illustrative of this.

Firstly, the Catholic school was not at the cutting edge of direct evangelisation but rather followed in its wake. It was not so much an instrument of missionary expansion as an agency of community consolidation. It was used not so much to preach to and baptize the unconverted, as to instruct and educate the converted.

Secondly, following on this, the medium of instruction at the beginning was in the vernacular, specially for religious and primary education of the neophytes, though the institutional model used for this was western. It was later that the language of the colonizer was imposed, more for political than pedagogic reasons. In competition then with the western model and the colonizer's dominant language, the indigenous education system collapsed and local languages languished.

Thirdly, post-school education was firstly a concern for providing an adequate clergy, but it did not stop there. However, it hardly reached beyond the upper castes and classes of Catholics and non-Catholics. Hence we find that while literacy levels are comparatively high among Catholics and school education quite widespread, college and university qualifications are proportionately lower than for other equally literate communities.

II.3 The Protestant Churches

Among the Protestants, "the missionaries to start regular schools in India for general education were the Danes working in the Madras Presidency".[29] In 1706 Ziegenbalg and Plutschou arrived in Tranquebar and by 1725 there were 17 schools for "Heathen and Muhammaden" children and 4 for Christians.[30] The first Protestant English Mission came to Madras with the Society for the Promotion of Christian Knowledge in 1727 and started schools in Madras, Tanjore, Cuddalore, Palamcottah and Trichinopoly. The Baptists came to Bengal in 1793, and the London Missionary Society in 1804; the Church Missionary Society and the Wesleyan Mission had far flung settlements at Surat, Meerut, Agra, Calcutta and Tranquebar already in the 19th century.[31]

One of the motivations of the Protestant missionary was their concern with "the removal of apprehended trouble owing to the predominance of Roman Catholics among the inhabitants of places where they settled".[32] But the mission to the non-Christians gained increasing importance, especially with the decline of Portuguese and French influence in India. For already the first Danish mission schools and very soon the famous trio of Carey, Marshman and Ward, began to use schools as a means of evangelization, and founded a school in 1818 at Serampore under Danish protection in the face of opposition from the East India Company, which was apprehensive of the effect of this education on the people, "lest it make them less docile".[33]

The beginnings of the Protestant mission to India in the 18th century were indeed small and not effectively supported by the East India Company, when not actively opposed by it. "It is doubtful whether in 1800 more than a thousand children were being educated in mission schools".[34] However, the first half of the 19th century saw a rapid expansion of Protestant missionary endeavour in education, specially after Macaulay's Minute of 1835, and when English replaced Persian as the official and court language in 1837, and again after the 1844 resolution of Lord Hardinge prescribed English as the preferred qualification for government service.

The Company Charter of 1813 granted the missionaries a new but restricted liberty, though in the one of 1833 "all restrictions were at last withdrawn".[35] Some of the Company's servants, like Martin Richard Gubbins of the Bengal Civil Service would even say that "the missionary is the true regenerator of India".[36]

But after Wood's Despatch of 1854, which encouraged government withdrawl from education in favour of other Indian agencies, and particularly after the 'mutiny' of 1857 the second half of the 19th century saw a change of emphasis from expansion to consolidation and quality in Christian education. This was specially after the Education Commission of 1882.[37] Thus some of the most prestigious institutions in higher education are still Protestant ones: Madras Christian College, 1839, St. John's, Agra, 1850, St. Stephen, Delhi,

1881, as also the Christian Medical Colleges at Ludhiana, 1894, and at Vellore, 1918. By 1931, the Lindsay Commission[38] found that Christian institutions had been displaced from the premier position in education in India by the expansion of governmental and other private resources committed to it.

But "for the most part of the 19th century, they dominated the Indian educational scene, not merely in regard to the magnitude of their educational enterprise but also in regard to the ideas and values inculcated through education. Even more importantly, from the 1870s the Protestant missions were seriously trying to influence the intellectual, religious and political awakenings of the educated Indian on the assumption that winning over the intelligentsia was the surest method to bring about the eventual conversion of India, as a whole".[39]

Once again the short historical sketch outlined here suggests some pertinent though tentative conclusions, which are mooted to carry the discussion further.

Firstly, in comparison to the Catholics, Protestant mission education was more clearly and decidedly evangelical in purpose. This is evident by the number of far flung schools and colleges in their mission territory, even where there was no sizeable Christian community to cater to as yet. The first to urge this evangelical purpose for Christian education was Alexander Duff (1806-1876), the founder of the Scottish Church College in Calcutta, who landed in India in 1830. He thought "that he was laying a mine which would eventually explode and blow Hinduism to pieces".[40] William Miller (1838-1923) of the Free Church Mission Society of Scotland, refined this somewhat crude approach and changed the purpose from direct evangelization to that of a *preparatio evangelica*, where education would be the Christian leaven for Hinduism in order to bring "Christ to India".[41]

Secondly, with regard to language the closer connection between the Protestant churches and the British government made the transition from the vernacular schools, of the early days of the Danish mission, to the English medium ones of missionaries, like Duff, quicker and more decisive. For English was seen not only as a positive gain for employment opportunities by the Indians, but also as a subtle though effective means of transmitting gospel and western values by the missinaries.

Thirdly, with the change of emphasis from quantity and spread, to quality and excellence, the allocation of resources for higher education and prestigious institutions followed quite inevitably. And even today many Protestant colleges have still held their ground here.

Besides the missionaries there were other agencies that formed the wider context of education in the country. From the beginning of the 19th century the government played an increasingly important role in education, while in the second half of the century other private Indian agencies entered into the field. Obviously each of these had their own interests and goals. Here we will be more concerned with the governmental ones, since these impinged more directly and critically on the missionary endeavour.

II.4 The Colonial Government

The India Act of 1813 was the first important landmark in the East India Company's education policy,[42] for it included a clause requiring the annual expenditure by the Directors of the East India Company of a lakh of rupees on education.[43] Earlier the Company had refrained from such commitments, but now the earlier ban on private enterprise in education in its territories was lifted in 1815. In 1833 the Company's allotment to education was increased to ten lakh rupees.[44] But the government's commitment was never adequate to the task.

For it adopted a 'downward filtration' approach as first proposed by Lord Auckland in 1839, and described by Nurullah and Naik thus: "the Company was expected to give a good education (which then necessarily meant education through English) to only a few persons (these may or may not be from the upper classes) and leave it to these persons to educate the masses (through modern Indian languages)".[45]

The implicit class and caste bias of such an elitist policy was inevitable. It was only strengthened further by the adoption of Macaulay's Minute of 1835 in favour of English as the medium for European learning. This effectively destroyed the old indigenous system of education and put the new western one decisively beyond the reach of the masses.

The Company's Education dispatch of 19th July, 1854, called the Wood Dispatch, rejected this theory in principle, but "replaced it with the doctrine of state withdrawl in favour of a system of grants-in-aid to privately managed institutions. The expansion of education became dependent on the private agencies who were willing to carry the burden which the government pleaded inability to bear".[46]

Subsequent to the grants-in-aid code, "about a third of the cost of education was borne by the private agencies, two-thirds by the government".[47] This relieved the government of some of the financial cost and much of the organisational initiative in education, but it led to "the *laissez faire* policy, enunciated by the Indian Education Commission (1882)",[48] also called the Hunter Commission.

The rapid expansion of education that resulted from this, caused serious concern to the government. Curzon tried to put some order and consolidate education with an emphasis on quality over quantity, but in spite of the Indian Universities Act of 1904, the Calcutta Universities Commission, chaired by Sir Michael Sadler in 1917 still found the system "fundamentally defective in almost every aspect".[49] The demand for education, especially western and English education, fuelled a rapid expansion by private agencies motivated by the desire of upward mobility for their respective caste and/or religious communities. Thus in 1967 J.P. Naik estimates that "85 per cent of our colleges and 65 per cent of our secondary schools are in the private sector".[50]

Following the missionaries, as each new group jumped on the educational bandwagon, the brahmins after 1882, the non-brahmins after 1921, the *dalits* with Ambedkar in the 1940s, and the *adivasi seva mandals* in the 1950s, government recognition and grants were demanded not on the basis of performance and quality, but on the principle of equality and non-discrimination.[51] Later with education coming under the provincial and state governments, the politicization and commercialization of education certainly has not helped more worthy pedagogic or democratic purposes, but it has rather coopted education to communal and consumerist ones.[52]

A unique feature of the official education policy in British India was its strict religious neutrality. This was according to some "absolutely without precedent or parallel elsewhere, besides being entirely opposite to the traditional idea of education in the East", or for that matter in Europe at the time as well.[53] The 'Pious Clause' for which Charles Grant agitated in England, was rejected by the Company's Charter of 1793, and though the Charter of 1813 and 1833 gave the missions greater freedom, the government retained its religious neutrality.

Thus in his farewell address to some missionaries Lord Bentick in 1835 reaffirmed that "the fundamental principle of British rule, the compact to which the government stands solemnly pledged, is strict neutrality . . . with the religious beliefs of the students".[54] The

Dispatch 1854 forbade any religious instruction in government schools, and the Education Commission of 1882 reinforced this. Queen Victoria's famous proclamation prohibited "all interference with religious belief or worship of any of our subjects, on pain of our highest displeasure".[55]

We are not arguing here that this religious neutrality was a question of moral conviction on the part of the government. Even people like Sir Charles Trevelyan, prominent in the educational controversies of the 1830s and Mounstuart Elphinstone, in Bombay, in spite of their secular credentials were more than just sympathetic to the missionary agenda in education. However, we would not agree that this religious neutrality was simply a matter of historical accident.[56] Given the diversity and depth of religious affiliations in India, this was an obviously pragmatic political necessity. Indeed "this was unquestionably one aspect of British policy in India. All reasonable men took it for granted that the government should interfere as little as possible with the manners, customs and ideas of subjects whose loyalty was not, and never could be more than precarious".[57]

Here again with regard to the wider contact of education in India we conclude with some tentative observations for further consideration.

Firstly, in spite of much liberal inspiration and many noble ideals, government educational policy failed in effective executive follow-up. It is interesting to note that although the Company officially accepted responsibility for public education in 1813, the government in England did so only in 1833.[58] But the difference in their delivery was one of the political will and vested interests involved. Other private Indian agencies in education were overly constrained by more narrow communal preoccupations, and though the nationalist movement was the inspiration for some, it was never quite strong enough, in spite of Gandhi's challenge, to break free from the system they inherited and operated within.

Even the religious neutrality of the formal system was less a committed secularism than a political expediency and this tended to follow whichever way the political winds would later blow. For the grants-in-aid code readily allowed the public good in education to be coopted by private interests in the community.

Secondly, the new western institutional model and the English language medium through which it was implemented, dismantled the old indigenous system of education and set back vernacular literacy. The overall literacy statistics tell the tragic story convincingly. Using literacy percentages as a vital indicator, we have the following figures for British India: 1881 – 4.8 per cent; 1891 – 5.6; 1901 – 5.3; 1911 – 5.9; 1921 – 7.2; 1931 – 9.5; 1941 – 16.1 per cent.[59]

Thirdly, not only was the expansion of the new education system unable to make up for the demise of the old one, it was itself inadequate to meet the needs of an industrial and an egalitarian society. The emphasis was on liberal not technical education, which existed more in intent than in effect. For as Lord Curzon himself admitted: "the plant of technical education in India, subsisted mainly on platitudes in vice-regal and gubernatorial speeches".[60] In sum, "the low rate of literacy neglect of mass education, as well as of technical and vocational education, and the methods of teaching, were all handicaps in the path of development".[61]

Moreover, higher education was extremely elitist, a small tip of a pyramid with a very inadequate base. The focus here was on the transmission of knowledge, not its creation, and that too more in the arts than the sciences, more generalists than specialist, more liberal than professional.

And so like much else in the country at the time, Indian education continued to be a colonial appendage to the British system. In spite of, and partly because of the contribution of the missionaries and the role of other various agencies involved, Catholic or Protestant, governmental or private, nationalist or communal, it remained "a colony, intellectually, culturally and even spiritually subordinate to the West and England".[62]

III.1 Discussion and Analysis

What was the contribution of the missions to this system of education in India? Certainly they were pioneers when there were few other agencies to shoulder the responsibility for education. The indigenous system lacked influential patrons and the Company held itself aloof from much ventures. Few would doubt that "the origin of the present system of English education in India is to be sought in the activities of early Christian missionaries".[63] But not just the beginnings, they were largely responsible for implementing and stabilising the western institutional model of education with English as the medium of instruction. They were in fact so successful that the demand for admission into Christian educational institutions by upper class/caste non-Christians was much greater than what could be made available.

Indeed, "for well over a century Christian educationists had stood at the top of the educational hierarchy, not only as pioneers but as leaders in that they excelled in the two principal functions of formal education – the imparting of knowledge and inculcation of values. Moreover, Christian educational institutions were among the best organized and best managed in the country. . . . All in all, Christian education stood on a pedestal during the British regime".[64]

However, mission education was very much part of the larger missionary venture, and always functioned within the ambit of the Christian enterprise. This connection may have been more or less explicit at times, but it has never quite been severed. For even when the content of its educational service was modern and secular, its inspiration still remained Christian and religious.

No wonder then that the perception of the educational needs of this country were filtered through their concern for their church, and the inevitable mismatch between an alien institutional system and indigenous pedagogic requirements could not be addressed. This of course was unavoidable as long as the school was used as an agent of evangelization. For if mission education was to be implemented and contained within the traditional structure of the church, it could hardly be expected to be non-sectarian in breaking new ground in a secular field, even one with as close an affinity to it as education.

The main contribution of Christian educators then was largely within the parameters of the colonial systems, and it served the Christian community within the churches rather well, even though its role as an agent of direct evangelisation for those outside it was increasingly challenged and marginalised. However, Christian educators, by and large, did not seriously question the basic features of the system for this fell outside the perview of their concerns. Perhaps too late did they recognize that "the alliance between the Christian colleges and the government and the University system while it has of course given the colleges great opportunities for service, has on the whole been bought at too great a price. Christian higher education has seemed to be a cheap form of missionary enterprise".[65]

A fortiori then this would hold true at the lower levels of government aided education as well. Christian education, then, was not prepared by its history for a new role in post-independent India. In fact, "the course of Christian education since independence does not impress the critical observer as a bold and spontaneous effort on the part of a mature section of Indian educators to lead the way in the crisis brought on by the changing times. It does not seem as if Christian educators have truly taken up the challenge of educational reconstruction for an Independent India".[66]

Even as late as 1967, a perceptive and sympathetic educationist like J.P. Naik, does not consider directly challenging Christian educators to the mainstream task of national development. Instead he proposes three purposes for Christian education in post-independent India: the reconciliation of religion and science, the provision of English teachers and a Hindu-Christian encounter.[67]

What could be the underlying reasons for the missed opportunities of Christian education in our country? We believe that these reasons must be sought in the debate within the churches regarding the role of mission education, to which we now turn.

III.2 The Ecclesial Debate

The discussion that preoccupied the missionaries with regard to the school as an agent of evangelism, involved a debate about two approaches to evangelisation in India: (i) evangelisation of India through education and intelligentsia; and (ii) evangelisation of India through the masses.[68]

It was a debate that began already in the 19th century and which the Protestants articulated better than the Catholics, who seemed less accustomed to discuss such issues publicly, at least from the source material available to this writer. But the importance of the issue to the goals and purposes of Christian educational mission cannot be gainsaid. For as bishop Newbigin insightfully observes: "The problem of stating our goals as Christian colleges is part of the wider problem of stating in clear terms the theological justification for the pursuit of secular goals".[69]

From the earliest missionaries the goals of Christian education were threefold: First, education of Christians themselves in a Christian atmosphere so that they could be good members of their church and occupy important positions in secular society; secondly, to render service to Indian youth at large; thirdly, to build evangelical bridges towards the country's intelligentsia and thus pave the way for an acceptance of the faith.[70]

In other words these were communitarian, service and evangelical, objectives, respectively. While the Catholics may have stressed the first and the Protestants the last, all three goals were present in varying degrees at different times in mission education. Much seemed to depend on what priorities the religious debate justified at the time.

In the first half of the 19th century, Alexander Duff, aggressively urged the use of English education to undermine Hinduism and thereby foster conversions. But it soon became apparent that Hindus stopped half way, accepting western education but not Christian beliefs. By the time of the Allahabad Missionary Conference in 1872, "a fresh apologia for Christian education and the educational missions became inevitable".[71]

This was provided by William Miller who argued for a *preparatio evangelica*, "to prepare the minds to be receptive to Christian principles",[72] and not merely adding numbers to the church. Hence there was now a change of "purpose and role from conversion to evangelic preparation through the diffusion of Christian principles".[73]

Thus began the 'mission to the educated'. This led to "multifarious religious tendencies, ranging from loss of faith, atheism, agnosticism, indifference, positivism, free-thought, neo-orthodoxy, revivalism, including its extreme aggressive forms of anti-Christian, anti-missionary undertones".[74]

Moreover, the very Christian principles the missionaries proposed of equality and brotherhood, etc., were used by the nationalists to oppose the colonial government much to the dismay of their teachers.

However, it was persons like T. E. Slater, who were sympathetic to this awakening of India, both religious and nationalist, describing it "as the Renaissance period in the history of the Hindus".[75] Slater's changed approach presented Christianity not antagonistically but as the fulfilment of all the higher and nobler truths of other religions.[76]

The Jesuit, Fr. P. Johanns, in Calcutta was very much within this perspective with his *To Christ through the Vedanta*, in the Light of the East Series, as also Stanley Jones' *Christ of the Indian Road*. More pragmatically, the objectives of Catholic schools and colleges have been "all more or less justified by their response to the needs of a particular time and place. They include: a Catholic education for Catholic children; the raising of the social and economic level of the Catholic poor; the socio-economic uplift of tribals and *harijans*; functional literacy and job-skills for the less literates; the establishment of centres for Catholic acceptability in major urban areas; the provision for the nation of highly literate and skilled leaders in professional life; inculcation of habits of moral integrity in a generation of leaders, natural elites. . . ."[77]

But the desire to evangelise this national awakening, put the missionaries in the dilemma of sympathizing with a movement which opposed a government on whom they relied for support. Slater, who represented the moderates, summed-up three main objectives justifying his support for the Congress party: in terms of the fusion of the peoples of India into one nation, regenerated morally and politically, and consolidated in a just, and healthy union with Britain.[78]

What we find here and also later at the end of the missionary venture in the colonial period is a still persistent paternalism. For the foreign missionaries were quite conscious of maintaining their identity as representatives of the ruling race.[79] As a cynical remark from some local Christians would put it: "The missionaries wanted them to become only their brothers but not their brothers-in-law".[80]

Obviously such a mind-set was quite inadequate to ride out the political storms that were brewing on the national horizons. For few missionaries would risk the political involvement of a C. F. Andrews or the cultural commitment of a Verrier Elwin. No doubt an appropriate theological justification was conveniently at hand! However, these remained an embarrassing aspect of the missionary mentality, the affinity between the Christian missions and colonial rule, which cannot be easily gainsaid. For "the principle of ecclesiastical establishment, for all that it was not formally recognised, yet played a quite important role in the expansion of the British empire and the Christian faith. Many problems facing the Christian Church in Asia and Africa today derive from this fact".[81]

All through these debates there are changing theological understandings underlying the issues being discussed. Beginning with an aggresive, almost imperialistic stance for religious conversion, it was modified into a more moderate view of diffusing Christian values and as a preparation for a full acceptance of Christian beliefs. The theology of fulfilment changed the emphasis from bringing 'India to Christ' to bringing 'Christ to India'. But at the end of the missionary venture, it is still a long way off from the religious dialogue and pluralism so much needed today.

The outcome of these exchanges would be relevant mostly to

those within the religious discourse in which it takes place. To those on the outside, it would seem more like a hot-house argument among an in-group. For all its very real impact on Indian society, "education did not help Christianity the way Trevelyan and Elphinstone, among others, had hoped".[82] They were mistaken in thinking that the liberal inspiration of Christian education would do in India, what the Church seemed to have done for the poor in England.[83]

For a more satisfactory explanation of the actual dynamics involved, we must enter into a socio-political discourse that provides a more pertinent perspective.

III.3 A Socio-Political Perspective

As we have remarked earlier Indians sought Christian education because it opened up preferred economic opportunities for them and not out of any religious preference. In fact they were rather suspicious of the missionary connnection of these institutions. This was pertinent enough to put a serious question to the assumptions underlying the very basis of these institutions., and thus it led to a "reversal of priorities" in favour of a more direct evangelization of the masses especially after 1910,[84] and later to the more secular approach of the social gospel.[85]

However, with the political awakening of India and of the freedom movement, there "was a growing awareness among British officials of the political dangers of English education".[86] This was a threat that put the government in an obvious dilemma with regard to education, specially at the higher level of the University. And yet, as Krishna Kumar insightfully argues, if "the concept of citizenship underlying the vision of the educated man in colonial India is examined in its ideological roots",[87] a fundamental "homonymy between the colonial and the nationalist views of the role of education"[88] is apparent.

For as the East India Company evolved into a colonial state, commercial exigencies had to be replaced by political socialization with regard to its subjects. Towards this end, colonial education was to be more than an assembly line producing clerks; it was to train the student in moral uprighness before the law and to be a loyal subject of the colonial order. "The emphasis it placed on the formation of dependable habits concerning the use of time and space was directly related to the demands of factory life".[89]

Moreover, the very elitism of the system especially in higher education, could not but make the educated Indian feel as patronizingly towards the illiterate masses, as the colonial sahibs felt towards him. The argument between bureaucracy and the Indian intelligentsia was in fact over the claim to speak for the Indian masses. Would it be a Curzon or a Gokhale![90] But at another level the "identification between the educated Indian and the colonial state consolidated the boundary walls around school knowledge"[91] and left the masses of India out.

Thus, in spite of the high-minded rhetoric, what the nationalists did really achieve was less a change of political structure than a 'circulation of elites', political *swatantrata*, not Gandhian *swaraj*. For the people, however, this only meant that the white sahibs were changed for darker ones. Indeed, "it is worth asking which of the two roles of education was more influential in shaping the cultural and political life of India at the turn of the century – the role of strengthening group solidarity among the educated, or the role of disturbing traditional hierarchies. The first is rarely acknowledged, whereas the second has been highly overestimated".[92]

For an elitist system is best able to do the first, but only a mass-based one can achieve the second. This has not as yet happened in our country, certainly not with secondary, or even primary education. On the contrary, the pattern of development has only accentuated the elitism and paternalism, the injustice and domination in the Indian state. In all this "the education system in independent India remained an agency contributing primarily to the maintenance of law and order".[93]

The nationalist promise of equality of opportunities for all Indians expressed itself in education as an irresistible demand for the expansion of the system, which was fueled by the class/caste bias of vested interests, "who exploited the code for missionary purposes, profit, communal advantage or political gain".[94] The social commitment to equitable access for weaker sections through reserved admissions for them is still being resisted on the grounds of 'merit', which is still defined by an examination system that in any case favours those, who already have a privileged access to the means to excel in it, with even further access and privileges. So "what really began as the dream of social transformation became a demand for avenues of upward mobility of individuals".[95]

The anti-brahmin, and other backward caste movements in western and southern India did mobilize and broaden the educational base in society somewhat, and this augured well for the breakdown of traditional hierarchies. But soon enough the "transformational force" of these movements "was subtly neutralized by utilitarianism and channelized towards the task of creating a market society".[96] Eventually, these too settled down to secure their own communal advantage, with the consumerist allure of the market-place, leaving the other underprivileged and disadvantaged groups behind.

The radical alternative urged by Gandhi's 'basic education', which wanted to validate local skills and knowledge to make education self-sustaining, and to integrate it with the lives of the masses, was never given more than lip-service and such a half-hearted implementation, that it was almost deliberately predestined to fail.

No wonder then the social equality and the economic development which education was to deliver for all, became increasingly problematic and is now in crisis. Hence, "the first conclusion we may draw from this review and social analysis of the educational developments over the last thirty years of independence is that the old pre-independence systems and structure of education have, by and large, been maintained and continued . . . the second conclusion that emerged is that while the system carries on its obsolete fashion, a considerable expansion – a wider spread of education – has taken place".[97]

Now given this fundamental continuity between pre- and the post-independence education, and the close identification of mission education with the system from its very beginnings, it was hardly likely that Christian education later would break free from it, given the advantages it had derived from this connection and still hoped to. Notwithstanding the soul-searching of a Lindsay and his Report[98] the consensus recommendation has been in favour, not of withdrawal, but of a reorientation, which has yet to prove effective.

We believe in this socio-political perspective, that it is, that we must look for the basic dynamics of the role of the school as an agent of evangelization. For it explains why mission education succeeded less at the Christianization of those it educated, than their embourgeoisiement.

IV. Conclusion

The religious discourse, we had outlined earlier, misses the issues of the larger social situation rather completely. It seeks to explain the impact of, and the response to Christian education in the context of other-wordly concerns and proves quite inadequate to deal with the this-worldly ones on the ground. For the implicit agenda and the real decisions, that influences the role which education plays, must be contextualized in the socio-political realities that obtain, even when they are legitimated in other-worldly religious terms.

What we urgently need then is a socio-political analysis of Christian education, which must be set in a secular discourse. But we also need as urgently a theology of education that breaks out of an exclusive religious discourse, to one which sees the school not only as an agent of evangelization, but rather, firmly legitimates it in terms of a theology of secular action and involvement. Only when both these are done will Christian education be able to fulfil its task and be truly 'good news' to people, and not just a limited edition of its more Catholic ideals.

In his perceptive report of 1931, Lindsay urged a plan for "Christian education as being distinctive but not exclusive".[99] But today, while Christian education is still striving to secure its evangelical purposes, Christian institutions have well-nigh achieved the opposite of Lindsay's recommendation, being rather exclusive without being quite distinctive!

For it seems to us that the neglect of the socio-political issues involved in mission education has allowed Christian efforts to be coopted by vested interests and integrated into the larger system in spite of its high-minded ideals, articulated by a "noble band of workers to whom India owes the beginning of English Education".[100]

Perhaps what we now need to make effectively, is a distinction between the church-related school, which is constrained to operate within the educational system, and Christian education that must reach out beyond to the very ones awaiting to be conscientised and liberated by it. Our educators cannot be just the apostles, scholars and gentlemen[101] as of yesterday. They must also be the prophets, activists, and witnesses for today !

NOTES AND REFERENCES

1. Talcott Parsons and Gerald Platt, *The American University*, Cambridge, Mass, Harvard University Press, 1972
2. Max Warren, *Social History and Christian Mission*, London, SCM Press, 1967, p. 164.

3. *Ibid.*, pp. 118-119.
4. Aparna Basu, *Essays in the History of Indian Education*, New Delhi, Concept, 1982, p. 91.
5. S. Nurullah and J. P. Naik, *A History of Education in India*, Bombay, Macmillan, 1951. Also J.P. Naik, *A Student's History of Education in India (1800-1973)*, Bombay, Macmillan, 1974.
6. T. N. Sequeira, *The Education of India: History and Problems*, London, OUP, 1939, p. 26.
7. J. Velinkar, "Jesuit Educational Style in Sixteenth Century Goa", *Indica*, vol. 21, no. 1, March 1984, pp 17-27.
8. *Ibid.*, p. 17.
9. Sequeira, *op. cit.*, p. 27.
10. Teotonio R. de Souza, *Medieval Goa: A Socio-Economic History*, New Delhi, Concept, 1979, p. 96.
11. *Ibid.*, p. 97.
12. *Ibid.*, p. 95.
13. Basu, *The Growth of Education and Political Development in India, 1898-1920*, Delhi, OUP, 1974, p. 131.
14. J. H. Gense, *Glimpses of the Past: St. Xavier's College, in the Making*, Bombay, 1964, p. 19.
15. *Ibid.*
16. *Ibid.*, p. 47.
17. *Bombay Miscellany of Western India*, cited by E. R. Hull, *Bombay Mission History*, (2 vols), vol. 1, pp. 140-141.
18. *Ibid.*
19. Gense, *The Church at the Gateway of India: 1720-1960*, Bombay, St. Xavier's College, 1960, p. 288.
20. Muktishree Ghosh, *The Concept of Secular Education in India*, Delhi, B. R. Pub., 1991, p. 50.
21. M. D. David, "Historical Development" in *Thoughts on Christian Education in India*, ed. J. W. Airan, Bombay, Wilson College, 1969, pp. 1-17.
22. A. Verstraeten, "Jesuit Colleges in India in the Restored Society", in *Jesuit Education in India*, ed. Gregory Naik, Anand, GSP, 1987, pp. 52-56.
23. *Ibid.*, p. 55.
24. Airan, *op. cit.*, p. 17. Comparative figures for Protestant colleges for the same years are 34, 35, and 46 respectively.
25. S. Chitnis, "A view of Christian Education", in Theophane A. Mathias, ed., *Not without a Compass: JES Seminar on Christian Education in the India of Today*, Delhi, JEA, 1971, p. 204.
26. Valerian Cardinal Gracias, "The Role of Christian Colleges in Indian National Development", in *The Christian College and National Development*, eds. Richard Dickinson and S.P. Appasamy, Madras, CLS, 1967, pp. 17-43, 21.
27. *Ibid.*, p. 24.
28. David. *op. cit.*, p. 2.
29. Mathias, "Christian Education in India — Meaning and Relevance", in Mathias, *op. cit.*, p. 3.
30. Sequeira, *op. cit.*, p. 29.
31. *Ibid.*, p. 30.

32. Narendra Nath Law, *Promotion of Learning in India by Early European Settlers*, 1915, p. 5. Cited by Sequeira, *op. cit.*, p. 28.
33. Syed Mahmud, *History of English Education in India*, pp. 11-13. Cited by Mathias, *op. cit.*, p. 4.
34. Basu, *op. cit.*, p. 4.
35. Stephen Neill, *Colonialism and Christian Missions*, London, Lutterworth, 1966, pp. 92-93.
36. *An Account of the Mutinies in Oudh and the Siege of the Lucknow Residency*, Richard Bentley, 1858, pp. 89-90. Cited by Warren, *op. cit.*, p. 104.
37. Nurullah and Naik, *op. cit.*, p. 252.
38. *Report of the Commission on the Christian Higher Education in India: An Enquiry into the Place of the Christian Institutions*, (Hereinafter *Report*), London, OUP, 1931.
39. A. Mathew, *Christian Missions, Education and Nationalism: From Dominance to Compromise, 1870-1930*, Delhi, Anamika Prakashan, 1988, p. v.
40. Leslie Newbigin, "The Secular-Apostolic Dilemma", in Mathias, *op. cit.*, p. 66.
41. Mathias, *op. cit.*, pp. 55-56.
42. Basu, *op. cit.*, p. 7.
43. *Report*, p. 63.
44. William I. Chamberlain, *Education in India*, New York, Macmillan, 1899, p. 32.
45. *op. cit.*, p. 113.
46. Rudolf C. Heredia, *Structure and Performance of College Education: An Organizational Analysis of Arts and Science Colleges in Bombay*, Bombay, Somaiya Pub., 1981, p. 15.
47. Neill, *op.cit.*, p. 102.
48. Basu, *op. cit.*, p. 10.
49. *Report of the Calcutta University Commission: 1917-19*, Calcutta, Government of India, 1919, vol. 5, p. 302.
50. "The Role and Problems of Private Enterprise in Education", in Dickinson and Appasamy, *op. cit.*, p. 123.
51. *Ibid.*, p. 127.
52. *Ibid.*, p. 125.
53. Arthur Howell, *Education in British India*, Calcutta, Govt. of India. p. 36. Cited by Ghose, *op. cit.*, p. 57.
54. *Ibid.*, p. 56.
55. *Ibid.*, p. 58.
56. Naik, *Educational Planning in India*, Bombay, Allied Pub., 1965, p. 85.
57. Neill, *op. cit.*, p. 86.
58. Nurullah and Naik, *op. cit.*, p. 270.
59. *The Population of India*, CICRED series, New Delhi, 1974, p. 64. Cited by A.R. Kamat, *Perspectives for Educational Reform in India*, Bombay, Himalaya, 1989, p. 70.
60. E. C. Buck's Report on Practical and Technical Education, 1901; Education, Proceedings, 1905, nos. 44-56. Cited by Basu, *op. cit.*, p. 57.
61. Basu, *op.cit.*, p. 21.
62. Mathias, *op. cit.*, p. 156.
63. Ghosh, *op. cit.* , p. 50.
64. Chitnis, *op. cit.*, p. 201.
65. *Report*, p. 121.

66. Chitnis, *op. cit.*, p. 203.
67. "The Role ....Enterprise", *op. cit.*, pp. 133-134.
68. Mathias, *op. cit.*, p. 5.
69. "The Spiritual Foundations of Our Work", in Dickinson and Appasamy, *op. cit.*, p. 236.
70. Mathias, *op. cit.*, p. 7.
71. Mathew, *op. cit.*, p. 75.
72. *Ibid.*, p. 56.
73. *Ibid.*, p. 228.
74. *Ibid.*, p 219.
75. "Report of Work among the Educated Classes", *The Harvest Field*, p. 137. Cited by Mathew, p. 95.
76. *The Higher Hinduism in Relation to Christianity*, London, Elliot Stock, 1903, and *Studies in the Upanishads*, CLS, 1897.
77. John Moore, "The Jesuit Christian Education and its Relevance in India", in Gregory Naik, *op. cit.*, pp. 66-83, p. 29.
78. "The Attitude of Missionaries Towards the Indian National Congress", *The Harvest Field*, March 1889, pp. 289-290.
79. J.W. Gladstone, *Protestant Christianity and People's Movements in Kerala: A Study of Christian Mass Movements in Relation to Neo-Hindu socio-religious Movements in Kerala, 1850-1936*, Trivandrum, Seminary Pub., 1984, p. 172.
80. Dick Kooiman, "Conversion from slavery to plantation labour: Christian missions in South India (19th century), *Social Scientist*, Vol. 19, nos. 8-9, Aug-Sep 1991, pp. 57-71, p. 67.
81. Warren, *op. cit.*, pp. 11-12.
82. K. Kumar, *Political Agenda of Education: A Study of Colonialist and Nationalist Ideas*, New Delhi, Sage Pub., 1991, p. 34.
83. Nurullah and Naik, *op. cit.*, p. 182.
84. Mathew, *op. cit.*, p. 158.
85. *Ibid.*, p. 194.
86. Basu, *op. cit.*, p. 66.
87. Kumar, *op. cit.*, p. 16.
88. *Ibid.*, p. 42.
89. *Ibid.*, p. 191.
90. Nurullah & Naik, *op. cit.*, p. 446.
91. Kumar, *op. cit.*, p. 15.
92. *Ibid.*, p. 36.
93. *Ibid.*, p. 19.
94. Heredia, *op. cit.*, p. 24.
95. Kumar, *op. cit.*, p. 194.
96. *Ibid.*
97. Kamat, *op. cit.*, p. 166.
98. *Report*.
99. *Ibid.*, p. 135.
100. C. Majumdar, *An Advanced History of India*, p. 70. Cited by Ghosh, *op. cit.*, p. 50.
101. Allan P. Farrel, *The Jesuit Code of Liberal Education: Development and Scope of the Ratio Studiorum*, Milwaukee, Bruce Pub., 1938.

11

DECOLONISING THE CHURCH

BENNY AGUIAR

Five hundred years of colonialism have left a legacy to the Church in India that is a mixture of lights and shadows. Christianity had come to India early in the first millenium, but it was only after the fifteenth century that it spread beyond Kerala to other parts of India and to Sri Lanka. Unfortunately along with the gospel message there came the veneer of a culture that tore the new converts from their roots, giving them new names, new habits and customs, even new languages. Their liturgy was the Latin liturgy, their churches were built in pseudo-Gothic and Baroque styles, their religious art, paintings and music were cheap importations from the West.

Foreign Christian missionaries had played a vital role in the development of some Indian languages. In Bihar they had made great efforts to better the social and economic conditions of the tribals. But it was mainly after second Vatican Council sent out a call to the Church to be involved in development and go to the help of the hungry and the needy that missionaries took up pickaxe and shovel to work in the fields. Besides distributing foodstuffs, they embarked on projects for digging wells, laying roads, loaning tractors for ploughing and harvesting, providing fertilisers and pesticides, constructing godowns for storage of grains, organising co-operatives and making surveys for long-term projects.

The divisions among Christians in India had long been a source of scandal to non-Christians. The spectacle of one denomination trying to rival another in making converts created confusion among other Indians. Mahatma Gandhi himself came almost wholly under Protestant influence. But with the critical food situation in the 1960s and the Council's call to go ahead with development, another of the Council's themes – ecumenism – got a great fillip. Catholics joined with Protestants in common prayer, exchanging pulpits and singing Christmas carols on the beaches. But it was on the food-front that they gave their best witness. Responding to the call of India's then health minister, Mr. Ashok Mehta, several Church-related and other voluntary agencies banded together to form one service agency. AFPRO (Action for Food Protection) was born, bringing together CRS, Caritas, Corags, the Indian Social Institute and the Indian Council of Churches (Protestant).

The first fruits of the Council were the reforms in the liturgy. Vernaculars replaced Latin and the altar was brought forward to look more like a table. But the norms for adapting the liturgy to the genius and culture of the people had still to be applied. The Council had set the Church in India on the path of inculturation and dialogue but this would quickly prove hardly less contentious an issue than that of population control which erupted after the publication of *Humanae Vitae*.

Some progress had already been made in the field of religious art. Christian themes were being depicted in the manner of ancient Indian and Moghul art by Agnelo da Fonseca, Angela Trinidade and Wesley. In the realm of Indian dance, music and drama, Fr. George Proksch, SVD, had achieved remarkable success. As regards philosophy and theology there had been attempts to show how Christ could be reached through a study of the *Vedas* and *Upanishads*, and through the works of philosophers like Shankaracharya and Ramanuja. The pioneering efforts of Frs. Johanns, Dandoy and Antoine in Calcutta as well as of Fr. H. O. Mascarenhas in Bombay (*Quintessence of Hinduism*), were remarkable in these fields.

As for dialogue Abbé Monchanin had started a contemplative monastic *ashram* on the banks of the Cauvery near Tiruchirapalli. Here he met Hindu *sadhus* and other holy men and mingled with the common people in order to learn how on the mystical plane, Christian beliefs like the Holy Trinity had been foreshadowed in the Hindu insight of *Sat-Chit-Ananda* or Being-Knowledge and Bliss. He was joined later by Swami Abhishiktananda (Dom Le Saux) and by Bede Griffiths.

As a result of the colonial mentality however, for the majority of Catholics in India, Hinduism was a religion steeped in mythology, superstition and error. Any idea that non-Christian religions could be ways of salvation and that they often reflected rays of that truth which enlightened all men, was alien to their minds. If God could have spoken through non-Christian scriptures, if the relationship between Hindu and Christians was to be marked by dialogue rather than by conversion, if the aim of Christian educational institutions was to make Hindus better Hindus or Muslims better Muslims, then where was the point of the vast missionary endeavour of the Church down the ages as crystallised in the apostolate of St. Francis Xavier in Goa, they reasoned. In other words, could mission and dialogue be compatible with each other?

The legacy of colonialism was so deeply ingrained in the minds of Catholics that Vatican II had at first little impact in India. A survey conducted in 1968, three years after the Council, concluded that Catholics in India had for so long lived in a ghetto that they were unaware of the changing reality around them.

All-India Seminar

The great breakthrough came with the Church in India Seminar in Bangalore in 1969. When it ended on Pentecost Sunday, 25th May, 1969, the 500 delegates broke out into a thunderous applause as Cardinal Gracias hailed it as a 'second spring and a new pentecost'.

The high point of the seminar was the resolution on rites. The coming of the Portuguese brought in its wake the Latin rite in the liturgy and the Portuguese *Padroado* system. Inevitably, there was a conflict between the then recent Catholic converts and the ancient Syrian Churches. Rome tried to bring them into line with its own theology and practices through the Synod of Diamper. Part of these churches reunited with Rome but a larger part refused taking what came to be known as the Coonan Cross oath. Ever since then there has been mistrust between Latins and Orientals including those reunited with Rome. Churches, hospitals and colleges were built sometimes across the same street vying with each other in splendour. Intermarriages were rare. At the preparatory seminar in Kerala, there had been a move for a merger of the three rites, the Syro-Malabar, the Syro-Malankara and the Latin. But a powerful section opposed it on the grounds that the decree on the oriental churches forbade any change in their structures. The Bangalore seminar resolution did not call for an outright merger but only for a study by a special committee of the areas where there was more than one jurisdiction to bring about a working arrangement. The hope was that as the three rites gradually Indianised, they would converge into a common Indian rite. The resolution was fiercely contested, but was passed amidst great applause and acclamation, when Syro-Malankara Archbishop Mar Gregorios announced he had persuaded members of his community to accept it. "We have awakened from a long slumber of two thousand years", he said. "We have to go forward hand in hand. I offer my wholehearted co-operation for the good of the Church in India".

A novel feature of the seminar was the Indian Rite Mass. Over one hundred priests walked barefoot to the altar, and the chief celebrant was vested in saffron shawl wrapped around his shoulders. *Anjali hasta*, *aarti* and *panchanga pranama* were some of the other distinguishing features of this mass. All were part of a package of 12 points which were approved by Rome for use as and when the episcopal conference or the local bishops thought it fit. But while there was unanimous approval to adapt the liturgy to India's cultural and religious heritage, there were considerable objections to the clause "integrating authentic forms of Indian worship". 168 voted for and 134 against, whilst nearly 200 abstained.

Thus, though technically the twelve points were approved, there was considerable hesitation to accept what seemed to many a gradual conversion of the liturgy into a poor imitation of Hindu temple worship. The decree on the mission – *Ad Gentes* – envisaged "a more thorough adaptation" to the culture and spiritual tradition of the people covering the whole extent of life. But why, the opponents objected, should this adaptation be confined only to Hindu worship ? Indian culture was a composite of many strands. Why not incorporate Muslim forms of worship as well? Moreover, could these gestures and symbols be extricated from the myths, superstitions and errors in which they were embedded ? The 'aarti' was not really an offertory, but a rite for driving out evil spirits. The *anjali hasta* was a salutation to human beings and lesser gods and could not replace genuflection. The mystic syllable *Om* which was used instead of 'Amen' was Shiva's cry of joy after relations with his wife.

Controversy round the twelve points raged for many years and took a serious turn when the All-India Laity Congress, a traditionalist organisation, launched a diatribe against what it called 'the hinduisation of the liturgy' and took Fr. Amalorpavadass, the then director of the National Biblical, Catechetical and Liturgical Centre (NBCLC), to court for having built a chapel in the shape of a southern Indian temple and with grill windows depicting the Hindu Trimurti and the dancing Shiva.

Still worse was the fate of the Indian anaphora or eucharistic prayer. Composed by students and professors of the Jesuit theological faculty at Kurseong, the text used phrases and expressions resonant of the Vedas and Hindu scriptures. At a meeting of the CBCI, Cardinal Parecattil endorsed it, but since the total count lacked one vote for the required two-thirds majority, the proposal was lost. In 1975, Cardinal Knox issued an instruction forbidding the use of the Indian anaphora, the reading of non-Christian scriptures in the liturgy of the word and unauthorised experimentation in the rites of the mass.

A resolution of the Seminar that fared slightly better was the one that encouraged the setting up of contemplative monastic *ashrams*. An ashram is a place of sustained intense spiritual quest, centred round a person of deep spiritual experience, the *guru*. The food is vegetarian and the lifestyle simple. It is open to all who seek peace and enlightenment through yoga and meditation. Christian ashrams already existed in Shantivanam near Tiruchirapalli where Bede Griffiths continued the attempts to make Monchanin's dream come true after Abhishiktananda left for Uttarkashi in the Himalayas to live with Hindu sanyasis. At Kurisimula in the high ranges of Kerala, Francis Acharya directed an ashram combining the Cistercian pattern of life and the Antiochene rule of the Syro-Malankara rite. As a result of the resolution other Christian ashrams sprang up in Pune, Madras, Varanasi and elsewhere.

These ashrams became centres of an ongoing dialogue with non-Christians, especially with Hindus. In Aikiya Alayam in Madras, Fr. Ignatius Hirudayam held monthly meetings for prayer, meditation and dialogue. In the live-ins at Shantivanam, participants shared their reflections on the Gospels and the *Bhaghavat Gita*.

Capitalist Legacy of Colonialism

"We must be humble, shedding all superiority complex in our approach to other religions. . . . In God's providence every religion has a part to play in leading men to their destiny", said Cardinal Parecattil at the World Conference of Religions held at Cochin in November 1981. The conference was a kind of summit meeting of all the dialogue groups that had sprung up in various parts of the country on the initiative of the CBCI Dialogue Commission. A similar experience was repeated recently in October 1988 when nearly 200 Hindus, Muslims, Christians, Buddhists, Sikhs, Parsis and Jains, 'lived together' and found that when confronted with each other's beliefs and spiritual practices the normal result was most often a deepening and enrichment of one's own faith.

Another legacy of colonialism was capitalism. After the industrial revolution, India's ancient art and craft fell into disuse and the country was mainly regarded as a source for raw materials for the industrialised West. After Independence the place of foreign capitalists was taken by Indians and a dualistic type of society emerged with a vast majority living in poverty and a minority group monopolising power, culture and economic consumption. A social analysis of the Indian situation revealed that the top 10 per cent spent 30 per cent of the country's income while the bottom 10 per cent only 2. Religion was too often looked upon as a legitimiser of the power structure.

The Asian Seminar on Religion and Development held at Bangalore in 1973 convinced many groups throughout the country that the task of the Church now was to disengage herself from the feudal ruling groups, the capitalist forces and structures and identify herself with the struggle of the oppressed. Development had not just increased agricultural production through self-help projects. Real development was a radical transformation of the economic and political power structures.

As the leaven began to spread, Jesuits in Bihar and Maharashtra were shocked at the physical and mental serfdom of the tribals and the low castes among whom they worked. They took up the struggle against bonded labour and broke the hold of moneylenders who had cheated the tribals of their land and of the fruits of their labour. In Goa priests spearheaded the struggle of the small fishermen against those who used trawlers and purse-seine nets that swept away fish roe during the spawning season. In Kerala a similar agitation became front-page news when priests and nuns who were leading it by remote-control jumped into the fray, courted arrest and went on hunger strikes in front of government offices.

The theology of liberation had thus come to the Indian scene with a bang. This was largely the result not only of some individual theologians like Frs. Samuel Rayan and S. Kappen, but also of the Indian Theological Association and the Ecumenical Association of Third World Theologians (EATWOT). Theology, they said, arises from a genuine encounter with God in the actual situation of human suffering. Traditional theology was too closely linked with western culture, capitalism, colonialism and male domination, and too heavily dependent on Greek philosophy. "Theology in Asia," said Fr. Aloysius Pieris, "is the Christian apocalypse of the non-Christian experience of liberation".

Latin Rite Domination to be Replaced with an Oriental One?

The recent history of the Church has been somewhat stagnant as even the CBCI had become bogged down in the internicine rivalry between the Latin, Syro-Malabar and Syro-Malankara rites.

True, the resolution on rites had been the high point of the 1969 Church in India Seminar. But as efforts towards greater inculturation proved increasingly fruitless, the prospect of the emergence of a common Indian rite receded from view. At the same time as a result of the Council documents, especially of *Orientalium Ecclesiarum*, the Syro-Malabar and Syro-Malankara Churches acquired a growing consciousness of their rights and equality with the Latin Church. They too were of apostolic origin, with their own liturgy, devotions, spirituality, theology and ecclesiastical administration, and they resented the fact that as a result of Portuguese domination, they had been prevented from undertaking missionary work outside Kerala. Seventy per cent of the missionary personnel in the country, they said, belonged to the Syro-Malabar Church but had to change their rite to evangelise. Twenty-four per cent of the India's Catholic population were members of the Syro-Malabar Church, but thousands had been lost when they migrated to the cities of the north. The report by the Apostolic Visitator, Mar Anthony Padiyara, painted a distressing picture of their spiritual condition. With no other choice but to follow an alien liturgy, tradition and practice, they felt themselves to be second class citizens.

The Indian Bishops' Conference thus became the battleground for the conflicting claims of Latins and Orientals, with the latter claiming jurisdiction over their faithful who had settled in Latin dioceses and the former clinging to the principle of 'one territory one jurisdiction' and pointing to the perils and confusion of 'double jurisdiction' as when Padroado and Propaganda fought their battles in Bombay and other places in India.

Bishops in Rome in 1985 were the Oriental bishops who claimed that the stand of the Latin bishops was clearly contradictory to that of the Vatican II decree on Oriental Churches and the Latin bishops insisted that in a missionary country like India there could be place for only one common Indian Church. Most of the priests and faithful of the Eastern rites who had settled outside Kerala would not like to return to their original church, they added.

The matter was submitted to a high-ranking pontifical commission of Cardinals and Bishops and on 28th May, 1987 Pope John Paul II announced that each of the three churches would have the right to form their own episcopal conferences though the national body could continue to look after common concerns. All the three would have the right and obligation to evangelise and the pastoral care of Eastern rite faithful settled in Latin dioceses would be entrusted to their own priests and where circumstances warranted, as in the Bombay-Poona region, to their own bishops.

Sociologically as a result of missionary work down the centuries most of the converts were poor and belonged to the lower castes, classes and tribes. Misssionaries did much to improve their lot. But unfortunately after Independence, though the Church had made a vital contribution through her educational and medical work, with an enormous increase in the number of health and educational institutions, yet more and more of these institutions were based in towns and catered for the Hindu upper classes. Unconsciously, perhaps the Church's institutions had been supporting the oppressive structures of society.

Today though Catholics of the lower castes and tribes, form over 60 per cent of Church membership, they have no place in her decision-making process. Scheduled or low-caste converts are treated as low-castes not only by high-caste Hindus, but by high-caste Christians as well. The total unconcern of the Church for the welfare of the converts has driven many highly qualified low-caste youth to revert to the Hindu fold. Only a superficial equality exists among the educated and the well-to-do low-caste Christians and that too only in metropolitian and large cities.

A sizable proportion of the Catholic population in the north of India is tribal. Though the Church has tried to improve their lot, yet its country-wide administrative system, its universal theology and its centralised authority structure have done much harm to the simple tribal communities. It is difficult to imagine how a priest born in Kerela or Mangalore and educated in a seminary in Latin or English can go to the tribal belt and tell them how to pray to God or reform their society. They take with them in their voices and lives, a cultural and religious authoritarianism worse than that of colonialism. When the scheduled castes and scheduled tribes accepted Christianity, it was not primarily a religious choice but a social and political one. Today more and more are feeling disillusioned.

Conclusion

The situation in the Church today is stagnant. The legacy of colonialism still persists. Yet the labours of so many in so many directions cannot be in vain. A ferment has been created by the numerous seminars, consultations and conferences that cannot but bear fruit in due time.

SECTION III

12

ASSETS AND INCOME OF THE RELIGIOUS ORDERS IN GOA AT THE END OF THE 16th CENTURY

ARTUR TEODORO DE MATOS

In numerous documents there is mention of the income of the Religious Orders in Goa which they received either from the royal exchequer (including income and land property) or from benefectors wishing to receive spiritual favours as a result.

There were frequent petitions made by the Orders to the king requesting favours and privileges to offset the heavy expenditures incurred by their activities, mainly in the fields of education and social welfare.

There were many inquiries into the increasing wealth of these Orders in Goa, mainly into that of the Society of Jesus, during the first half of the sixteenth century.[1] In 1587, D. Duarte de Menezes acting on a petition from the bishop of Cochin, had suggested to the king that the *Dizimos* privilege required by him should be granted only *por tempo limitado* (for a limited period). The viceroy explained that *estas merces, a tempo feitas a eclesiasticos destas partes elles as fazem logo perpetuas, e em lhe falando alguem nisso, publicão que tem encorrido na exconunhão.*[2] In order to probe the accuracy of these accusations, one needs to check accurately the figures of their income and expenses. Were the loans advanced to particular people and officials by the Jesuits burdensome ?[3]

We are well aware of the importance of the Orders in Goa regarding cultural adaptation and their efforts in the formation of the first Christian societies in India.[4] Clerics and Franciscans were on board the armada of Pedro Alvares Cabral, to lay the foundations for missionary work in the East. Their efforts eventually led to the setting up of the diocese of Goa in 1534. 1542 marked the end of the first phase of the history of the Portuguese missions in the East. With the arrival of Francis Xavier in Goa that year, all missions were to experience a change organizationally and methodologically.[5]

The missionaries needed resources for their missions and for their own maintenance. Although I do not have all the data at hand, yet I will attempt here to present a picture of their income during the 16th century.

In 1596, Manuel de Abreu Mouzinho, judge at the High Court of Goa, at the request of D. Francisco da Gama, count of Vidigueira, worked out in detail an inventory of the land properties belonging to members of the Orders in Goa.[6] This is indeed an important source. Together with the *Tombo das Rendas* from Ilhas, Bardez and Salcete prepared a year earlier by Francisco Pais, Goa's surveyor of the *Casa dos Contos*[7] and the budgets for the end of the fifteenth century,[8] one will have an outline of the assets as well as financial situation of the Orders in Goa at the time.

For 1596, the individual income of the Jesuits, Franciscans, Dominicans and Augustinians (totalling 9.418$ 438 *reis*) was as follows:[9]

Jesuits	6.686$438	(71%)
Franciscans	874$400	(9.5%)
Dominicans	1.238$400	(13%)
Augustinians	619$200	(6.5%)

While studying the *teres* and *haveres* (Assets and Income) of these Orders, we realize that part of their income (money, food as well as other goods) came from leasing assets belonging either directly to them or to establishments founded and administered by them, from a few taxes granted by the crown or from donations granted every year by the royal exchequer from Goa.

It would be interesting to enquire into the assets of these Orders, and to find out which sums were usually available to them. We will begin by studying the Jesuits who had the heaviest expenses. The college of St. Paul and the novitiate had at that time a fairly important estate consisting of thirteen single-floor and a few multiple-floor structures for rent, almost all of them located well in the city,[10] three *boticas* (shops) and four plots.[11]

The rents from these were not very much. St. Paul's received annually 132$684 *reis*. Besides, according to Dr. Abreu Mouzinho *as casas tem os seus gastos de consertos* (there were the maintenance costs) and that most certainly reduced the college's income further.[12]

317$ 150 *reis* was the annual rent for the Novitiate. It got its profits mainly from its palm groves, small farming grounds and one *Cunto*,[13] as well as from jack fruits, mangoes, palm trees and estates formerly owned by temples in Salcete.[14] Its other revenues came from landed properties (farming grounds, vegetable gardens, groves of palm trees, etc.) which could be found on Goa's islands, Divar and Chorão and also in Salcete. In addition, the *namocins* included many non-specified possessions whose rents were once bestowed to the temples and the village's officials.[15]

There were the revenues from the estate on the Goa islands (1.115$ 132 *reis*) and Chorão (1.038$ 330 *reis*). Part of these revenues met the ordinary expenses of the College (516$ 960 *reis*). The temples in Goa island had been destroyed in 1540. Those in Salcete had similar fate in 1564-1566.[16]

D. Sebastião, on the 21st March, 1569 had transferred income pertaining to the temples of Salcete and Bardez to the churches and to the priests in charge of them.[17] In 1541 the same misfortune had befallen the Hindu temples on the Goa islands.[18] Thus, the Jesuits to whom the Salcete's churches had been entrusted, enjoyed the revenues from these.

The *haveres* (assets) of the Franciscans, the administrators of the Bardez parishes, also came from taxes gathered from the estates which had formely belonged to the temples. In 1596, these amounted to 874$ 400 *reis*.[19]

According to Francisco Pais, the methods chosen by the Jesuits and the Franciscans to encash these amounts were different. Notwithstanding the fact that there were tax collectors and clerks appointed by the viceroy as *Cristãos da terra*, the priests of the Society *se apossarão [...] de tal modo desta Renda que não ha darem copia della* so that the income and expenditures of the parishes are unrecorded *e o que sobeja para se dispender nas maes couzas que o Padrão del Rey nosso Senhor declara*.[20] But, *não ha tomar se lhe conta nem quem possa pedir rezão do cressimento desta Renda por os Padres não darem copia, e se apegarem ao foro ecleziastico*.[21]

The methods of the Franciscans were very different from that of the Jesuits. Similar rents were collected by the tax collectors and clerks who paid for the church services and afterwards rendered the accounts in the *Casa dos Contos*. However, the same purveyor states (partially or not one could not be sure) *não se intremete nesta arecadação nenhum ecleziastico por Rezão de os ministros da conuerção destas terras serem Padres de Sam Francisco que se não intremetem com dinheiro*.[22]

The Augustinian estate included 14 houses for rent, 6 *boticas* (shops) and a portion of a palm grove and the income amounted to 619$200 *reis*.[23]

The convent of St. Dominic had 12 *marinhas* (salt-pans) along the river of Santana in the parish of Batim, and a small farming ground near the *marinhas* which got them an annual income of 272$400 *reis*.[24] Nevertheless, according to the above source *por as ditas marinhas estarem danificadas* (because the salt pans were damaged) it only amounted to 193$ 800 *reis*.[25]

The Dominican estate also included 52 single-floor as well as multi-floor houses for rent. Some of them were near the convent, and others on the Rua do Mandovi, Rua do Japão, Rua Direita and two in Chaul. Almost all of these houses were acquired as legacy, while a small residential quarter *de 25 casinhas terreas* (houses with ground floor only) were built by the convent at its own expense on grounds that belonged to Pedro Godinho. It was, in fact, some sort of investment as these houses had been rented right away.[26]

The purchase of houses for rent was a paying proposition to the convent. Six houses on the Rua do Japão were acquired in the auction of Ambrosio Ferreira in order to pay for the maintenance of the chapel of Antonio de Vivar. The Dominican convent also had 28 *boticas* at the market of St. Francis,[27] where dates, rice, spices as well as other products could be found. It also owned a few palm groves. These possessions brought in 799$ 800 *reis* each year and the inmates of the convent were duty-bound to perform a number of long religious services.[28] The author ends by stating that *os rendimentos dos alugueres de tais casas e buticas palmas, marinhas despendem os padres parte delles nas benfeitorias e concertos e mais repairos e no foro que pagavão.*[29]

The convent of St. Thomas, belonging to the same order, collected each year four caskets of wine from Portugal, olive oil, rice and wheat, owned several shops inthe neighbourhood, besides two houses on the Rua Direita and others on Rua de S. Jorge rendering 166$200 *reis.*[30]

Each year, India's royal exchequer provided for the clergy. Simão Botelho has specified the sums (available in the *Tombo* of 1554) and as regards the other Orders from Goa, the amounts are indicated, as follows:[31]

Monastery of Holy Faith – 854$000 *reis*, 2 casks of wine, (400$000) and some rents from the temple.

Monastery of St. Dominic – 800$000 *reis.*

Monastery of St. Francis – 135$000 *reis* in wine and olive oil.

The budget for 1571 shows that at a time when the archbishop's ordinary expenses had almost tripled, St. Francis' collected the usual 600$000 *reis*, St. Dominic's 800$000 *reis* and St. Paul's 800$090 *reis*.

The budget of 1588 shows that the endowments had increased, thus absorbing 21.3 per cent of the amount spent on the church in Goa.[32]

Dominicans	1.098$000	*reis*
Augustinians	129$000	*reis*
Franciscans	1.000$000	*reis*
Jesuits	1.340$000	*reis*

The *Regimento* of 1576 fixed the amounts for each parish and religious community.[33] That explains why the budget for 1588 specifies the amounts stating, however, that the expenses of the Salcete parish had to be paid from the income of the temples. This enables us to assume that perhaps the other parishes, although collecting the same revenue, could not support their own expenses.

The Orders, therefore, looked out for other financial resources. Trade was an obvious alternative. Prof. Boxer in *Portuguese India in Mid-Seventeenth Century* explains some of the financial affairs of the Jesuits in Asia. He states that there was not one branch of economic activity in Portuguese Asia in which the Jesuits did not have a hand, directly or indirectly.[34]

Yet only a look at their accounts would enable us to know and quantify with accuracy. In the sixteenth century, the Orders in Goa, the Jesuits and the Dominicans in particular, owned important estates. Besides, they had a yearly income along with the revenues granted to them by the royal exchequer, and other sources which assured them a life neither too poor nor too ostentatious.

NOTES AND REFFERENCES

1. Arquivo Historico Ultramarino (AHU), *India*, cod. 205, fl. 177v. Letter from D. João V to the Chancellor of Goa, Lisbon, 24 March 1750 and cod. 513, fls. 168v-169. Letter from the king to the archbishop, Ajuda, 10 April 1761.
2. Arquivo General de Simancas, *Secretarias Provinciales*, cod. 1551, fl. 54v. Letter from D. Duarte de Menezes to the king, Goa, 23 November 1587.
3. Historical Archives of Goa (HAG), *Cartas e Ordens*, n. 880 fls 49-49v. Letter from the Marquis of Tavora to the Jesuit Fr. Provincial, Panelim, 3 October 1750. *Monções do Reino*, n. 125 C, fls. 691-691v and 695. Letters from the Jesuit Fr. Provincial to the viceroy, 14-17 June 1753.
4. E.R. Hambye, "Goa" in *Dictionnaire d'Histoire et de Geographie Ecclesiastique*, ed. R. Aubert, Paris: Letouzey et Ane.
5. A. da Silva Rego, *Curso de Missionologia*, Lisboa, Agencia Geral do Ultramar, 1956, p. 359; A. Mathias Mundadan, *History of Christianity in India*, Vol. I, pp. 242-278 and 429-475; and J. Thekkedath, Vol. I, 1984-1988. See also John Correia-Afonso "As missões catholicas no Oriente (1500-1650) em particular na India" in *Portugal no Mundo*, ed. Luis de Albuquerque, Vol. IV, Lisboa, Alfa, 1989, pp. 223-236.
6. Biblioteca Nacional, Rio de Janeiro, 2, 2, 19, n. 17, fls. 313-324v, *Titulo das Propriedades que tem os Religiosos das Ordens de São Domingos, São Francisco e de Nossa Sra. da Graça e da Companhia de Jesus e do collegio de São Paulo nesta cidade de Goa, e suas ilhas e nas mais aiacentes a ellas e nas terras de Salsete e Bardez que mandou o Conde da Vidigueira no anno de 1596 feita pelo Manoel d'Abreu Mousinho Dezembargador de Goa*. D. Francisco da Gama was appointed viceroy of India on 2nd December 1597 but he took office on the 25th May 1597. *Tratado de Todos os Vice-Reis e Governadores da India*, Lisbon, 1962, pp. 131-132.
7. "Tombo da Ilha de Goa e das Terras de Salsete e de Bardes organizado em 1595 por Francisco Pais, Provedor-mor dos Contos de Goa", *Boletim do Instituto Vasco da Gama*, Bastora, n. 62 (1945), 66 (1950) and 68 (1952).
8. Those from 1588 and 1589 can be found at the Arquivo Historico Ultramarino, cod. 500 and at the British Library, *Add.*, 28433, fls. 101-106v.
9. Biblioteca Nacional (Rio de Janeiro), 2, 2, 19, n. 17, fls. 313-324v, *Titulo das Propriedades que os Religiosos das Ordens [...]*.
10. The three *boticas* were located on the road along the Mandovi whereas the houses could be found on the Rua da Ourivesaria, Rua dos Pintores, Pelourinho, near S. Tomé, opposite St. Paul's.
11. One small farm in Mapusa, one palm grove in Bardez, and one *chão marinho* in S. Tomé.
12. Biblioteca Nacional (Rio de Janeiro), *op. cit.*, fl. 313v.
13. Income owned by the community. From the Konkani *khunt*. Cf. S. R. Dalgado, *Glossário Luso-Asiático*.
14. Biblioteca Nacional (Rio de Janeiro), *op. cit.*, fls. 318-319.
15. *Namocim* or *namacim*, farming land owned by a community. Its profits were kept for cult services or for the sustenance of the village officials. From the Konkani *namas*, plural *namaxi*. Cf. S.R. Dalgado, *Glossário*.

16. "Tombo da Ilha de Goa" in *BIVG* (Bastora), n. 62 (1946), pp. 139-150. P.S.S. Pissurlencar, *Regimentos das Fortalezas da India*, Bastora, 1951, pp. 34-35.
17. *BIVG*, n. 62 (1946), pp. 169-172.
18. *Ibid.*, p. 94.
19. Biblioteca Nacional (Rio de Janeiro), *op. cit.*, fls. 320-321.
20. *Ibid*, p. 94.
21. *Ibid.*, p. 94. It says that there was no way of demaning an account of the income, and the priests would fall back on the legal dispensations and privileges to justify their refusal.
22. *Ibid.*, p. 96. The Portuguese quotation says that the Franciscans did not personally handle the money matters. They left it to a lay person to do that.
23. Biblioteca Nacional, *op. cit.*, fls. 319v-320.
24. *Ibid.*, fls. 321-324.
25. *Ibid.*, fl. 323.
26. *Ibid.*, fl. 323.
27. *Ibid.*, fl. 323.
28. *Ibid.*, fl. 323.
29. *Ibid.*, fl. 321-324v. The income was spent partly in maintenance and development of the property and in paying the State taxes.
30. S. Botelho, "Tombo do Estado da India," in *Subsidios para a Historia da India Portugueza,* Lisbon, Academia Real das Sciencias, 1868, pp. 68-71.
31. Biblioteca da Ajuda (BA), 51-VII-31, fls. 18v-20, *Orçamento do que rende o Estado da India, e o que despende ordinariamente e asi o extraordinario, que se pode alcansar por contas orçado huns annos por outros, o qual se fez por mandado do Senhor Vice Rey Don Antonio de Noronha, aonde se declara miudamente o em que se fez tal despeza.*
32. AHU, cod. 599, *Titolo da recepta e despeza da cidade de Goa,* tls. 4-11.
33. Pissurlencar, *Reigmentos*, p. 17.
34. C.R. Boxer, *A India Portuguesa em meados do século XVII,* Lisboá, Edições 70, 1982, p. 73.

13

MISSIONARY EXPANSION:
Cultural and Agricultural Contacts between Colonial Goa and Brazil

PHILOMENA S. ANTONY

Portuguese colonial expansion was motivated by spiritual priorities: the conversion of natives, the expansion of the church and the spread of the true faith. King John III told Tomé de Souza, the first Governor of Brazil, that the reason that had led him to colonize Brazil was the need to convert its people to the faith.[1] In short, the colonizing process was regarded as part of God's design to let all people know the true faith. Missionaries therefore, played a key role in consolidating the work of explorers and administrators. In the process of missionary expansion various parts of the empire got closer to one another. The object of this paper is to bring out the missionary interaction between two of Portugal's colonies, Goa and Brazil, and see how this affected them.

Right from the beginning of the sixteenth century when the riches of India were the prime concern of Portugal, the underlying religious emphasis was evident. Here, the St. Thomas tradition was a convenient tool. When Pedro Alvares Cabral landed at Cochin in 1500, he and his men claimed to have come across some St. Thomas Christians.[2] In 1517 the Portuguese claimed that they had found the tomb of St. Thomas at Mylapore. Similarly, in Brazil (whose ultimate value was then largely unknown) the legend of this apostle found favour with the missionaries in the sixteenth century; footprints of St. Thomas were believed to have been found in Brazil; and some corrupted vestiges of his teachings were discovered among the natives. Soon after his arrival in 1549, Fr. Nobrega reported that some natives had a vague memory of the passing of St. Thomas (whom they called Zome) through their land.[3] Ultimately, not only were all Portuguese Indiamen forced to touch São Tomé during their voyage to and from Lisbon, but in each of the Indian, Brazilian and African possessions places were named after the missionary apostle.

D. Pedro Fernandes Sardinha, the first bishop of Brazil (1551) provided the next link in the Goa-Brazil missionary relations. His experience and efficiency as the vicar-general of Goa was regarded as an advantage and the Jesuits themselves had recommended him to the king. But he envisaged in Brazil, a dual society of the kind he had known in India. Yet his earlier experience proved to be prejudicial in his dealings with the primitive Amerindians.[4] Little did Sardinha realize that despite its own difficulties, European culture and religion could be far more easily imposed on the Brazilians than on the Indians, who had a strong cultural background, a deep-rooted religious tradition and social customs and habits.

Role of the Jesuits

It was there that the Orders took over. In Brazil, the Society of Jesus took charge under Fr. Manuel de Nobrega in 1540, that is, a little before the Jesuit entry into Goa. From then on, until the time of its suppression in 1759, the Jesuits formed the vanguard of the Portuguese missions. However, along with others, they became responsible for the introduction of the cross, which implied spiritual instruction of the natives, their education in some way, leading to indoctrination and the physical welfare of the sick and the needy. Along with their Portuguese confreres, the Luzo-Brazilian missionaries accomplished their duty with a deep sense of dedication, and with significant impact. In the course of their endeavour to 'save' souls by showing them the 'right' path, secular tasks were not ignored. To the latter idea, I shall return later.

The India-Brazil missionary contact was two-fold: (a) Through letters which were detailed on information about the spiritual work, as also on the character of the region and the people among whom they worked. As these letters were sent to various missions, the zeal of the Jesuits in one part of the empire, inspired those in others. Since those in India were called upon to face greater challenges than in Brazil, the enthusiasm aroused by letters from India was equally great, and (b) Another means was by expeditions. When ships sailed from Lisbon to Goa and back, they generally put in at Bahia, and many missionaries on board would give accounts of their work so convincingly that many would offer to serve in the distant Indian missions.[5] Evangelical work in the East was so extensive that, in their little way, missionaries from Brazil extended a helping hand to their religious brethren.

Fr. John de Brito, after being procurator of the Malabar Province, while returning from India to Lisbon in 1687, reached Bahia. He was put up at the Jesuit college there. His narration of the Jesuit work in India inspired the young students around, and two of them, Francisco Soares and Agostinho Correa, both Portuguese, offered to serve at the Malabar Mission. Their requests were not conceded as their services were urgently required in Brazil.[6] Yet, the movement from Brazil to India, initiated by de Brito continued to show results in the years to come.

Already, Luzo-Brazilian Jesuits had left their mark in India. The outstanding among them was Fr. Francisco de Souza, missionary and historian. Born at Itaparica near Bahia in 1649, he entered the Society in 1665. The same year he came to Goa, and studied at St. Paul's College. Later he held several important offices as spiritual director at the Holy Spirit Church at Margão, rector of the colleges at Chaul, Rachol, and Goa, and prepositor of the Professed House. He died at Goa on 17th June, 1712.

Fr. de Souza was a pre-eminent historian as well. His monumental work, *Oriente conquistado a Jesu Christo pelos padres da Companhia de Jesus da Provincia de Goa*, is a mine of information and narrates the deeds of Francis Xavier and his companions and successors from 1542 to 1585. He refers to Goa, to the rulers of Bijapur, Cochin, Vijayanagar, Travancore, Madurai, Mughal India and to the first Jesuit mission there.[7] He condemns certain social practices and complains about the prevalence of female slave prostitution in Portuguese Asia, and the excesses of the Portuguese soldiers with native women, as being irremediable abuse.[8] Whether his fear was because the loose morals of the Portuguese deterred the natives from embracing Christianity or not, he is critical in his approach. The clarity of his narration and details on geography and chronology make his work an outstanding piece of history.

Another Luzo-Brazilian who attained fame in India as a great missionary was Fr. Laureano de Brito who was born at Recife and joined the Society in Bahia where he was a preacher. When an India ship called at Bahia with many Jesuit missionaries on board, and as the master of novices happened to be dead at the time, Fr. Brito offered to go to India. He taught theology at St. Paul's. Later, he opted for the Malabar Mission, where he arrived in 1705. He converted many to Christianity at Travancore. His services lay mainly in educating the young spiritually and intellectually. In fact, some of the natives who were trained by these and other Jesuits, carried on extensive work. Fr. Jose Vaz, a Goan, contemporary of Fr. de Souza, and trained by the Jesuits, converted over 30,000 to Christianity and is today known as the apostle of Ceylon. Frs. José Agostinho and José Teotonio, both natives of Bahia, lived at Goa and were victims of Pombal's decrees. They were deported and died in exile in 1760.[9]

Fr. Serafim Leite provides us with a list of missionaries from Brazil who worked in India. When Fr. John da Costa, procurator at Malabar, visited Bahia in 1696, three years after the martyrdom of St. John de Brito, three Bahians wished to come to India. They were John de Silva, Antonio de Guisenrode, and Jose de Viveiros. Guisenrode became rector of the college at Goa, and procurator at Rome. He was to be be nominated as Fr. Provincial of Brazil in 1729. However, he returned to Bahia as rector of the college there, where he died on 9 April, 1737. Fr. John da Rocha opted for the Indian mission in 1701. He was born at Sergipe in 1654, and was a popular preacher. But he felt a greater urge to work in Goa and Malabar than in Brazil. He boarded the ship for India, but died on the way on 5th May, 1702.

During the visit of Fr. Francisco Laines, procurator at Malabar, to Rio de Janeiro in 1706, Fr. John Tavares and Bro. Manuel da Luz, expressed their wish to work at Malabar. The former was a professor of theology at the college at Maranhão and the latter, a pharmacist at the college of Rio de Janeiro. He believed that through corporal treatment he could help cure souls. However, the desire of both of these did not materialise.

Between 1725 and 1732, the missionary expedition of Jesuits consisted of students like Alexander Correia of Bahia, Antonio Ferroz of Rio, Eusebio de Matos of Bahia (he became the superior of the Professed House at Goa), Luiz Vieira of Bahia, and Manuel Monteiro of Espirito Santo. In the second expedition (1747-49), the novices were accompanied by two priests. Many Jesuits from Brazil faced persecution and exile during the suppression of the Order. Fr. Diogo de Albuquerque of Pernambuco, Fr. Vicente Xavier Caturro,

Fr. Inacio Francisco of Rio de Janeiro, Bro. José Duarte of Bahia, Fr. José Xavier of Recife, Fr. Luiz da Silva of Pernambuco, and Fr. Manuel Xavier de Burgos of Bahia were all members of the apostolic movement initiated by Fr. John de Brito in Bahia in 1687.[10]

These Jesuits who worked in India were responsible for the trans-continental dissemination of ideas and culture. During their stay in India they learnt the vernaculars and familiarised themselves with the local culture in accordance with the directive of the Society. They made up in quality of activity, what they lacked in numbers. The strategy of these missionaries might not have been different from those of other Jesuits, as most of them were trained in Brazil where Jesuit justification of, and participation in, slavery was commonly known, along with the temporal power of the missions.

Nevertheless, whether their work was confined to the portals of spiritual learning, or involved dealings with the rank and file, their presence in India created a ripple in our society. In these missionaries was found another example of the glaring racial discrimination so prominent among the Jesuits in India before 1759. The Luzo-Brazilian Jesuits[11] had the doors of the Indian missions opened to them, while the *mestiços* and *castiços*, let alone the native Indians, were less fortunate, even if they wished to lead the Gentiles to the right path. In retrospect, it appears to be a kind of moral drain, the full implication of which was either not fully realised at the time, or could not be given expression. In short, the East had to walk in the shadow of the West.

Details of work by members of other Orders are not easily available. Around 1800, Fr. Domingos dos Dores, a Bahian, was in the Franciscan convent of Madre de Deus of Goa. He served there for about 14 years.[12]

Missionaries as Spice and Drug Mediators

The missionaries were as much ambassadors of the kings as messengers of the good news of Christ. As men supporting the secular arm of royal administration, they utilised their organising ability, their contacts with their brethren in other areas, and their easy access to natives, to become instruments in the strategy of transplantation of Indo-Brazilian flora. This role was clearly visible in the consequent exposure of men, modes and techniques of cultivation to each other, bringing drastic changes in bio-diversity both in India and Brazil.

The Jesuit *Quinta do Tanque* at Bahia was the first model nursery, where the Jesuits had sought permission to plant ginger, assuring the crown that they would send to Portugal 20,000 quintals in 15 years, or else, would put it to medicinal use.[13] By 1682 cultivation of *Sinhalese cinnamon* and Malabar pepper was introduced.[14] The initial experiment was highly encouraging, hence annually plants of various spices were shipped to the Jesuit College at Bahia,[15] from where they were taken to Maranhão and other places. In 1690, two *canarins*, Lourenço de Noronha and Salvador de Távora, both 30 years of age, and residents of Serula in Bardez, were sent to the *Tanque*.[16]

In 1690, Fr. John de Brito was sent to India, entrusted with the task of procuring two men, experienced in spice cultivation. The Fr. Provincial at Malabar was also to assist in this project.[17] Meanwhile, the work of Jesuits like Fr. Miguel do Amaral had borne fruit. By the end of the seventeenth century, about four barrels of fine cinnamon of the new cultivation were sent to Lisbon.[18]

The Oratorians were also brought into the picture. Fr. Joseph Vaz, who was known for his selfless service in the Ceylon mission, was asked to select expert cinnamon cultivators from among the Christians around him and bring the men along with him to Goa, to be sent to Bahia.[19] The reputation of Fr. Vaz was expected to provide the cover for the project, which had to be executed with the utmost secrecy in view of the political and religious hostility of the Dutch dominating that island. It appears that the project was still-born. In 1706, Fr. John de Assunção, a Franciscan, was sent from Goa to Bahia to teach the cultivation of cinnamon and pepper.[20]

Success of the Jesuit experiment led to the introduction of a variety of oriental fruit-trees like jackfruit and mango, trees of commercial value like teak and sandalwood and a number of flowering plants which were acclimatised in Brazil.[21] The pioneering effort of the Jesuits, supported by other missionaries, broadened the basis of Brazilian tropical flora. Besides bringing about a change in the occupation of people, it changed the techniques of cultivation. Today Brazil competes with India in spice production though in a small way.

While the culinary and medical applications of spices were popularised by Jesuits in Brazil, one of them brought (it is believed) tobacco, a product native to America, into India. It is said that Luis de Goes (brother of Pero de Goes, donatory of the captaincy of Paraiba do Sul), who, after many years in Brazil, came to India, brought tobacco here, entered the Society of Jesus, and worked here till his death in 1567.[22] Though opinions vary as to when exactly tobacco was introduced in India, smoking was begun by natives approximately around 1605 or at the end of Akbar's reign.[23] It gained such popularity that it appeared to travellers that the poor devoured more smoke than anything else.[24]

Tobacco was initially used by the Jesuits as a curative. Its smoke facilitated digestion and cleansed the phlegm from the stomach,[25] but gradually it was so widely used by them that in 1638 the Fr. Superior-General referred to the necessity of checking this abuse among the Indian Jesuits.[26] In Goa, it was daily consumed or smoked by men, women and children alike.[27] Its trade provided employment to numerous natives. It came to be grown in Gujarat, the Konkan region and the Coromandel coast.[28] Today, large quantities of it are produced in Rajasthan, Bihar, West Bengal, and Karnataka. India is the sixth largest exporter of tobacco in the world, and the largest producer of unmanufactured tobacco.[29]

The Other Kind of Missionaries

I would also like to refer to the role played by the less known, but equally important missionaries of culture. When Portugal was faced with manpower crisis to govern her vast empire, one of the strategies adopted by her was to deport to Goa, the *degredados* who were (a) Military personnel accused of desertion and indiscipline, and (b) Civilians sentenced to serve in India for various crimes committed in Brazil. Age was no bar for such banishment. Hence, we have a large number of such men, even children in their teens, coming to Goa to serve their sentences.[30] They were employed in various branches of the military, and some of them stayed on for a few more years. There were also those who volunteered to serve in India, as sailors, commanders, soldiers and administrators.[31] Besides performing their official duties, they unconsciously served as carriers of culture into their new homeland. It is through interaction with such men (and at least one known woman who worked in Goa as a soldier for 13 years in the guise of a man, Ursula de Abreu de Alencastre of Rio de Janeiro, registered as Baltazar de Couto Cardozo, and known as Senhora de Panjim), that exchange of ideas, customs and manners took place. As inheritors of the luzitanian culture, they mingled with people in the Estado da India, freely making themselves comfortable, and finding themselves at ease. Perhaps, the introduction of *Para*[32] in the Goan cusine owes much to these men. In return the Goan balchão entered the Brazilian menu along with the uses cf the coconut and preparation of Goan curries.

NOTES AND REFERENCES

1. Eduardo Hoonaert, *História da Igreja no Brasil*, II/1, 3rd ed., Petropolis, 1983, p. 24. A similar opinion was expressed by Fr. Nobrega in a letter to Tomé de Souza in 1559, pp. 165-166.
2. Carlos Merces de Melo, *The Recruitment and Formation of the Native Clergy in India*, p. 4.
3. Teotonio R. de Souza, "Tradition of St. Thomas in India: Some Opinions", *CCBI News* (Goa), 1 (n. 4-6, 1990), pp. 64-66.
4. Leslie Bethell, (ed.), *Colonial Brazil*, p. 23.
5. John Correia-Afonso, "Indo-American Contacts through Jesuit missionaries", *Indica*, 14 (n. 1, 1977), p. 33.
6. Leite, Serafim, "Movimento missionario do Brasil para a India (1687-1748), *Boletim do Instituto Vasco da Gama*, (n. 69), p. 109. Also, "Suma Historica da Companhia da Jesus no Brasil (1549-1760)", p. 107.
7. Correia-Afonso, *Jesuit Letters and Indian History, 1542-1773*, pp. 123-125.
8. Charles R. Boxer, *The Portuguese Seaborne Empire, 1415-1825*, p. 305.
9. Antonio Paulo Fernandes, *Missionários Jesuitas no Brasil no tempo de Pombal*, pp. 9-22, 150.
10. Leite, *op. cit.*, pp. 108-118.
11. The steady increase in the number of Brazilian born Jesuits in Brazil until the expulsion in 1759 is as follows: 1549 (6 Jesuits — all foreign); 1574 (110 — 14% Brazilian); 1610 (165 — 17% Brazilian); 1654 (170 — 34% Brazilian); 1698 (304 — 37% Brazilian); 1732 (362 — 45% Brazilian); 1757 (474 — 44% Brazilian). *Source*: *Cambridge History of Latin America*, Vol. 1, p. 543.
12. Historical Archives of Goa (HAG), *Monções do Reino (MR)*, no. 180-A, fl. 157.
13. Arquivo Historico Ultramarino (AHU), Lisbon, *Ms. Baia*, catalogued loose papers (clp), n. 955.
14. Leite, *História da Companhia de Jesus no Brasil*, Vol. IV, pp. 156-7.
15. HAG, *MR*, no. 51-B, fl. 236.
16. *Ibid.*, no. 57, fl.349; AHU, *Baia* (clp), n. 3199. Luis Ferrand de Almeida, "Aclimatação de plantas do Oriente no Brasil durante os seculos XVII e XVIII", *Revista Portuguesa de História*, Tomo XV, 1975, p. 387. As the *canarins* were not found proficient, they were sent back to Goa.
17. HAG, *MR*, n. 55-B, fls. 348-9. However, Fr. John de Brito died a martyr at the Malabar mission in February 1693.
18. Biblioteca Nacional (BNL, Lisboa), Ms. *Collecção Pombalina (CP)*, n. 495, fl. 37.
19. HAG, *MR*, n. 59, fls. 320-321.
20. *Ibid.*, n. 68, fl. 234; n. 70, fl. 29. He was paid 400 *reis* daily for his work. He had a hard time fighting the menace of ants; Leite, *op. cit.*, p. 157.

21. HAG, *MR*, n. 180-A, fls. 83, 85; n. 181-A, fls. 83-84.
22. Peixoto Afranio, *Historia do Brasil*, p. 87.
23. *O Oriente Portugues*, VI, 1909, pp. 161-162.
24. G.B. Scammell, *The First Imperial Age*, p. 129.
25. Leite, "Os Jesuitas no Brasil e a Medicina", *Revista Petrus Nonius*, I, Lisbon, 1936, pp. 5-16. Similarly, pineapple was found to be useful in relieving pain of kidney-stone.
26. Teotonio R. de Souza, *Medieval Goa*, New Delhi, Concept, 1979, p. 160.
27. HAG, *MR*, n. 159-C, fl. 691v; *Documentação Ultramarina Portuguesa*, V, p. 98.
28. W.H. Moreland, *From A' bar to Aurangzeb*, p. 80.
29. India — 1991. A Reference Annual, ed. Research and Reference Division, Government of India, New Delhi.
30. Here is a sample of the list of *degredados* sent to Goa in 1748. Tomaz Domingos de Barros (aged 25) died in Goa 1 Oct., 1786; Martinho John (24); Raimundo Pereira (28) died in Goa 11th July 1790; Antonio Jose de Sta. Anna; Paulo Primeiro; John de Maceno Barbosa (21); Paulo Carneiro (37); Manoel Monteiro (16); Thomaz de Aquino; Manoel Carneiro de Azevedo (14); Vidal Pereira; John de Moraes Sarmento and Jose Duarte Contuiras. Source: HAG, *MR*, n. 164-G, fls. 1986-2006.
31. A. de Silva Rego, *O Ultramar Portugues no Seculo XVII*, pp. 78-80.
32. *Pará* is a fish pickle named after the Brazilian city of Para. *India Portuguesa*, I, Panjim, 1923, pp. 172-182.

14

TEACHING METHODS IN GOA (1750–1800): Jesuits and Oratorians

MARIA DE JESUS DOS MARTIRES LOPES

Though Portuguese discoveries in the fifteenth and sixteenth centuries had given an impressive stimulus to various trade ventures, yet Portuguese cultural contacts with the people of Asia, Africa and America were no less impressive. Their more distinctive impress, however, lay in the spiritual field. In this essay I intend to concentrate on Asian culture in particular. Being older, it was the more resilient of the three and resisted till it could any outside western influence. The missionaries (Franciscan, Dominicans and Jesuits in particular) played an important role in their evangelisation and educational work.

The Jesuits

In Goa, Jesuit religious zeal had led to a spiritual renovation of the then corrupt Portuguese officials.[1] The Jesuits had within a short span acquired intellectual as well as spiritual recognition at the various Indian courts, with their knowledge of languages and their insight into the social structure. They were at home in the local society, introducing new strategies for missionary work, publishing Konkani books, and laying great store by good preaching.[2]

The Society of Jesus stood out with her emphasis on education, and worked alongside other Orders in Goa. One could ask: What were the problems related to education and Jesuit teaching methods in the sixteenth century? Related to this is a study into the educational problems that followed Jesuit suppression in 1759.

Since the early fifteenth century, parochial schools functioned in the parishes of Goa, owing their origin to the efforts of Francis Xavier. D. João de Albuquerque, the first bishop of Goa encouraged the process further. A royal order of 1545 set up schools for the teaching of catechism, liturgical chants, arithmetic, art and craft, and Portuguese language.[3]

At the Seminary of Holy Faith (Santa Fe) and at the College of St. Paul's (both under the care of the Jesuits), students studying for the priesthood, learnt music, grammar, rhetoric, philosophy and theology. St. Paul's had classes in Latin, courses in art, and lectures in theology. It became the inspiration for similar schools in the East. Its fame led to its being termed 'the University of Goa'. Pyrard de Laval considered it the most important in India, and it had two thousand students, both Indian and Portuguese, on its rolls.[4]

The Jesuits set up a school in 1574 in Salcete and later permanently established it at Rachol in 1610. Here, besides the local hospital, there was also a seminary for poor children, a house for catechumens and two other schools, one where children learned catechism, and the other where Jesuits learnt Konkani.[5]

Jesuits devised a specific teaching method for their schools which they synthesized in the *Ratio Studiorum* in 1599. The method was used most likely in Goa too. The courses taught consisted of theology (four years covering scholastic and moral issues), philosophy (logic and sciences in the first year, cosmology, psychology, physics and mathematics in the second, and ethics in the third), and humanities (rhetoric and grammar).[6]

Scholastic theology was Thomistic, and philosophy Aristotelian (except in those matters that went against the Christian faith). Physics and mathematics were Euclidean. In humanities, rhetoric was Aristotelian, and oratory, style and erudition Ciceronian. Latin was cumpulsory and had to be spoken by all students of humanities. Methodology and dissertation were important teaching procedures, meant to be the dynamic analysis of model systems. The teaching method overall was an interaction between teacher and student with a system of reward and punishment.[7]

Jesuits scored ahead of others in their teaching methods, yet other Orders had their respective educational institutions too, all of which continued throughout the eighteenth century. The Dominicans had the college of St. Thomas, the Franciscans a college at Reis Magos, college of St. Bonaventure (where philosophy and theology was taught for their own candidates), and the Seminary of St.

Jeronimo for orphans. The Augustinians at their college of Populo had public classes in Latin, philosophy and theology, with many graduates passing from their ranks. Yet one is in the dark about the teaching methods employed at these places.[8]

In Portugal, Illuminism was popular in Jesuit schools. Inacio Monteiro, according to the *Elenchus Quaestionum* (1754), followed philosophical eclecticism rather than Aristotelian metaphysics, and maintained that the search for truth ought to be attained through reason and experimentation. His ideas were at first received with mistrust, yet the acceptance of his theories and pedagogical methods points to the new thinking at Jesuit schools in the latter half of the eighteenth century.[9]

The suppression of the Jesuits in 1759 raised the problem of finding suitable replacements for them in the various schools since they had been indispensable to some degree. The educational reform came under the *Directoria Geral dos Estudos* – The Directorate of Studies (1759 to 1771) and *Real Mesa Censoria* – The Royal Board of Censors (1771-1777). Jesuit books were banned, and the overall purpose was to follow unquestioningly the dictates of the Marquis of Pombal who had initiated the reforms in the first place. Yet the violent methods used for the purpose elsewhere did not have their same sting here.[10]

Latin, Greek and rhetoric continued to be taught with Latin the most important course, as had earlier been the case at Jesuit schools. Latin grammar enabled students to speak Portuguese with perfection.[11]

The reform remained unsuccessful since qualified teachers were few and funds insufficient. In Goa, teachers were available, usually the locals, and the idea gained ground that the earlier measures had been too harsh for this land.[12] The *subsídio literário* was paid for through revenues collected on wine and meat.[13] Education in public schools was free, private schools were allowed, and there was a department for education established. The system of appointing *mestres* and *professores regios* was current also during the reign of Maria II with public schools set up in Salcete and Bardez, each province with one *mestre de ler* and one Latin teacher. At the end of the century, ten *cadeiras régias* were taught in Goa.[14]

Public schools were started in several Goan villages in answer to the needs of the people.[15] Private schools were funded by local benefactors and confraternities, and not from the *subsídio literário*.

Escolas régias as well as private and parochial schools worked side by side.[16]

The Oratorians

The Oratorians were entrusted with teaching in Goa after 1759. They were a new congregation, Brahmin by caste and Pombal wishing to ensure a speedy educational system picked on them.

Questions surface as: Which were the cultural patterns and educational methods that they employed while they substituted the Jesuits? Was there a *guerra surda* between them and their predecessors with matters like Luis Antonio Verney, Latin grammar, and experimental philosophy at the centre? Verney had in his *Verdadeiro Metodo de Estudar* come down heavily on Jesuit pedagogy and their Latin courses. The Oratorians had admired Verney and his fascination for Illuminism.[17]

Portuguese and Latin were now taught using the dialogistic method rather than the Jesuit one as mentioned in Fr. Manuel Alvares' *Arte*. It was believed that Jesuit students gave up orality in favour of Latin grammer.[18] Many Oratorians agreed on the need of a slant in philosophy towards applied sciences. It is interesting to know that Verney and Antonio Pereira de Figueiredo corresponded and sent books to the Oratorians in Goa.[19]

In 1761, the Oratorians started a seminary at Chorão, a year later one at Rachol, and another in 1781 at Bom Jesus, yet this time along with the secular clergy. At Chorão they taught courses in theology, philosophy, rhetoric and Latin grammer.[20] In physics, they taught Gassendo, Descartes and Leibniz, and Fr. Antonio Pereira's Latin grammar, thus replacing Jesuit methodology outright. Oratorian methods were accepted since they paid more attention to the mother-tongue, to simplification of Latin grammar study, to greater stress on study of history and geography, and to their openness to some sort of experimentation and rationalisation in teaching of philosophy.[21] This was the Oratorian contribution of Illuminism to the people of Goa.

Rachol followed Chorão closely in the courses given, the duration for them, and in the methodology, since the above two seminaries and the one of Bom Jesus most likely too, used the same manuals and followed the same authors, thus having a certain academic solidarity. Yet the short-lived existence of the Oratorians prevented them from leaving a lasting mark on the education of Goa.

The *aulas regias* were closed in 1798 and secondary education came to be associated with the diocesan seminaries.[22] They played an important part in the educational system of Goa and in the shaping of an intellectual climate. Public schools gave many an access to education and other cultural pursuits.

The suppression of the Jesuits in 1759 had led to a reformulation of the educational system. The result was the acceptance of the ideals of Illuminism and the need to keep abreast with the rest of Europe scientifically. The setting up of the Academy of Sciences, was an answer to these reforms.

Goa responded to the prevailing cultural movement. The *aulas regias* and the seminaries taught modern literature and the system of enlightenment (*luzes*). Much of present-day Goan culture owes its origins to these movements. The transformation was undoubtedly forwarded by priests (Jesuits, Oratorians and the secular clergy). Their respective roles in cultural adaptation are an important point while reviewing the importance of their missionary work.

NOTES AND REFERENCES

1. Sebastião Gonçalves, *Primeira Parte da Historia dos Religiosos da Companhia de Jesus*, ed. Jose Wicki, Vol. II, Coimbra, 1960, pp. 43-45, 186-287; E.R. Hambye, "Goa", *Dictionnaire d'Histoire et de Geographie Ecclesiastiques*, ed. R. Aubert, Paris, p. 287.
2. A. B. de Bragança Pereira, *S. Francisco Xavier: Esboço Historico*, Panjim. Tomas Estevão, *Doutrina Cristã em Lingua Concani*, 2nd ed., ed. Mariano Saldanha, Lisbon, 1945, pp. 6-9.
3. Historical Archives of Goa (HAG), *Monções do Reino (MR)*, Livro 180-A, fls. 168-169v. Maria de Jesus dos Martires Lopes, *Goa da Segunda Metade De Setecentos: Esboço de Ensaio Socio-Cultural.* (forthcoming).
4. *Viagem de Francisco Pyrard de Laval*, II, trans. by Joaquim Heliodoro da Cunha Rivara, Porto, pp. 45-46.
5. Francisco de Souza, *Oriente Conquistado*, I, pp. 12-15.
6. Leonel Franca, *O Método Pedagógico dos Jesuítas: O Ratio Studiorum*, Rio de Janeiro, 1952, pp. 41-2, 47-48.
7. *Ibid.*, pp. 47-8, 152, 155, 159, 215-16.
8. Martires Lopes, *op. cit.*
9. Antonio Alberto Banha de Andrade, *Contribuições para a Historia da Mentalidade Pedagogica Portuguesa*, Lisbon, 1982, pp. 648-652.
10. *A Reforma Pombalina dos Estudos Secundarios (1759-1771). Contribuição para a Historia da Pedagogia em Portugal*, Vol. I, Coimbra, 1981, pp. 70-72, 83.
11. Romulo de Carvalho, *Historia do Ensino em Portugal*, Lisboa, 1986, p. 429.
12. Banha de Andrade, "A Reforma Pombalina dos Estudos Secundarios no Arquipelago dos Acores (1759-71)," in *Arquipélago: Revista da Universidade dos Açores*, 1983, pp. 219-220, 781-2.

13. Francisco de Souza, *op. cit.*, pp. 83-84.
14. *Ibid.*, pp. 87, 90; Menezes Bragançã, "A Educação e o Ensino" in *India Portuguesa*, Vol. II, Panjim, 1923, p. 74.
15. ANTT (Lisbon), *Junta da Real Fazenda do Estado da India*, L 63, fls. 145v-146v, 148v-149, 151v, 152v-153v, 158, 165-165v; L 73, fls. 79-79v.
16. *Ibid.*, L 74, fls. 155v; L 78.
17. Eugénio dos Santos, *Para a História da Cultura em Portugal no século XVIII.*
18. Banha de Andrade, *Contributos para a História da Mentalidade Pedagógica Portuguesa*, pp. 497-508, 518, 537, 539, 544.
19. *Cartas de Luis Antonio Verney e Antonio Pereira de Figueiredo aos Padres da Congregação do Oratorio de Goa*, ed. da Cunha Rivara, Panjim, 1883; L. Cabral de Moncada, *Estudos de Historia do Direito*, III, Coimbra, 1950, pp. 441-443. Quoted by Banha de Andrade. Luis Antonio Verney, "Soldado na India", *Boletim do Instituto Vasco da Gama*, Bastora, 1958.
20. Antonio Caetano Pacheco, *Plano Geral da Instrucção Publica nos Estudos Portugueses da India Precedido de uma Exposição*, Lisbon, 1848, p. 7.
21. Eugenio dos Santos, *O Oratorio no Norte de Portugal: Contribuição para o Estudo da Historia Religiosa e Social*, Porto, 1982, p. 302. HAG, *MR*, L. 180-A, fls. 170-173v.
22. Francisco de Souza, *op. cit.*, p. 88. HAG, *MR*, L. 177-B, fls. 547-548.

15

SECONDARY TOOLS OF EMPIRE: Jesuit Men of Science in India

R.K. KOCHHAR

The arrival of St. Francis Xavier at Goa on 6th May, 1542, is an event of singular importance. He was the first Jesuit in India, and many others were to follow him for the next two hundred years. Although the spread of the Christian faith was the most important plan of the Jesuits, their activities had a scientific dimension about them also, being the first European men of learning in India. In this paper I will describe their scientific activities and discuss their impact on later political developments.[1]

The Portuguese arrived in India even before the Mughals did. While the latter entered through the traditional north-western landgate, the former came by sea and settled on the west coast. The Portuguese introduced a new parameter, navy, in India's geopolitical equations, placing the Mughals at a permanent disadvantage for all times to come. The year of Xavier's arrival in India was also the year of Akbar's birth. The latter's fascination for elephants was legendary. We can compare the Mughal empire itself to an elephant, which is powerful on land. The Portuguese were the crocodile which controlled the waters. Because of his interest in comparative theology and probably also due to his apprehension about the Portuguese sea-borne power, Akbar invited in 1580, a Jesuit mission to his court. This led to the establishment of a church and a Jesuit mission at Agra which continued till 1803.

As long as the Mughal empire was powerful, the Europeans remained confined to the coastal regions, outside the imperial zone of influence and minded their business. They did take an interest in botany.[1] This is natural, because after all it was the lure of the culinary plants that had brought them to these parts in the first place. Interest in plants was beneficial and profitable, because of their medicinal, commercial, and curiosity value in Europe. While the European traders had a good idea about India's coast-line, they were ignorant about the country's interior, having had no reason to venture there, nor being equipped for the task. Geographical exploration was left to the Jesuits, who had the training, the time, and the opportunity to criss-cross the country. They had also the necessary discipline to make careful observations, to record them faithfully, and to transmit them regularly. In Europe, these reports were dutifully preserved, yet ignored. Europe was not as yet ready for India.

In the eighteenth century, the collapse of the Mughal empire produced a political vacuum. The European *vaishya* outfits developed *kshatriya* ambitions, and knowing post-Plassey India became a paying proposition. Jesuit data were now dug up and put to use. Colonial geographers avidly scanned the 34 Jesuit volumes of *Lettres Edifiantes et Curieuses*. Interestingly, an abridged translation in two volumes was edited in London in 1743 by John Lockman entitled, *Travels of the Jesuits into Various Parts of the world*. He deleted accounts of conversions and miracles, as being 'quite insipid or ridiculous to most English readers, and indeed to all persons of understanding and taste'. English readers were interested undoubtedly only in those parts of the work which furthered their overseas interests. A fresh edition was published in Paris between 1780 and 1783 in 26 volumes by Querboeuft, who conveniently arranged the letters in geographical order. Volumes 10 to 15 give information about India. This compilation is however largely devoted to the French missionaries, with the Mughal Mission being very poorly represented.[2]

Traditionally, the conquerors entered India from the north-west and moved eastwards, leaving the southern part alone. (Aurungzeb brought an end to the Mughal power by needlessly trying to subdue the south, and the Marathas ruined themselves by trying to extend their hold right up to Delhi). In contrast, the Europeans, coming as they did by sea, were first interested in south India, and later in the eastern, central and northern parts. This is therefore the order in which geopraphical information about India was sought and incorporated into the main body of European knowledge, irrespective of the order in which this information was first obtained.

Fr. Anthony Monserrate (1536–1600)

Chronologically speaking, the first Jesuit geographer in India was Fr. Anthony Monserrate even though his work was unnoticed for 200 years.[3] Born at Vic de Ozona, 30 miles from Monserrate in Catalonia (Spain), he joined the Order in 1558 and left for India in 1574. He was chosen to be a member of the first Jesuit mission to Akbar's court and was asked by his superiors at Goa to keep a diary. This he did most faithfully, adding greatly to its value by his geographical and astronomical observations. On his journey from Surat to Fatehpur Sikri in 1580, he made a survey and took observations for latitude. When in 1581, Akbar marched to Kabul against his half-brother Mirza Muhammad Hakim, he took him along for continuing the tuition of his second son Murad (1570–99). He encouraged Monserrate to take observations en route, which he did as far as Jalalabad.

Akbar however did not seem to have shown any interest in the data collected by Monserrate, who kept it with himself when he returned from the mission.

On the basis of his observations, Monserrate prepared in about 1590 a small map, 5½" X $4^1/_8$" in size. This little map was a tremendous improvement on all previous efforts. It was based on actual observations rather than on travellers' tales. It gave a better idea of the Himalayas and of the upper course of the Punjab rivers than Rennell had done nearly 200 years later. Expectedly, Monserrate did not have any knowledge about regions east of the Yamuna. Studied today, one notices that he had placed Surat east of Goa instead of west of Goa, and that the map is four degrees too far to the east. But keeping in mind the times when it was first prepared and when it was first used, its value cannot be under-estimated.[4]

Monserrate's geographical endeavour belongs to the category of historical romance rather than to that of historical compulsion. The Jesuit Mughal Mission operated under the Portuguese patronage, but the latter soon became redundant in the European power-game. Indeed, ironically, Monserrate's work done when the Jesuit mission was established, came to light only when the mission ended.

The French who were the last of the Europeans to arrive in India and became semi-finalists in the power-game, acted as patrons to the French Jesuits. Thanks to the Jesuits, French werre more successful on the scientific front than on the colonial.

Fr. Jean-Venant Bouchet (1655–1732)

The first dependable map of the interior of the southern peninsula was due to the efforts of Fr. Jean-Venant Bouchet who had the distinction of arriving in India from the east rather than from the west.[5] Born at Fontenay-le-Comte in France, he joined the Society in 1670 and was a member of the expedition sent to Siam in 1687 by king Louis XIV. There were 14 Jesuits in all, formally designated as 'The Mathematicians of the King'. They arrived in Siam in 1688, but were expelled the same year as a result of a revolution that overthrew the king. The missionaries left for India, but only three survived the ordeal and reached Pondicherry on 17th February, 1689, two of them being Fr. Bouchet and Fr. Jean Richaud. It is not clear who the third Jesuit was. On arrival in India, Bouchet joined the Madura Mission, but left it in 1702 to set up the Carnatic Mission.

Bouchet covered the Coromandel coast on foot, made astronomical observations at Pondicherry, and prepared maps and sketches. In 1719 Bouchet sent to France his map of Madurai and the neighbouring kingdoms, extending it to slightly north of latitude 14° N. Obviously there was some sort of coordination between the Jesuit data collectors on the one hand, and the French commercial and political interests, on the other. Because of the map being drawn by a small scale of not quite an inch to one degree of latitude and consequently not capable of giving the countries in any considerable detail, the Jesuits sent over several manuscript charts, and other materials, from which D'Anville composed a new map. It was drawn by a scale nearly twice as large as the former, and was a great deal more particular as well as accurate, and extended further north.[6] D'Anville published his map of the southern Peninsula in 1737 and followed it by his famous *Carte de L'Inde* in 1752. An important feature of this map was that he left blank very conscientiously those parts of India, about which he did not have authentic knowledge. The significance of D'Anville's efforts can be judged from the fact that his Memoirs were translated, annotated, and published with a reprint of his map in London in 1754 and 1759.[7]

Bouchet's companion Fr. Richaud discovered in 1689 that the bright southern star Alpha Centauri was in fact a double star. This was the second binary ever discovered. Earlier in 1685 another Jesuit, Fr. Fontenay, had discovered from the Cape of Good Hope the first binary Alpha Crucis. Richaud's was the first credited astronomical discovery from India.

Fr. Claude Stanislaus Boudier (1686-1757)

The next stage was the geographical exploration of Hindustan (North India) undertaken by Fr. Claude Stanislaus Boudier. Born at Sens in France, Boudier left France for Chandernagore in Bengal in 1718. His chance to traverse north India came about as a result of astronomical pursuits of Raja Jai Singh Sawai of Jaipur, who wanted the Jesuit to visit him for scientific consultations. Accordingly, Boudier and another Jesuit, Pons, set out from Chandernagore on 6th January, 1734. 'On their arrival they seem unfortunately to have wasted much time in disputing with the local Brahmins as to the extent to which Indian astronomy was indebted to the ancient Greeks'. The two Jesuits worked at Jaipur during August and September 1734 and returned to Chandernagore about a year later.[8]

The Jesuit mission was no doubt a failure from Jai Singh Sawai's point of view. But seen from the colonial angle it was a huge success. During his journeys to and fro, Boudier fixed the longitude and latitude of many important places, and kept a survey of his route between Agra and Allahabad. His Memoir gave 'the description of places on this road (between Agra and Bengal) . . . with the computed distance of each from the course of the Gemne (Jamna) and the Ganges'. Boudiers' work was used extensively by D'Anville and by his British counterpart, Rennell. D'Anville used Boudier's value for the latitude of Madras in preference to any other. Rennell depended on Boudier for his 1774 general map of Bengal, and used his values as late as 1793.[9]

Fr. Joseph Tieffenthaler (1710–1785)

A rather pathetic figure was Fr. Joseph Tieffenthaler who survived the dissolution of the Society of Jesus in 1773 by working under the British auspices.[10] Born at Bolzana in the Austrian Tyrol, he joined the Order in 1729, and left Germany for Spain in 1740. In 1742 he sailed from Lisbon for Goa by way of the Philippines. He reached Goa in 1743. He was apparently intended originally for the Jaipur Observatory, but Raja Jai Singh's death in 1743 cut short these plans. He was accordingly sent to Agra to work at the Jesuit College there. Shortly afterwards, he began his wanderings to Mathura, Delhi, Narwar, Goa, Surat, Jodhpur, Ajmer, Jaipur, Gwalior, and to innumerable other places. In 1747, he commenced service as a priest at the Bourbon Colony at Narwar, where he remained for about eighteen years.

Meanwhile, in 1759 the king of Portugal had banished all Jesuits from Portuguese dominions. Consequently, the Jesuit presence at Goa ceased, and with this the Mughal Mission as a Jesuit enterprise 'may be said to have come to an end.' Tieffenthaler found himself in such financial straits that in 1756 he boldly decided to appeal for financial help to the 'famous English nation so well known for their humanity, liberality and charity to the poor'. He travelled to Calcutta keeping surveys of the way. Apparently he found the help he needed and settled in Oudh for the rest of his life, making Lucknow his headquarters. Till 1771 he was continually on the move making astronomical observations and surveys, employing also one or more local assistants 'versed in geography', whom he sent to explore the sources of the Ganga and the Gogra.

Tieffenthaler was a tireless explorer. 'Next to the salvation of souls, and their conquest for God, nothing has afforded me greater pleasure than the study of the geographical position of places, the variations of winds, the nature of the soil, and the character and manners of the regions through which I am travelling'. The publication history of his works makes interesting reading. In 1772 or 1773 he sent a voluminous collection of his works in Latin to a Prof. Kratzenstein through the agency of a Dutch doctor, whom he had met in India. He sent other material to the French orientalist Anquetil Duperron, who was in India betwen 1755 and 1764, three of which he had spent at Surat collecting Parsi manuscripts.

In 1771 Duperron published the first European translation of *Zend Avesta*.[11] In 1759, when he was at Surat and Tieffenthaler at Narwar, the two were in correspondence with each other. Suddenly in 1776, Duperron received from Tieffenthaler (then at Faizabad) a packet of maps (including a 15-ft long map of Ganga) and some loose papers. Duperron very promptly prepared a treatise on these maps and in 1776 itself published it in the *Journal des Savants* making it a point to mention Tieffenthaler's unattended Copenhagen works. This publication spurred the German astronomer and mathematician Joseph Bernoulli, at the time professor at Berlin. He obtained Tieffenthaler's geographical work *Descriptio Indiae* from Copenhagen, and collaborated with Duperron on its translation and publication along with that of an expanded version of Duperron's treatise. The work was published in three volumes in German (1785-

87) as well as in French (1786-89). Bernoulli's publication reached Rennell in England in time for Tieffenthaler's work to be incorporated into his map of 1788.

Thomas Call in India had already received copies from Tieffenthaler himself. Call's *Atlas of India* embodies *Routes taken between Goah and Agra by Padri Tieffenthaler; A Survey of the country N.W. of Delhi by Padries Windell and Tieffenthaler.*

Fr. Francis Xavier Wendel (d. 1803)

The sad state of the last days of the Moghul Mission is best epitomised by the rather shadowy Fr. Francis Xavier Wendel who along with Tieffenthaler survived the mission. He came to India in 1751 and resided at Agra and Lucknow for the greater part of his life. Though many of his flock were French, he was pro-British in his leanings to the extent that the Commandant at Chandernagore wrote to the Minister in Paris accusing him of being a British agent.[12]

Wendel was closely associated with Tieffenthaler in geographical pursuits. In 1764, he sent Duperron a map showing the strategic position of the Mughal and British armies at the time of the battle of Buscar. He was the author of *A Memoir on the Land of the Rajputs and other Provinces to the South and South West of Agra*, with a map which he drew up in 1779, and presented to Rennell, who was much indebted to Wendal in the preparation of his own great map of Hindustan. In 1780, Wendel met a Russian named Czernichef who had travelled from Bukhara through Kashmir to Lucknow, and communicated his diary to Col. Francis Wilford at Benares.

Wendel died on 20th March, 1803, and like Tieffenthaler was buried at Agra. With his death, the last links with the Mughal Mission were snapped.

Monserrate revisited

In the very early years of the nineteenth century, more than 200 years after its completion, Monserrate's work was dusted out of the archival shelves and incorporated into the corpus of geographical knowledge. The time was not fortuitous. The struggle for territorial control over India was almost over, and the British were finally at Delhi. The territory west of Delhi was now of strategic importance. In 1804 Francis Wilford of the Bengal Engineers brought out a valuable *Map of the Countries West of Delhi*. This map was a tremendous improvement on any thing that had been produced before. It stretched as far as Sukkur and Dera Ghazi Khan on the south-west, Kabul on the west, and to Chitral and Gilgit in the north. For the collection of the material he employed a surveyor, Mirza Mogul Beg between 1786 and 1796, and made use of Fr. Monserrate's manuscript.[13]

It is reasonably certain that a copy of Monserrate's manuscript journal was kept at the Jesuit college at Agra, from where it was taken by Tieffenthaler, who may have passed it on to Wilford in 1784 one year before his own death. Monserrate's work thus neatly brackets the Mughal history. It was prepared when the Mughal empire was first established. It was made use of by the British when they reached the Mughal capital and formally deprived the titular emperor of his sovereignty.

Conclusion

The eighteenth century saw a bitter struggle between the two European powers, Britain and France, for territorial control of India. The European military might could have been of decisive use against the native kings only if the lay of the land was known to the foreigners. Accurate geographical information of the country came from the Jesuits who had the training, time, and the opportunity to criss-cross the country. The French were more successful on the geographical front than on the colonial. The first reliable map of India was the work of D'Anville, achieved no doubt because of his easy access to the meticulous field-work done by the Jesuits.

Interestingly, the history of the Agra-based Jesuit Mughal Mission tells us much about the history of the increasing European involvement in India. In 1579 when Akbar invited Jesuits to his court from Goa, there were apprehensions that he, incensed at Portuguese affrontry on the sea, might hold the Jesuits as hostages. Two hundred years later in 1765 Tieffenthaler, already disowned by Portugal and soon to be disowned by the Pope, successfully appealed to the British at Calcutta for financial help for his geographical and exploratory pursuits. And finally Wendel, the last remnant of the mission, was openly accused by the demoralized French of being a British agent.

We have seen that the geographical work done by the Jesuits in India was of great value to the French and British colonial interests. It will be interesting to find out whether these interests directly or indirectly influenced the Jesuit aims in India and whether the Jesuits perceived the use to which their work was being put to.

NOTES AND REFERENCES

1. R. K. Kochhar, "Science in British India". I. Colonial tool, *Current Science*, 1992, pp. 63, 689.
2. E. Maclagan, *The Jesuits and the Great Mogul*, London, 1932, p. 15.
3. *Ibid.*, p. 148.
4. R. H. Phillimore, *Historical Records of the Survey of India*, Vol. I, Dehra Dun, 1945.
5. Kochhar, "French Astronomers in India during the 17th-19th Centuries," *J. Br. Astr. Assoc.*, 1991, pp. 95, 101.
6. Phillimore, *op. cit.*, p. 238.
7. *Ibid.*, p. 210.
8. Maclagan, *op. cit.*, p. 134; Phillimore, *op. cit.*, p. 314.
9. *Ibid.*, p. 314.
10. *Ibid.*, p. 137; Phillimore, *op. cit.*, p. 388; Noti, S., *Joseph Tieffenthaler, S.J.*, Bombay, 1906.
11. *Sacred Books of the East*, Vol. 4, p. xv.
12. Maclagan, *op. cit.*, p. 141; Phillimore, *op. cit.*, p. 395.
13. Phillimore, *op. cit.*, p. 395.

16

THE BRITISH ANTI-SLAVERY DRIVE AND ITS IMPACT ON INDIAN OCEAN COMMERCE, 1815–1885

ANIRUDHA GUPTA

Christian Missionaries Arrive

Half way through the nineteenth century, the missionary movement in Africa began to gather momentum. First came the evangelical Church Missionary Society, which was to develop important fields of work in West and East Africa. Next followed many Protestant missionary societies, of which the most important for Africa were the Methodist Missionary Society, with missions in West and South Africa; the Basel Society in West Africa; the Berlin Society, with missions in South and later in East Africa; the Universities Mission, a High Anglican Society, with its field in central parts of East Africa; and the Mission of the Scottish Presbyterian Churches in South, West and East Africa.

By around the 1850s, the Roman Catholic missions too made an impressive debut. Members of the Congregation of the Holy Ghost (refounded in 1848) set up work in West Africa, in the Lower Congo, and in the coastal regions of East Africa. They were followed by Cardinal Lavigerie's foundation in 1868, of the Society of Our Lady of Africa, with missions deep into the interior of the continent, from Uganda in the north to northern Rhodesia in the south. Both these Orders were to be joined in due course by contingents from the older Orders, the Benedictines, Franciscans, Dominicans and Jesuits.

Missionary Indignation

In Europe, radical Christian movements had succeeded in arousing great public indignation against maritime slave-trading across the Atlantic. As a result, the British Parliament was prevailed upon to pass a law in 1807, which made trading in slaves illegal for British subjects, and four years later another Act imposing heavy penalty on those who continued in it. Under British pressure, most other maritime nations followed suit, and by around 1842, transportation of slaves across the Atlantic had been technically accepted as an illegal activity by almost all European and American nations.

It was around this time that Christian abolitionists turned their focus on Arab slave-trading in the Indian Ocean area. Being in the forefront of the anti-slavery drive, Britain was called upon to hunt and punish the offending Arab traders and their rulers who indulged in slave trafficking. Britain was particularly well-placed to undertake such actions for, in the first place, it had emerged, at the close of the Napoleonic war, as the paramount naval power in the east; second, it had to oversee that British subjects in India and those in East Africa and the newly acquired island territories of the Indian Ocean strictly obeyed the parliamentary laws; and third, quite independent of the missionary factor, Britain had sound commercial reasons to prosecute slave drivers, "since the trade in slaves was so much easier and more profitable than any other African trade, it had to be internationally suppressed before legitimate commerce between Africa and Europe could develop".[1]

A New Crusade: Fresh Alibis

But the success of the whole enterprise depended on the imposition of naval surveillance by British cruisers, which could intercept and search both Arab and other slave-ships sailing under European flags. This was a right European nations were unwilling to grant. As a result, although the British crew could arrest and destroy Arab boats carrying slaves (*dhows*) and force African rulers to outlaw the export of slaves, European trafficking, with Arabs acting as their intermediaries, not only flourished but also took a virulent form and penetrated into the very heart of Africa. A spill-over effect, but perhaps more damaging, was the total disruption of Afro-Asian commerce in the area. For, wrote the British Consul in Zanzibar in 1860, "the news has travelled far over the interior that the white man is now best customer to the slave dealer, and that he pays good price in ready money. . ."[1a]

All this is shocking; yet the question arises, "What could have brought about such results?" Was the missionary zeal, which contributed in large measures to the suppression of trans-Atlantic slave trade, found to be lacking – or misconstrued – in the eastern hemisphere? Or, did the mixing of philanthropic and commercial interests blunt the British anti-slavery drive? Or, was this inevitable in view of the refusal of other European powers to support an apparently humanitarian cause? Further, why did native societies and commerce of the area crumble in the face of British naval campaign against slave trade? If the economic health and prosperity of these societies rested on trade in slaves only, they had no reason to incur losses as this trade increased manifold *precisely* as a result of British campaigning. On the other hand, if Afro-Asian commerce was legitimate, how did it fail to take advantage of the favourable climate created by Christian abolitionists?

Historical Pretentions

These are difficult questions, and perhaps more difficult to answer (for since when has history been trained to give right answer?). In the pages that follow, we will simply make an attempt to show how strangely history functions to frustrate even the noblest of human endeavours.

But, first the historical setting:

In 1846, Lord Palmerston wrote to the British Resident in Zanzibar: "You will take every opportunity of impressing upon these Arabs that the nations of Europe are destined to put an end to the African slave trade, and that Great Britain is the main instrument in the hand of Providence of the accomplishment of this purpose, etc."[1b] This, it is believed, introduced an evangelical note in British foreign policy. It helped appease the Christian emancipationist movements on the one hand, and created the image of all Europe engaged in a war against the Arab practice of slave trade in the East. Above all, the "war" paved the way for British paramountcy in the whole of Indian Ocean area.[2]

There is perhaps an element of truth in this assertion. But the motive behind the British anti-slavery drive was suspect in the eyes of rival European powers right from the outset. The French, in particular, "suspected Britian's campaign to abolish the slave trade as a decorous cover for the profitable extension of commercial connections by the contemptible shopkeepers".[3] The Portuguese and the Germans also shared and expressed the same view. What is, however, disturbing is the fact that despite British injunctions and naval surveillance of Africa's east coast, European involvements in slave trade, sometime in competition and sometime in collaboration with the Arabs, continued as late as the beginning of this century. Worst, it pushed slave trade far and wide into Africa's interior, laying waste to settled communities and cultures.[4] The French and large American shipping companies offered higher price for Africans captured by Arab intermediaries. The whole economy of Portuguese-held Mozambique turned into "men-stealing and men-selling".[5]

Two other consequences followed. First, the French device of exporting "free" labour from Africa. This device was audacious and simple: ships with French flags visited east African ports, obtained assurances from slave-dealers that Africans in their charge were not slaves, and took them aboard for Bourbon, Reunion and Mayotte. This was not slavery in the technical sense, and hence allowed free passage by British ships ! Second was the British practice of engaging contract labour from India, called *coolies*. From 1833 onwards – with but a few years interruption – *coolies* were engaged for sugar plantations in Mauritius, Fiji and West Indies and later in South Africa. This gave birth to a floating population of skilled or semi-skilled workers – technically free but tied wholly to the plantation economy of British colonies.[6] The basic advantage of the system was that it was cheap, abundant enough to replace the supply of African slaves, and morally not outrageous to Christian missionary sentiment.

The worst effect of the anti-slavery drive was, however, on Asiatic commerce and civilization. Muscat in the Gulf of Oman and Madagascar on the outer Cape route, which had been the centres of traditional Asiatic trade – a meeting point of Arab, Indian, Chinese and African (Swahili) businessmen – were ruined by remorseless competition among European powers for post-industrial commerce and colonies.

Mixture of Roguery and Morality

It is not the purpose of this paper to establish any *conscious* pattern in the manner in which Western domination of the Indian Ocean ruined traditional Afro-Asian commerce in the Indian Ocean area. Nor, in this sense, it is concerned with any formulation of dependency schools, which usually – though paradoxically – give subjectivity a higher place than objective factors in history. Its aim, on the contrary, is very modest viz., to show how despite noble ideals, gaps between policy and practice can produce opposite – even disastrous – results. In this particular case of British anti-slavery campaign, a mixture of roguery with morality – and the failure of the British imperial apparatus to carry out what were deemed as historic decisions by British public opinion – ruined Siddi Sayyid's dominion based in Zanzibar.

Why Zanzibar? Because it was there that the Omani Sultan, Siddi Sayyid had shifted his capital in 1840 and made it the "most important trading centre along the East African coast".[7] In time, Zanzibar became a clearing house of supplies from Africa's interior, e.g. ivory, gum, copal, coconut oil, hide, tortoise shell, etc. for European and Eastern merchandise in cotton, flour, sugar, spirit, glassware, and arms. On all such imports, the Sultan imposed a flat rate of five per cent for tax collection. At his death, in 1856, Zanzibar's total custom receipts were estimated to be about 50,000 pounds per annum.[8]

Secondly, despite the fact that most subjects of the Zanzibar sultanate were Arabs, slave trade constituted but only a marginal element in its world trade.[9] Zanzibar's economic prosperity depended on large-scale plantation of cloves for export. This laid the foundation of a commercial empire which European companies of all sorts and sizes wanted to covet and win over.[10]

Yet, the much prized anti-slavery campaign initiated by the British knocked down by stages the foundations of this commercial empire. After a quarter century of association with European powers, in particular the Sultan's willing co-operation with British efforts against slave trade, Zanzibar had neither the officers, nor seamen, nor ships. Instead, wrote Captain Richard Burton in 1873, "rats and cockroaches compose (Zanzibar fleets') live stock; the ammunition is nowhere, and everything below is foul with garbage and vermin".[11]

How did this rapid dissolution come about? Not because of any deliberate policy pursued by Britain or any other external powers, and yet *because* of the support Zanzibar gave to Britain's campaign against Arab slave trade. We shall try to illustrate this by examining the progress of two anti-slavery treaties the Sultan signed with the British government in 1822 and 1845.

The Anglo-Zanzibar Treaties

Britain had both strategic and commercial interest in Zanzibar. Strategic because with its northern outpost in Oman and southernmost point at Kilwa, Zanzibar held sway over the entire coastal belt of east Africa. It had extensive diplomatic and trade relations with native princes in Kathiawad and Nizam of Hyderabad.[12] More specially, Zanzibar provided a close point for watching French activities in Bourbon, Madagascar and the French-held islands off Mozambique coast. A close alliance with the Zanzibar Sultan was also indispensable in order to discourage active commercial expansion of rival European powers into the East. All in all it was necessary to keep the Sultan solidly on British side without *undermining* his alleged claim on vast stretches of territory on the east coast. The mode the British adopted was negotiating a series of anti-slavery treaties with Siddi Sayyid which (a) appeased the evangelists, (b) could not be faulted by other European powers, in particular France, and (c) allowed the Royal Navy to act as "maritime policemen" to guard and inspect every Arab vessel which plied the Indian Ocean.

The first agreement with the Sultan was negotiated by Capt. Fairfax Moresby, RN, then a senior officer in Mauritius. Acting under orders of the Mauritius Governor, Robert Farquhar, Moresby secured Sayyid's agreement (8th September, 1822) on the following proposals: (1) abolition of foreign slave trade in his dominion; (2) all Arab boats "attempting the foreign slave traffic" be seized and their crew punished; (3) Arab vessels found with slaves "without passes" could be seized by British cruisers; (4) such vessels could also be seized if bound eastward of a line drawn from Cape Delgado, passing 60 miles east of Socotra and to Diu at the western end of the Gulf of Cambay, and (5) appointment of an Agent in Zanzibar "for the purpose of having intelligence and watching the traffic in slaves with Christian nations".[13]

By accepting these proposals of what came to be known as the Moresby Treaty, Siddi Sayyid also admitted British surveillance on his commercial transactions. British captains and crewmen could search any Arab vessel without fearing "reciprocal search" or court of adjudication for deciding the fact of captured slaves. Such an agreement was to lead to abuses, as it often did when the Royal Navy interfered with Arab ships loaded with cloves and other merchandice. Such interference increased when, in 1833, *prize and bounty* money were announced to add a practical incentive to "piracy on high seas" indulged in by average British sailors.[14]

On the other hand, the extensive zone defined in the Moresby Treaty for slave trade provided opportunity to smuggle slaves on forged passes. Also, once it became known that vessels flying the French flag could not be searched by British cruisers, the situation changed dramatically. In ever increasing numbers, northern Arabs invaded the east African coast to transport slaves on French vessels.

What could Sultan Sayyid do? More than the emancipationists, he was perhaps anxious to put a stop to slave-smuggling from his dominions. For, trans-shipment of slaves by illegal means deprived him of customs return. But, under the agreement his navy could not search or seize Arab boats even when found loaded with smuggled slaves. Sayyid was expected to obey decisions of HM officers, which is what he did quite willingly. Yet, the British Government constantly accused him of passivity – even duplicity – in the pursuit of a noble cause. By 1840, British agents from the Persian Gulf were reporting that about 20,000 slaves were being smuggled annually to Egypt, Arabia, Persia and Makran coast. Reacting to such reports, the Governor-General of India expressed his regret in a despatch of 14th February 1841, that the "Imaun of Muscat (also Sultan of Zanzibar) is apparently not acting with fairness in the matter."[15]

Obviously, the HM Government faced a dilemma. It could neither use force against slave ships owned by the "civilizing" Christian powers, nor could it – for reasons of financial stringency – expand its own fleet in the Indian Ocean. Clearly, a scape-goat had to be invented, so it twisted the arms of the Sultan to accept another slave treaty in 1845.

The Second Treaty

The treaty which came into force in January 1847, bound Sayyid to (1) prohibit export of slaves from his *African dominion*; (2) ban importation of slaves from any part of Africa into his possession *in Asia*;

(3) use his utmost influence with the chiefs of Arabia, Red Sea and Persian Gulf to observe this prohibition; and (4) permit British navy and East India Company to seize and confiscate every vessel of the Sultan's subjects engaged in slave trade except between the port of Lamu in the north to Milwa in the south.[16]

Here, the question may be asked: "Why did not the British prohibit the illegal trade even from one point to another within the Sultan's dominion?" The reason was primarily strategic. By allying with Muscat (Zanzibar) the British hoped to keep rival European powers – particularly France – away from the sea-routes to India. A total ban on slave transportation on east African coast, it was feared, would have weakened Zanzibar's authority over the coast. This was strategically inconceivable.

The treaty, however, did nothing to discourage East African slave trade. It merely restricted the Sultan's sea-borne commerce to a mere strip on the coast. In the years that followed, Arab and European boats infested Zanzibar waters to seize and carry away even his own Negro subjects. "Zanzibar," wrote Col. Rigby in 1860, "resembled a city with a hostile army encamped in its neighbourhood".[17]

The fear of Christian and Arab slaves affected Zanzibari commerce. "Not half the usual quantity of iron, hide, gum, and other produce of the interior," wrote Rigby to Bombay on 13th December 1858, "has arrived here this year from Keelwa and other ports of the South".[18] In the meanwhile, the high price offered on smuggled slaves turned a large number of Zanzibaris to the contraband trade. "Even members of the royal family", Rigby reported, "engaged in traffic in slaves with the Persian Gulf".[19]

Faced with such odds, the Sultan's authority in Africa began to collapse. A stage came when he had to depend on Baluch guards for his own protection! And, after his death, the sultanate of Oman and Zanzibar was divided into two, with the latter being obliged under the Canning Award to pay an annual subsidy of 9,000 pounds to Muscat.[20] Thus, ended the house of Siddi Sayyid.

Consequences

Twenty years later, a Select Committee of British Parliament (1871) found to its own dismay that larger vessels owned by French, Spanish American companies transported slaves to trans-Atlantic ports. The

role of Arabs and Swahilis became one of intermediary – a middleman between European merchants and African chattel![21] The business of "head-hunting" now called for a larger supply of guns and ammunition. Between 1856 and 1859 – just three years later – American sale in arms increased fourfold from $ 22,000 to $ 68,000. The French followed with a net sale of $ 21,000 from guns in 1859. The Germans sold guns worth $ 4,250. Matchlocks and guns thus replaced the traditional, peaceful commerce of the Indian Ocean.[22]

The Whiteman's "civilizing mission" had perhaps a focus – as well a justification. But to Arabs and Africans, this mission turned out to be drastically different from the one preached by missionaries and philanthropists. Wrote Col. Pelly to Bombay in 1862, "We have exhibited the power of civilization without its mercy".[23] That, in all probability, sums up the result of British drive against slave trade in the east.

NOTES AND REFERENCES

1. Ronald Oliver & J. D. Page, *A Short History of Africa*, London, 1964, p. 136.

1a. See General Rigby's Deposition before Select Committee of Parliament 1871, reproduced in C.S. Nicholls, *The Swahili Coast*, Edinburgh, 1971, pp. 342-75.

1b. Cited in Reginald Coupland, *East Africa and its Invaders*, OUP, 1938, p. 298.

2. For an exhaustive study on this theme see G.S. Graham, *Great Britain in the Indian Ocean 1810-1850*, London , 1967.

3. *Ibid.*, p. 2.

4. For a vivid account see Macgregor Ross, *Kenya from Within*, London, 1923.

5. Col. Rigby's Deposition before the Select Committee of Parliament in 1871. Copy, Indian Archives, New Delhi. Also C.S. Nicholls, *The Swahili Coast*, Edinburgh, 1971, pp. 324-75.

6. Hugh Tinker, *The New Slavery*, London, 1978.

7. Kenneth Ingham, *A History of East Africa*, London, 1966, p. 73.

8. J.S. Galbraith, *Mackinon and East Africa 1878-1895: A Study of New Imperialism*, London, 1972, p. 19.

9. Appendix of Select Committee Report excerpted in G.L. Sulivan, *Dhow Chasing in Zanzibar Waters*, London, 1968.

10. Captain Roberts, an American, who visited Muscat in 1833, wrote that Sayyid possessed a "more efficient naval force than all the native princes from the Cape of Good Hope to Japan". Quoted in Coupland, n. 1, p. 298.

11. Richard Burton, *Zanzibar: City, Island and Coast*, London, 1972, Vol. I, p. 77.

12. A large number of Zanzibar businessmen visited Hyderabad. Sayyid had a special regard for the Nizam's family. In 1850, acknowledging "the extra-ordinary good treatment all Arabs received in Hyderabad", Sayyid sent a leathered upholstered carriage to the Nizam he had originally received from Queen Victoria. (Graham, n. 2, p. 172).

13. Quoted in John Gray, *The British in Mombasa 1824-26*, London, 1957, p. 202.
14. Graham writes: "Every captain realized the necessity of indoctrinating his crew with something of the piratical spirit. . . And, "as soon as the slave was taken, the less disciplined were off like bloodhounds in search of loot, whether money or trinklets". (n. 2, pp. 140-42).
15. *Ibid.*, p. 212.
16. Coupland, *East Africa and its Invaders*, OUP, 1938, p. 519.
17. Quoted by Brig. W.K. Coughlon in his letter to Chief Sect., Bombay, 1st November, 1860. *Indian Archives.*
18. No. 55 of 1861, *Indian Archives.*
19. C.E.B. Russell, *General Rigby, Zanzibar and Slave Trade*, London, 1935, pp. 107-24
20. *Ibid.*
21. Rigby's deposition, n. 5.
22. C. S. Nicholls, *The Swahili Coast*, Edinburgh, 1971, pp. 24-75.
23. No. 113 of 1862, *Indian Archives.*

17

THE MISSIONARY MUSCULAR CULTURE IN MODERN INDIA

M.D. DAVID

Origins of YMCA

Among the various Western missionary organisations that came to India in the nineteenth century, the Young Men's Christian Association (YMCA) had the distinct objective of bringing salvation to the youth of India. It strove to achieve its objective through health and physical development programmes and by promoting playground culture and sport-consciousness in the country.

Born as a mid-nineteenth century urban Christian enterprise, the YMCA attempted to meet the spiritual and human needs of the modern city, a product of the industrial revolution. Modern capitalism produced wealth by exploiting man and machine. In the first half of the nineteenth century, in London the worst and the best of the modern industrialised society could be seen. It was an age of religious revivalism in England and the YMCA was a product of this Christian zeal.[1]

It was in London that the YMCA movement was founded in 1844 by George Williams, a God-inspired businessman, in order to cater to the spiritual and human needs of young men who came from rural Britain to find a living in the oppressive conditions of urban society. Today, the YMCA, with its 10,000 local associations in 118 countries, serves more than 30 million members irrespective of their caste, creed or colour.

It was the Greeks who gave a new dimension to physical training required for a soldier by adding to its goals the ideals of religion, education and art. Various physical activities gradually came to be centred around what came to be popularly known as the *Olympic Games*.[2]

The concept of physical education originated in Greece. Though Europe learnt during the Renaissance the significant role played by athletics in Greek national life, it was the American YMCA that developed the modern concept of physical education based on the Greek model. It was the American YMCA secretaries who brought this concept to India.

In the West, the Church before the mid-nineteenth century did not encourage the development of sports, play and athletics. Prior to 1895, no one could openly play games in the USA without violating the established prejudices and Church dogmas and without a sense of personal shame.[3] The concept of "Muscular Christianity" was not a viable alternative to religious work in the consideration of conservative European YMCA secretaries.

The YMCA movement was born in America at Boston in December 1851 at a time when religious revivalism and moral reform programmes were taking hold of the people. Under the circumstances the revivalists thought that "Muscular Christianity might be the means of salvation of the errant youth". During the pre-civil war period, most YMCA leaders in America had emphasised *Bible* study, intellectual activities and social visitations. They had learnt by experience that it was necessary to maintain a proper balance between work and play.

Pioneer of Sports Culture

The American and British YMCA leaders finding that they had been only partially successful in attracting youth by evangelistic approaches debated among themselves about the ways of serving young men as a Christian agency keeping in view the concept of 'total man'. Specific adaptations were made to meet certain social, spiritual and intellectual needs of the young men who were alone and adrift in large urbanised centres away from the stabilising influence of their homes. They soon realised that it was the physical education, recreation and sports activities of the YMCA that became the most sought after. However, when physical education was first introduced, it was not regarded as a legitimate activity or function of the YMCA as a religious organisation.[4]

The American YMCA took the initiative to include physical

education as one of its programmes while European YMCAs were slow to respond. The New York YMCA was the first to amend its constitution in 1866 to read: "The object of the YMCA shall be the improvement of the spiritual, mental, social and physical condition of young men".[5]

Halls of Health

In the 1870s and 1880s, the YMCAs health and physical education programme received a boost under the effective leadership of Robert J. Roberts of the Boston YMCA, who became its first Christian physical director in 1876. Roberts advocated strict obedience to the laws of health, particularly those pertaining to rest, relaxation, bathing, diet and air. For the purpose, he advocated light exercises which were conducted in gymnasiums called 'Halls of Health' run by the YMCAs. This new-found interest in physical education led the American YMCAs to organise in their gymnasiums in 1870s, for some time, circus acrobatics, aerial trapeze, parallel bars, jumping, club swing, giant swing, horizontal bar, weight lifting and the like.

By the end of the nineteenth century, the YMCA had succeeded in making sports a popular culture in the USA so much so that in the twentieth century sports became a cultural phenomenon of great magnitude, permeating art, business, education, law, politics, mass communication and international diplomacy. Thus the YMCA became the pioneer in popularising physical and sports culture in its multi-dimensional character. Through sports the YMCA began to inculcate in young people the ideals, value structures and behavioural patterns implicit in the Christian way of life. Guided recreation, play and physical education were found to contribute to the all-round development of the personality and promote sound Christian character.[6]

Realising the importance of training physical directors, institutes came to be established at Springfields, Massachusettes and at Chicago. In the early days, physical education directors had to be medical graduates with a proper grounding in anatomy and physiology. Dr. J.H. Gray and Dr. A.C. Noehren, the missionaries who pioneered physical education in India, were medical graduates.

In India

Though India had its *Vyayam Shalas* and sports competitions, they were of a different kind and were limited in scope. Before the advent of the YMCA concept of physical education, the British had introduced the army type physical drill in Indian schools and colleges. The Indian YMCA, which was largely supported and influenced by the American YMCAs had no hesitation in adopting the physical education programme developed in North America by the YMCA, considered to be the best in the world. The government of India seeing the advantage, not only supported the Indian YMCA in promoting it but also adopted it as a national policy.

The YMCA's programme of 'Play for everybody' and 'sound physical education' came to be greatly appreciated in India. Since it had a truly social basis, many ancient Indian games and exercises could be easily incorporated in its programmes.

Dr. Gray, attached to the Calcutta YMCA for five years since his arrival, had so popularised physical education that the National Council of YMCAs decided to open a new department and appointed him as the full-time physical director in 1913.

The government of India requested the YMCA to make available Dr. Gray's services on a part-time basis and gave a grant of Rs. 2,760 a year to the Calcutta YMCA. Gray's services were now partly at the disposal of the education department of the government. He instruced drill teachers in school about physical development and toured the province inspecting the teaching. This brought an end to the practice of employing gymnastic teachers trained by military gymnasts.[7]

The government of India was so pleased with what had been achieved in Bengal under the advice of Dr. Gray, that its joint secretary wrote to the education secretaries in different provinces and suggested that physical directors be appointed in other states as well.[8] For instance, the government of Bombay created a post of director of physical education in 1925 and appointed Mr. Weber of the YMCA to it.[9] The government also set apart a sum of Rs. 1,60,000 for the promotion of hygiene in schools and colleges under the guidance of Dr. Gray.

Physical Education in India

This certainly marked the beginning of a new era in the history of physical education in India. It can be called the 'physical awakening' of India. It was in one respect a part of a world-wide phenomenon which was directly inspired by the revival of the Olympic Games in 1896. "The world-wide movement is an expression of race restlessness; an attempt of the human species to adjust itself to make conditions of living – a natural reaction against the comparatively sedentary life of today. India is not yet deeply involved in the current stream of physical renaissance".[10]

When Corporation Sports Meets were organised all over Bengal in 1912, Dr. Gray taking advantage of the sportive mood of Calcutta, helped to organise the first inter-collegiate sports meet of colleges affiliated to Calcutta University. Likewise the first inter-collegiate sports meet in Bombay University was organised by the Bombay YMCA.

Some of the pioneering activities Dr. Gray undertook in 1912 were the introduction of basket-ball tournaments, lecturing on practical gymnasium work at the YMCA Training School and bringing a proposal before the Corporation of Calcutta for the inauguration of a public playground and athletic fields. He also initiated a thorough discussion in the press on organising an Olympic team for the 1912 Olympics, but the matter could not be taken up for lack of time.[11] By 1916 there were fourteen men working full time in physical work, of whom four were in Calcutta and the rest in other areas.[12]

Health Education

Dr. A.G. Noehren, who had joined as the Physical Director of the Madras Association in December 1915, did a thorough job in making people conscious about the importance of maintaining good health. He began to understand the problems of youth in Madras when he started examining them medically. Reporting about this work he wrote: "Up to date, I have examined 284 men . . . it is seldom you examine an Indian who could be pronounced normal; either he suffers from chronic malarial attacks, hookworm, alimentary troubles, diabetes, nephritis and the like, or shows of malnutrition often due to tuberculosis. The mortality among students as well as the depressed classes is appalling, and we welcome this opportunity for giving sound advice together with an invitation to take some form of regular exercise. My office is now equipped adequately not only with the necessary anthropometric apparatus, but with all the conveniences for making clinical diagnoses, and I have come to regard my medical training as a most valuable asset of my work".[13] None, till then, had undertaken the promotion of health education in India by such thorough methods.

Playground Culture

As Dr. Gray had popularized playground culture in Calcutta, Dr. Noehren also made every effort to popularize the playground movement in Madras and attempted to open a model playground in Madras. Such playgrounds run under expert supervision were to be taken over by the government or municipal corporations all over India. Emphasising the crying need for playgrounds in India, to improve the health of young people, he wrote: "If America, in a temperate climate has demonstrated the utility of such recreation centres in preventing disease and promoting health, not to mention the valuable products of these community centres, what about India with its frightful mortality and low vitality".[14]

In order to make physical education popular in schools and colleges, group games, athletics and gymnasiums were introduced. Western games like football, hockey, badminton, basket-ball, table-tennis and tennis were introduced and organised by the YMCA. These games provided ample recreation and vigorous exercise and were so popular with young people that not only did the YMCA organise them as a part of its regular programme but also developed them in schools, colleges and universities.

The revolution in physical education brought about by the YMCA under the direction of Dr. Gray could not be carried on to cover the country without an adequate number of trained physical directors. Dr. Gray therefore pioneered the idea of establishing the first well organised physical training institution in India which today is called the YMCA College of Physical Education. In his opinion, India needed first, as a model, modern types of physical training equipment, and secondly, an adequate physical education training college.

In consultation with Schaetti, he prepared a tentative scheme for land and buildings as well as a course of instruction. The building was meant to accommodate one hundred students with staff quarters and student hostels.[15] The entire expenditure of the project was estimated to amount to Rs. 600,000 or $ 200,000. Dr. Gray placed the plan before the government of India and asked them to meet half the cost. But it did not materialise.

The efforts of the YMCA to promote playgrounds under trained

supervisors were appreciated and local governments at Madras, Bombay, Delhi and Calcutta had already taken up the responsibility of running them as model centres.[16]

Lack of Physical Vitality

The task of developing physical education to its peak was left to H. C. Buck who arrived in Madras in September 1919. Dr. Noehren had done such splendid spade work that Buck was spared many initial efforts: "He found, however, that much work still needed to be done for the laying of the foundation for national vitality through proper campaigns for health and hygiene, sanitation, proper diet and sex education. Physical education was something like preventive medicine".

From his preliminary observations of India, her people, their diet and their low vitality, Buck concluded that India badly needed help in these areas which the American YMCA alone had developed. Commenting on the situation, Buck wrote: "Madras might well be called the Boston of India. Her schools, colleges and universities under Government or Mission control make her our great education centres. From July until April, the city teems with students; our hostels are overcrowded and every YMCA activity is full of life. But with teachings of centuries back to the effect that all physical labour is degrading, India's boys grow up enjoying the very minimum of physical exertion. There is none of the healthy "hardy boy" life which we know in America, and as a result students come to us with constitutions and habits which would cause grave anxiety if the same conditions prevailed among our student bodies at home. Whereas in American YMCAs, the physical director might be privileged to expend most of his energy on purely physical activities, knowing that his subjects are normal well-nourished individuals, here we must first lay the foundation for enduring strenuous physical exercise by removing those many devitalising influences, which have been for so many years a hindrance to India in attaining the national vitality which she so much needs".[17]

Diagnosis of India's problem of lack of physical vitality by Gray, Noehren and Buck showed that the root cause was an unbalanced diet which was mainly carbohydrate-rich and that an average Indian boy or man was 10 to 30 pounds lighter for his height than the average men and boys of the West.

Lack of physical vitality seems to bother India today as well, even after 70 years. No wonder that India, despite its large population, has failed miserably to win medals and make its mark in Olympic Games.[18]

It was to remedy this situation that the National Council of YMCA decided to open India's first training school for Indian physical directors on the 1st August, 1920 in the Madras YMCA building, with the first five earnest and dedicated young men under the direction of Buck.[19]

Physical directors trained by the YMCA school of physical education begun to fan out in schools and colleges all over India – in the Punjab, Baroda, Central Provinces, Patna and Madras. Provincial governments sent graduates to this school for training. Recognising the all India significance of this school, the National Council asked the YMCA Building Commission to prepare plans to erect a school and gymnasium in the compound of the Royepettah YMCA specially suited to Indian needs. A provision was made for a hostel, lecture rooms, library, bathing and other facilities.

College of Physical Education

After the first four years in the Madras Central YMCA, the school shifted to its own premises in Royepetta YMCA in 1924. The library and lecture hall were housed in the thatched hut. A portion of the Principal's residence was converted into the school office. An adjoining building was rented as a hostel for students and the spacious land of the Royepetta YMCA was put to the fullest use.

The school of physical education in Madras acquired further credibility when the Indian govenment accorded recognition to it in 1923 as the Official Training and Certification Centre for students who wished to obtain a Public School Physical Training Certificate. During the first five years, from 1920 to 1925 no less than 146 young men were trained. The college at Royepetta made rapid progress during the next seven years by popularising physical education all over the country. Madras University made physical education compulsory in all colleges. The same was done in schools. The physical directors trained by the college and employed in various provinces popularised the physical education programme. Meanwhile, N.K. Mia was appointed on the staff as Associate Physical Instructor and was placed in the permanent cadre of secretaries. The demand for more YMCA trained physical directors in all parts of India increased and more and more candidates began to seek admission to the college. The premises at Royepetta became inadequate. The National Council was asked to write a letter to the government of Madras for a free grant of a site for the school near Saidpet Teachers' College. The National Council approved the suggestion and asked the Principal and the National Physical Director to make an application to the Government in the name of the Council.[20]

In response to this, the Madras government which had taken a keen interest in the development of the YMCA college of physical education gifted it 63 acres of land at Saidpet in April 1932. In July that year the college was shifted to Saidpeth where thatched huts rose up to house classrooms, offices and hostels.

Frantic efforts were made to find funds to construct the college building. Even the central government was approached for assistance. But it was John R. Mott, one of the greatest among modern missionaries and the guardian angel of the Indian YMCA, who came to the rescue in finding funds to erect the college building at Saidpet. He urged his millionaire friend Col. Vincent Massey of Toronto, Canada, to make a donation of 35,000 dollars from the Massey Foundation towards the cost of the college building, which thus came to be named Massey Hall.[21] With Buck as the Principal and with a permanent building of its own surrounded by a vast land, the college developed into a fine All-India Institution of Physical Education that drew students from every region of India.

Buck's dream of making the Physical Education College at Madras serve as a demonstration centre and a laboratory from the stand-point of training physical directors had finally come true.[22] With the opening of the YMCA College of Physical Education, the government of Madras closed down its various other physical training centres where drill masters were trained. All those aspiring to be physical directors were sent to the YMCA school. The typical Indian physical education teachers, known as drill masters, had most often lacked the esteem and respect normally accorded to teachers. But now the age of the slighted drill masters was over.

Buck's Rules

Equally significant was Buck's contribution to creating a consciousness among the sporting public in India, particularly among young men and leaders of sports, that rules were a pre-requisite and to play the games according to rules was necessary for the orderly conduct of play and for development of understanding and friendship.

His *Book of Rules* was meant for both indigenous and western games. There had been different rules followed in different parts ofthe country. Buck was the first to introduce uniformity and bring Olympic standards through his *Book of Rules.* "It was not only the first of its kind, but Herculean in its magnitude. The success that he achieved and the reputation that he built thereby will be borne out by both the manner in which sports organisations in India still look to Buck's *Rules* for authority and the immense popularity the book has enjoyed in successive editions from 1928 onwards".[23] The book is still popular as a standard work and had run into 22 editions by 1986.

Buck had devised programmes and courses which combined both Indian and Western physical exercise so that the YMCA college offered the best of the East and the West. He made *yoga* an integral part of the YMCA physical education programme and taught coaching methods appropriate to the sports he introduced. In the summer of 1929 he launched the first sports journal in India known as *Vyayam*, and served as the founder editor of this all-India quarterly. His wife, Mrs. Marie Buck, not only helped her husband in the whole venture, but was also a teacher of physical education in her own right and trained the first women physical education teachers in India with the opening of Women's Wing in the college in 1940. She also wrote articles on the subject.[24]

The YMCA College of Physical Education continued to make rapid progress. Beginning with an enrolment of 5 in 1920, by 1930 it had 75 of whom 40 were university graduates from all parts of India. In those ten years, 152 men who had secured the diplomas of the college were employed in government and missionary schools and colleges, municipal playgrounds, YMCAs and in the administrative work of government educational departments.

It is necessary to mention the significant role played by the Physical Education Department of the YMCA in promoting playgrounds in congested urban centres in the early 1920s. In Bombay, Madras, Calcutta and other cities, YMCA supervised playground programmes became conspicuously successful because of the enthusiastic support of the local municipal corporations. The first experiment of its kind was made in Bombay in 1923 under a YMCA secretary, on a small ground less than the size of a football field, in one of the most congested chawl sections of the city. Nearly 1,000 children of all communities played under a YMCA trained supervisor. The Bombay Municipal Corporation opened two more such playgrounds to be run by the YMCA. Similar ones were opened in Madras and Calcutta and they became models for cities in the rest of India. In Bombay, the playground movement especially in areas where the industrial workers lived, served as a counter-attraction to the evil of drinking. Government also assisted in improving the lives of the workers by comprehensive schemes of recreation to wean the workers away from alcohol.[25]

Such programmes were taken to rural India as well. Buck drew up a programme in the Madras Presidency whereby YMCA trainees demonstrated in villages the value of recreation in order to counter the evil of drinking. A scheme of Rural Recreation drawn up by the YMCA was launched by the government and it became highly popular as it brought joy and new life among rural youth.[26]

Olympic Games

The most significant contribution of the Indian YMCA was to make it possible for India to be represented in the World Olympics for the first time in 1924. How did the YMCA come to play such a key role in promoting the Olympic Games in India? Following the 1920 Olympic Games at Antwerp, the International Olympic Committee under its President Baron de Coubertin discussed the question of getting those countries to participate which so far had not been represented. At this meeting Elwood S. Brown, physical director, International YMCA, submitted a plan according to which YMCA physical departments in various countries like China, Japan, the Philippines and India were invited to select competitors to represent their countries at the Olympics. In response to this, the YMCA national physical directors of these countries were appointed as special representatives of the International Olympic Committee.[27]

Dr. A.G. Noehren, the national physical director of the Indian YMCA attended the International Olympic Committee meeting as India's representative. He prepared the YMCA and its physical directors in India to commit themselves to the promotion of the Olympic idea in India. As a representative of the International Olympic Committee in India he set about organising the All India Olympic Association, Provincial Olympic Committees and Provincial Athletic Meets in preparation for the All India Athletic Meet which was planned to be held in Delhi.

The Viceroy of India agreed to be the chief patron of the All-India Olympic Association. Sir Dorab J. Tata, who had knowledge of athletic games both in India and abroad, was made the President of the first Indian Olympic Association created in 1920 and attended the International Olympic Committee meeting held in 1920 as India's representative.

Every youth in British India was eligible to compete for a place in India's team provided he was domiciled in India and was an amateur. The following ten official events were listed:[28] 100 yards run, 220 yards run, 440 yards run, one mile run, three miles run, running long jump, running high jump, 16 lb. shot put, modified marathon (10 miles), and 120 yards high hurdles.

In his notification, Dr. Noehren clarified that though the YMCA would help to organise competitions to select and then train the Olympic team for the VIIIth Olympiad, it could not undertake any financial responsibility. He therefore, appealed to all public-spirited people in the country to contribute generously for the success of the Indian Olympic team and send the money to the honorary treasurer of the Provincial Committees. Provincial Olympic Committees were organised in Bengal, Bombay, Baroda, Madras, the Punjab, the United Provinces, the Central Provinces, Mysore, Bihar, Orissa and Hyderabad.

Dr. Noehren sent out bulletins and announcements regarding the VIIIth Olympiad to all concerned, including therein the Rules and Regulations in force at the Olympiad. All Provincial and State Athletic Meets were held between the 10th and 15th of December, 1923, and the final Meet was organised at Delhi, in February 1924, presided over by the Viceroy himself. In all, more than 7,000 competitiors participated at different provincial and inter-state competitions.

At the Delhi Sports-Meet conducted under the leadership of Dr. Noehren from the 9th to the 11th of February, 1924, the first ever Olympic team to represent India was selected. It included Dalip Singh, a Sikh from Patiala and a graduate of Panjab University; Hinge, an orthodox Brahmin from Maharashtra; Pitt and Hall, two Anglo-Indian sprinters from Calcutta; Pala Singh, a sepoy from Meerut, and Laxman, a medical graduate from Madras. Hildreth of Calcutta, who was in England, joined the team in Paris. "These six gentlemen representing five different communities and as many widely separated sections of the country, had won the right to be acclaimed the greatest track and field athletes in the Indian Empire, by defeating all other aspirants to the title in a fair and open competition held at Delhi".[29]

It was decided to place the first Indian Olympic team under the charge of H.C. Buck, an athletic coach and Principal of the YMCA Physical Training School at Madras. In a short span of two months, each member was so well trained by Buck that each of the competitors broke his own record at the Olympics. Buck did an excellent job despite the fact that he was dealing with inexperienced athletes who did not know the niceties of form and training necessary for a championship performance.

The entire team assembled at Madras for a month's rigorous training before departing for Paris on board the ship *Lancashire,* expected to sail from Colombo on 29th May, 1924. That would have given the team a month in France to get acclimatised. However, the departure of the steamer was delayed due to a dock strike in Colombo. The team which rested for a week agreed to participate in an exhibition sports meet in Colombo.

The team which arrived at Marseilles was received by a representative of Tata Sons and taken by train to Paris and then brought to the Olympic village. Buck took the team out for training twice a day. At the inaugural ceremony on the opening day, the Indian team, smartly dressed with the work INDIA printed in bold capitals across the chest, marched proudly carrying their banner. The credit for building the morale and discipline of the team at Paris should go to Buck and his wife. The team conducted itself so well that even the newspapers showered the highest praise on the demeanour of the Indian team.

On their return to India, the team was given a reception at Madras by S.V. Ramaswamy Mudaliar, honorary treasurer, All-India Olympic Committee, before each athlete went home.

The significant result of this was the growth of sports consciousness among the Indian people. Buck handed over to the Indian Olympic Association Rs. 8,000 he had saved. It was used as seed money for organising the Indian Olympic Association of which Dr. Noehren was the secretary. Buck promoted the Madras Provincial Olympic Committee.

The story of the maiden appearance of the Indian team at the Olympic Games can be best concluded in the words of its main architect, Dr. Noehren himself. He wrote, "We close this final account of India's venture into world athletics by reference to a most valuable by-product of the whole enterprise. Way down in Trivandrum, an enthusiastic Olympic Committee is now planning to create . . . a *pucca* quarter-mile track with accessories for conducting all athletic events in a central location in the city. The city fathers of Bombay are now considering proposals for establishing supervised play centres in certain congested areas in the city. The Madras Corporation has approached us for advice on the utilisation of twenty open spaces as playgrounds, one of which is to take the form of a central athletic field where track and field sports can be conducted according to Olympic standards. The average annual sports meet conducted by most high schools and colleges, has but rarely been managed on proper lines as far as strict adherence to universally accepted rules is concerned. The publication and wide dissemination of these rules, together with the definition of amateurism, in our Olympic bulletins has already helped to standardise such contents throughout the country. The future is full of promise, no country in the world is more in need of a stimulus that will promote physical vigour among the masses".[30]

In 1926, the YMCA was again commissioned to organise Provincial and All-India Meets to select an Indian team to participate in the Far Eastern Games. The All-India Competition was organised at Eden Gardens, Calcutta, in February 1927.

In organising the Olympic Association in India, the YMCA was the prime mover and provided the first honorary secretary of the Central Committee, viz. Dr. Noehren himself. With his resignation from this office in 1927, the YMCA lost contact with Central Olympic Committee but continued to be closely associated with Provincial Olympic Committees. It had its full share in conducting the All-India meet at Allahabad in 1930 to select a team for the Far Eastern Games to be held at Tokyo. S.K. Mukerji of the Calcutta YMCA was selected to lead the team.[31]

NOTES AND REFERENCES

1. M.D. David, *The YMCA and the Making of Modern India*, New Delhi, 1992, p. 1.
2. These games were held every four years at Elis and named after the god Olympus or Zeus. To begin with, they were funeral games held for the purpose of thanksgiving, praise and satisfaction of the deity. Expensive prizes were awarded to the winners during the first Olympiad but were soon after substituted by merely the award of the Olive Wreath. Gradually, these games became inter-tribal and inter-city-state contests upholding the heroic ideal and they celebrated local events or national victories. These games enjoyed national importance for decades and declined and disappeared with the downfall of the Greek city-states.
3. Johnson Elmer, *History of YMCA Physical Education*, Chicago, 1979, p. 31.
4. *Ibid.*, p. xiii.
5. David, *op. cit.*, p. 12.
6. *Ibid.*, p. 13
7. *YMCA Review*, 1914, p. 59.
8. Letter of H. Sharpe, C.I.E. Joint Secretary to Government of India, dated 24 February 1913, to secretaries of education in different provinces, p. 21.

9. *A Review of Education in Bombay State 1855 — 1955*, Poona, 1958, p. 370.
10. *YMCA Review*, 1914, p. 251.
11. *Report of Dr. J. H. Gray, M.D.*, Physical Director, Calcutta for the period from 1st October, 1911 to 1st January, 1913, pp. 5-6.
12. *Young Men of India*, 1916, p. 739. National Physical Director, or Secretary for Physical work of the Indian National Council, Calcutta; J. Henry Gray, M.D., M.P.E.

    Senior Physical Director, Calcutta YMCA, especially related to the Chowringhee and Wellington Branches, and Advisor to the Government of Bengal C.P. Segard, M.D. Supervisory Physical Director for the North Calcutta Association Work: W. Sarkar, M.B.

    Physical Director, at the College and Boys' Branches: P.K. Biswas, Indian YMCA Training School.

    Physical Director, Hyderabad associations, and related to H.H. the Nizam's Government: H.G. Beall, B.P.E. Physical Director, Lahore Associations and Advisor to the Government of the Punjab: J.S. Robson, B.A., Physical Director, Jubbulpore Associations: P.A. Bassinger, Indian YMCA Training School.

    Physical Director, Bombay Associations; Donald Munro, North American YMCA College, Springsfield, Mass.

    Physical Director to the Madras Associations and Advisor to the Madras Government: A.G. Noehren, M.B., B.D., Associated at Madras for Special Training.

    Alexander, M.B., Physical Director, Bangalore Associations: L. Hoxsey, YMCA College, Chicago, USA.

    Physical Director, Colombo, Ceylon Associations: R.W. Cammack, B.Sc., YMCA College, Chicago, USA. Physical Director, Trivandrum Association, Travancore. E.B. Saunders, YMCA College, Chicago, USA. Physical Director, Allahabad Associations: G. Law, M.B.
13. A.G. Noehren's Annual Report from Madras for the year ending September, 1916, p. 3.
14. *Ibid.*
15. Dr. J. H. Gray's Annual Report of 30th September 1918, p. 8. Dr. J. R. Mott also took a similar memorandum to the Viceroy of India.
16. *Ibid.*, p. 7.
17. Report Letter of H.C. Buck, M.P.E., Director of Physical Education, YMCA, Madras, 1919, p. 1.
18. *Ibid.*
19. *Ibid.*, p. 2.
20. Executive Committee Minutes of 26th August, 1927, p. 7.
21. Letter of Vincent Massey from the Canadian Legation, Washington to John R. Mott, dated 7th December, 1929, pp. 1-2.
22. H.C. Buck's Annual Report for 1924-25, p. 1.
23. Govindarajula, L.K., *Buck Commemoration Volume*, Madras, 1949, pp. 59-60.
24. David, *op. cit.*, p. 325.
25. Physical Department Report to the Twelfth National Convention, 1927, p. 68.
26. Govindarajulu, *op. cit.* p. 105.
27. *Young Men of India*, 1923, pp. 360-361.
28. *Ibid.*, p. 536.
29. *Ibid.*, 1924, p. 598. Hildreth, from Calcutta, was the seventh athlete who joined the team at Paris but could not take part in the games as he pulled a muscle during practice and could not run. *Ibid.*, p. 600.
30. Noehren, "Indian Athletes at the Olympic Games" in *Young Men of India*, 1924, p. 604.
31. *Report of the 15th Annual Convention*, pp. 116-117.

INDEX